sexopedia

everything you wanted to know…

sexopedia

everything you wanted to know...

ANNE HOOPER

A DORLING KINDERSLEY BOOK

To Albert Z. Freedman,
love and thanks for starting me off

LONDON, NEW YORK,
MUNICH, MELBOURNE, DELHI

Dorling Kindersley Limited

Category Publisher Corinne Roberts
Senior Managing Art Editor Lynne Brown
Senior Editor Peter Jones
Senior Art Editor Rosamund Saunders
Designer Carla De Abreu
Production Heather Hughes
Picture Research Anna Grapes

Photographers
Luc Beziat, James Muldowney, Peter Pugh-Cook

Produced for Dorling Kindersley by
studio cactus ⓒ

13 SOUTHGATE STREET WINCHESTER HAMPSHIRE SO23 9DZ

Senior Art Editor Sharon Moore
Senior Editor Polly Boyd
Project Art Editor Laura Watson
Project Editor Kate Hayward
Managing Editor Mic Cady

First published in 2003 by
Dorling Kindersley Limited,
80 Strand, London WC2R 0RL

2 4 6 8 10 9 7 5 3 1

A CIP catalogue record for this book is available
from the British Library.

ISBN 0 7513 4394 3

Colour reproduction by GRB, Italy
Printed and bound by Mondadori, Italy

For our complete catalogue visit

www.dk.com

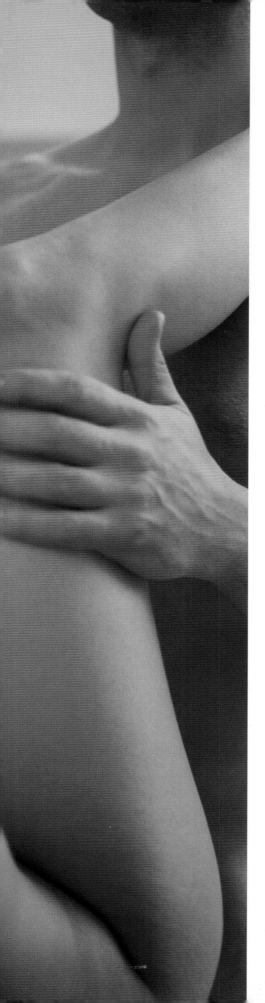

CONTENTS

Introduction   8

1. Sexual Chemistry

Gallery	12	Intimate relationships	28
Falling in love	14	Casual relationships	30
What drives us to be sexual?	18	Learn to love yourself	32
Human sexual behaviour	20	Presenting yourself	34
Male and female attitudes to sex	22	Meeting a new partner	36
Innate sex role differences	24	Early relationship issues	38
Learned sex role differences	26	What do you want from a relationship?	40

2. How Sex Works

His sexual anatomy   44

Her sexual anatomy   46

Hormones   48

Reproduction   50

3. All About Foreplay

Gallery   54

Setting the scene   56

Sensual massage   58

Erotic massage   64

The art of kissing   66

Self-touch for him   68

Self-touch for her   70

Mutual exploration   72

Increasing sensation   74

Mutual masturbation   76

Oral sex   78

Food games   80

4. The Art of Good Sex

Gallery	84	Rear-entry positions	108
Sexual response in both sexes	86	Side-by-side positions	110
His sexual response	88	Kneeling positions	112
Her sexual response	90	Sitting positions	114
Orgasm techniques for men	92	Upright positions	116
Orgasm techniques for women	94	Sex tricks	118
Multiple orgasms	96	Tantric sex	120
Controlling orgasms	98	The tao of sex	122
Man-on-top positions	100	Anal sex	124
Woman-on-top positions	104		

5. Sex Without Limits

Gallery	128	Sex boosters	146
Beyond the bedroom	130	Dressing for sex	148
Sex outside the home	132	Sensual materials	152
Exploring fantasy	134	Fetishes	154
Submission and domination	138	Alternative sexual lifestyles	158
Bedroom toys	142	Transvestites and transsexuals	160

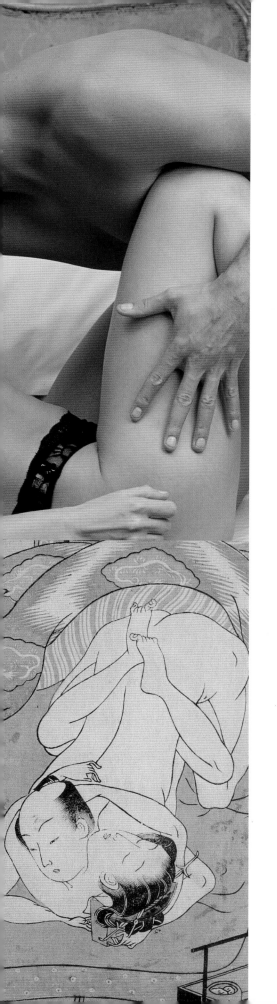

6. Gay Sex

Gay issues	164	Why are some people gay?	168
Dealing with the outside world	166		

7. Sex for Life

Gallery	172	Sex in adolescence	188
Sex exercises	174	Sex drive during pregnancy	190
Diet and food supplements	176	Sex during pregnancy	192
Personal care	178	Sex after childbirth	194
Medical check-ups	180	Sex in the middle years	196
Safer sex	182	Sex in later life	198
Contraception	184		

8. When Sex Goes Wrong

Common sex problems	202	Discovering orgasm	229
Men's problems	206	Coping with infidelity	230
Women's problems	210	Erections in later life	231
Illness and sexuality	212	Communicating under stress	232
Medicinal drugs	216	Balancing mismatched libidos	233
Recreational drugs	218	Controlling premature ejaculation	234
Sex-related diseases	220	Rekindling sexual excitement	235
HIV and AIDS	223	Understanding selective impotence	236
CASE HISTORIES:		Dealing with a partner's depression	237
Managing anger	224		
Adapting to life with a baby	225		
Rediscovering intimacy	226	Restoring sexual confidence	238
Learning to assert yourself	227	Overcoming inhibitions	239
Overcoming grief	228		

9. History of Sex

Gallery	242	India and Arabia	250
Pre-history	244	China and Japan	252
Classical sex	246	Exploration and imperialism	254
Christianity and the medieval age	248	The Victorians	256
		Sex in the 20th century	258

Further reading	262	Index	266
Useful addresses	263	Acknowledgments	272

INTRODUCTION

SEX CAN BE THE GREATEST source of pleasure and happiness in our lives – it can boost our personal sense of well-being and health, and it also fosters precious feelings of intimacy with a partner. While sexuality used to be viewed as a "private matter", today it is featured in magazines, newspapers, movies, and now on the Internet; indeed, our exposure to the subject is greater than ever before. While this is generally a good thing, information is not always correct or adequate, and it can give confused messages. With so much apparent interest in sex, I felt what was needed was a reliable source of detailed and accurate information

on the topic, so I set to work on compiling this sexual encyclopedia, incorporating all the exciting new developments and the latest facts and figures.

Since I first started in sex therapy 30 years ago, there has been a great surge of scientific and academic research. Drug companies have made huge advances in the treatment of sexual problems, particularly those of men, such as impotence. There is still less known about female sexuality, but this is changing. There's now a drug that reduces inhibition in women, so those who've never climaxed before can do so for the first time. We've also learned more about the benefits of men and women taking the hormone testosterone to boost a low libido.

In addition to these remedial solutions, the sex-toy industry has boomed in recent years. Many men and women who previously wouldn't have dreamed of buying sex aids now shop by mail order or online. Thanks to a revolution in battery technology, stimulatory devices are now smaller, more discreet, quieter, and more powerful than ever before. Radio-controlled sex toys are currently being researched, and in future you'll be able to stimulate your partner from the other side of the street. Perhaps one day, with the use of satellite technology, we'll even be able to stimulate a partner from the other side of the world!

I've done my utmost to ensure that all the facts in this book are up-to-date and accurate. However, sex research is in a state of continual renewal, and if you know of anything I've left out I'd really like to hear from you. My website, www.annehooper.com, has become a clearing house for new sexual information and I, and ultimately my readers, grow richer for your contributions. So please drop me a line – I will investigate further, and may include the information in my next volume. Here's wishing you a wonderful sex life,

Anne Hooper

CHAPTER 1

Sexual Chemistry

ATTRACTION

rapport

flirtation

TEMPTATION

FALLING IN LOVE

FOR SOME PEOPLE, falling in love is an instantaneous thing ("love at first sight"). But falling in love can be gradual, too. You might be in a relationship for months before one day you look at your partner and the truth dawns on you. But what actually happens – why do we feel so great when we fall in love? The explanations are both emotional and chemical. What's happening in your mind is bound up with hormones at play in your body, so let's start at the beginning.

The closeness that most of us experience with our parents, that knowledge of unconditional love and sense of security that we get from snuggling up to our mother or father as children, is a wonderful thing. As we grow older, however, the physical side of love with our parents subsides – we grow out of it. We begin to seek that security and physical closeness elsewhere – from a partner. We all need to feel cared for and looked after.

Finding a mate

Attraction is the first phase of love, and men and women are attracted to each other for a number of reasons (see p.16). One major factor is that they tend to be drawn to the "familiar" in the other partner. They perceive something in the new lover that feels well known and this offers a sense of comfort and pleasure. Brain studies show there is a good reason for this. When we have an emotional experience, the amygdala – two small nut-shaped sections

---

FAMILIAR LOVE

TO IDENTIFY your familiar love, ask yourself the following questions:

1 What was your early experience of love? Was it from parents, siblings, grandparents, or significant others?

2 What family or friendship package did it arrive in? Did your parents show each other love or antagonism?

3 What did it feel like? Did it feel warm, sensuous, matter-of-fact, or dangerous?

THREE KINDS OF LOVE

THE WORD LOVE encompasses a range of different emotions. However, generally speaking there are three main types of love: storgic, ludic, and erotic. Two matching love types may pair up (in which case the relationship is often harmonious). Alternatively, one type of lover can fall in love with another type (the differences may be interesting but they may also lead to problems!).

STORGIC From the Greek word *storge*, meaning "natural affection", this type of love is characterized by affection and companionship rather than great passion.

LUDIC From *ludos*, the Latin word for "game", this is a playful, pleasurable kind of love with free commitment. It is a lot of fun but lacks the intimacy of erotic love and the security of storgic love.

EROTIC Named after the Greek god of love (Eros), this kind of love features physical attraction, intimacy, rapport, passion, sensuality, and confidence.

of the brain – trigger a hormonal rush. When that experience gets stored in the neo-cortex, the part of the brain that works as a kind of super filing cabinet, then it is associated with both the emotion and the hormonal rush. When we come across something familiar in someone, those emotions and hormonal responses can be triggered all over again.

Your earliest experiences are likely to have come from your family background. So, if your parents were sad, gloomy, or hostile, you may find that when you meet someone sharing those characteristics your buzzer will be pushed. Possibly to your dismay, you are likely to feel a warm hormonal response and an exhilarating wave of feeling – suddenly you are inexplicably attracted.

Attraction of opposites

Not everyone unconsciously wants exactly what they've experienced in childhood. Sometimes we want what we didn't get as infants but wish we had. It is for this reason that we occasionally get interested in people who on the surface seem unsuitable because of their apparent extreme differences. This other person may have developed parts of his or her character that you have not and that you somehow feel you are lacking. An association with him or her is therefore seen as a way of "acquiring" these traits. For example, if a child was not "allowed" to be angry at home, that child when grown-up may seek someone who is angry and "does" the angry bit for him or her.

Freud's view on love

Viennese psychoanalyst Sigmund Freud (1856–1939) proclaimed a number of highly controversial and influential theories relating to the nature of human love and sexuality. He declared that it is our "love affair" with our opposite sex parent during childhood that spurs most of us on to seek love and affection from an opposite sex lover when we develop sexually. He claimed that a heterosexual man makes a reality of his subconscious desire for his mother when he enters into a loving sexual relationship with a woman (this he called the "Oedipus complex"). Similarly, a heterosexual woman satisfies her desire for her father when loving a man friend.

Stages of love

Falling in love gives rise to a range of intense feelings and emotions, particularly at the start of a relationship. The process can be divided loosely into three basic stages – initial attraction, infatuation, and attachment.

- **Initial attraction** is the first phase of love. For the most part, it is purely physical. Most men and women tend to be attracted to people who are of the same level of conventionally perceived attractiveness as themselves, people who are "in their league".
- **Infatuation** is the second phase of love and consists of the chemical addictive rush provided by the love chemicals that flood the body (see right).
- **Attachment** is the third phase of love, forming at around the same time as the infatuation phase dwindles. Ideally, by the time all the effects of the euphoric love chemicals have worn off (usually around the two-year mark) a strong bond will have grown between the couple, substituting attachment for love's first flush.

Love chemicals

So what's happening in our bodies when we fall in love? A plethora of neurotransmitters and chemicals come into play, giving us intense physical feelings. Probably the first of these chemicals to affect us are pheromones.

- Pheromones – These are chemicals secreted by men and women that have the effect of drawing people together. If you've ever felt wildly attracted to someone but aren't sure why it may be that you're picking up on their "scent", or their chemicals of attraction. Women produce more pheromones during ovulation, which in theory makes them more attractive to men during this period.
- Adrenaline and dopamine – As initial attraction develops and sexual desire increases, adrenaline begins to course through the veins, adding to feelings of excitement and desire, and making the heart beat faster. Rising levels of the feel-good chemical dopamine in the blood stream cause sexual feelings to further intensify.
- Phenylethylamine (PEA) – This is the stimulating chemical that is responsible for the delirious dizziness, churning feeling, shortness of breath, and palpable quickening of the heartbeat when we fall in love. It generally creates a euphoric state, raises the libido, and accounts for the incredibly positive outlook most of us experience at the start of a relationship. Unfortunately, this chemical starts wearing off after about six months and dwindles over the next 18 months, leaving you ready for the next stage of love – attachment.
- Oxytocin is a chemical generated by the experience of orgasm and during breast-feeding and is thought to generate feelings of attachment.

The need for intimacy

Sex brings couples closer together, in both a physical and an emotional sense. As well as forging a connection between bodies, the successful sex act fosters a sense of intimacy and attachment. Although intimacy can be achieved with close friends who are not lovers, the intimacy of two lovers, brought together in sexual union, tends to be greatest. Intimacy is an integral part of falling in love. For this reason, even though we may no longer feel the same intense sexual buzz in a long-term relationship, intimate feelings act as a reminder of those special early days and continue to bond us.

INTIMACY IS VITAL for a healthy, long-term relationship, helping to reinforce feelings of love, attachment, and sexual interest.

STAGES OF PHYSICAL CONTACT

OBSERVATIONS OF SEXUAL BODY LANGUAGE demonstrate that there are very specific stages of physical closeness experienced by men and women as they grow more sexual with each other:

HAND TO HAND Hands are usually the first points of touch at the early stages of a relationship. Holding a friend's hand is the least "threatening" type of physical contact.

ARM TO ARM There is a natural progression from holding hands to touching each other's arms and embracing. Such touch brings you much closer together, both physically and emotionally.

MOUTH TO MOUTH People today often kiss out of friendship. This makes it easier to venture towards the first serious kiss, since such intimate touch feels relatively secure.

MOUTH TO FACE Once the ice has been broken, the lover then feels free to move on to other erotic parts of the face, neck, and shoulders, denoting a build-up of trust and sexual interest.

HAND TO HEAD When men and women begin to hold or manipulate parts of another person's body, this shows a growing sense of freedom and power.

HAND TO BODY Stroking and caressing the body is a natural progression from stroking the face, made possible by an increased sense of intimacy and trust.

MOUTH TO BREAST There's no mistaking this body language. The breasts are a prime sexual organ, and kissing or sucking here denotes acceptance of sexuality and possible arousal.

HAND TO GENITALS Genital touch signifies serious sexual intent. This means it needs to be sensitively timed in order to be fully acceptable to the other person.

GENITALS TO GENITALS This is the ultimate point of the touch cycle, denoting trust and openness. Intercourse is probably the prime way of giving and receiving love in stable, long-term relationships.

WHAT DRIVES US TO BE SEXUAL?

AT A PURELY BIOLOGICAL LEVEL, sex obviously exists for the continuation of the species. But there is certainly more to it than that. The question, minutely examined by the great psychologists of the last 100 years, is "what drives human beings to be sexual?" Inspired thinkers have come up with a selection of potential reasons, some of which have influenced generations of people.

SIGMUND FREUD (1856–1939) had a major influence on human sexuality in the last century.

Austrian psychoanalyst Sigmund Freud was probably the most influential of all the psychologists concerned with human sexuality in the early part of the 20th century, even though several of his theories have subsequently been disproved. He invented the idea of "drives" as something that compels people to behave in a certain way and believed that the primary source of human behaviour was the libido. In other words, he considered that we are driven by our sexuality and that it is relevant to all human achievements.

Balancing this is Freud's other theory that a healthy, mature personality is dominated by the "ego" – the "grown-up" part of a personality which has learned to make rational judgments instead of acting only on instinct as a child does. He believed, therefore, that we are driven to satisfy our sexual needs as a result of our libido but in a socially appropriate fashion as controlled by our ego.

Adler's theories

Alfred Adler (1870–1937) was a colleague of Freud, working in Vienna at the same time. He broke with Freud however because he did not believe that the sex drive was the primary one. He claimed that humans are social creatures born into a family group where they strive to feel of importance, and that it is this need for importance that is the primary drive. He asserted that there are at least three major life tasks in which humans need to succeed in order to feel important and complete – work; friendship; and love, intimacy, and marriage. Therefore, if you follow Adler's theory, you are driven to achieve satisfaction in sex and relationships – a different premise from the Freudian drive to satisfy your sexuality.

Behaviourist theories

From the mid-1930s onwards a school of thought developed that stated all human behaviour is strongly influenced by learning. These theorists do not deny the importance of biological drives but believe these drives are strongly directed by what they learn from those around. Where sex is concerned, behaviourists agree that humans are born with sexual drive but contend that the drive is expressed according to the environment they are exposed to.

Thus, they believe, people learn to be homosexual, heterosexual, or bisexual. They learn to be celibate, to restrict themselves to few partners, and to associate erotic sensation with certain sights or smells. Another theory is that children develop traits by being unconsciously rewarded for doing them. For example, it has been found that some mothers of transvestites reward their sons for dressing in girls' clothing. Nor is the avid learning phase of adolescence left out of the picture. Certain behaviourists believe that girls and boys are shaped by the opinions and behaviour of their friends.

The growth of sexology

Sexology is the scientific study of human sexuality and it is only during the last half of the 20th century that actual laboratory studies of sex were carried out. These were fascinating because they disproved some of the Freudian theories that had been so influential in their time.

Evolutionary psychology

Evolutionary ideas are the latest theories in sex psychology. The evolutionary belief is that we do what works best for the survival of the species. On an extremely basic level, if sex in the missionary position is the best way of doing sex for survival of the species, this is why it has survived so successfully today. There is also a theory that just as behaviour has survival value so too have many ideas. Ideas about sex are transmitted from generation to generation and are responsible for our sexual attitudes. You might believe, for example, that:

- Sex should be confined only to the partner you marry
- You shouldn't experience sex before the wedding

- Sex should be done in the privacy of the marital bed
- Sex is just one of many aspects of family life

All these ideas are very influential and possess great evolutionary value. They are all about ensuring that *your* line of descent, *your* children, and hopefully *their* children will carry your genes through from one generation to the next for as long as possible.

SEXFACTS

INFANTILE SEXUALITY

Freud was the first to assert that infants are sexual from birth. He argued that since we are born with erogenous zones, infants experience innocent sensuality. (NB: He did *not* mean infants are consciously sexual.)

HUMAN SEXUAL BEHAVIOUR

IT IS NATURAL to be curious about sex. Most of us like to know what other people do so that we can reassure ourselves that we are similar and therefore "normal", whatever that may mean. But how do we know what "normal" or "average" behaviour consists of? Where do we get this information from? The brief answer is from the sex specialists.

The sexologists of the 20th century have had a major impact on how we view ourselves. Their detailed research tells us about human sexual behaviour and, over the years, as they have altered and evolved the idea of what is normal, they have altered our ideas as well. For example, when Sigmund Freud (see p.18) asserted his theory of the female orgasm, stating that clitoral orgasms are "inferior" to vaginal ones, women felt that they were failing. It was only with further research, 50 years later, that we learned the clitoris played a key part in all orgasms and that any division laden with judgment, such as whether an orgasm was "superior" or "inferior", was not just erroneous but harmful. What follows here is a breakdown of the most salient research and theory by sexologists over the past 60 years.

The Kinsey Report

Zoologist Alfred Kinsey (1894–1956) was the first scientist to survey real human beings methodically and find out what they did sexually. Although he did not make laboratory measurements, such were the size and scope of his surveys of the US population in the 1940s that they constituted an invaluable part of our sexual knowledge. Kinsey shocked the middle-class English-speaking world

BRITISH SEX SURVEY

THE NATIONAL SURVEY of Sexual Attitudes and Lifestyles, conducted in 1994 and based on interviews with 18,876 men and women, established the following about sexual behaviour in Britain:

SEX FREQUENCY

The following measurements were taken over a four-week period:

- For women aged 20–29 and men aged 25–34, the maximum number of times people had sex was 5 times
- The numbers then gradually decline with age until for men aged 55–59 it was twice, while more than 50% of women in this age group had no sex

The maximum number of times someone had sex during that period was 130 times.

SEX PRACTICES

- The most frequent type of sex recorded was vaginal intercourse
- 75% experienced non-penetrative sex not leading to intercourse
- 70% had experienced oral sex
- Anal sex was reported by only 13.9% of men and 12.9% of women

HOMOSEXUALITY

- 6.1% of men had some homosexual experience
- Only 3.4% of women had any lesbian experience

This figure was considerably less than the Kinsey figure and is presently considered to be a more accurate statistic.

when his famous *Kinsey Report* went on sale in bookshops in 1948 and 1953. He stated:

- over 96 per cent of men and 85 per cent of women masturbated
- masturbation improved the eventual quality of married life
- women were capable of pleasure and orgasm, something which had previously been doubted
- 14 per cent of women were capable of having multiple orgasms
- pre-marital sex was common for both men and women
- 37 per cent of males had or will have had at least one homosexual experience during their lifetime

Kinsey's theories about sexual preference were also controversial. He saw sexuality as a sliding scale with homosexuality at one end, bisexuality in the middle, and heterosexuality at the other. Where you are placed depends on the number of sex acts you have had with men or women.

Masters and Johnson

Also controversial were US sexologists William Masters and Virginia Johnson who, in the 1950s, observed people having sex in their laboratory, wired up to record any body changes. It was the first time anyone had tried to discover what happens inside us during orgasm. They confirmed that:

- women could have multiple orgasms
- a man's sexual performance is not related to his penis size
- there is a distinct pattern to sexual response which they defined as excitement, orgasm, and resolution
- sexual response is remarkably similar for both sexes
- there was no evidence to support the Freudian theory that a vaginal orgasm is better than a clitoral one

The Hite Report

In 1974, US feminist Shere Hite brought out her controversial *Hite Report on Female Sexuality*. The fact

that gave courage to many women was her finding that although only 29 per cent of women were capable of experiencing orgasm regularly during intercourse, 82 per cent of women could do so through masturbation. The effect of this was for women to stop feeling pressurized over climaxing during intercourse, which up until then had been thought of as the "right" way for women to climax.

HISTORY FACTS

SEX VOLUNTEERS

Masters' early research was done on prostitutes, since it was so difficult to get other women to take part. He soon realized that prostitutes were not typical (their profession meant they were more easily aroused), so he hired Virginia Johnson to help him recruit "respectable" volunteers.

MALE AND FEMALE ATTITUDES TO SEX

SEX IS NOT JUST A PHYSICAL THING – it also takes place in the mind. Our bodies respond to physical sensation and pleasure, but without an emotional connection to sex we would not be human. It is generally acknowledged that emotional attitudes towards sex differ between men and women, but how do they vary, and why?

Male and female sexuality develops differently for the very obvious fact that male genitals are easily accessible while female genitals are hidden away. Little boys become familiar with genital sensation almost immediately after they are born. Quite unconsciously they rub and play with their penis and learn that the mere act of touch leads to sensuality. By the time they reach puberty, that rubbing and touching will result in orgasms. In most young men this process is simply a spontaneous physical event, which is not necessarily linked to a person.

Women, by virtue of having their genitals "hidden" in infancy, do not discover them as easily as boys. For this reason many tend not to experience genital sensuality until much later and, as a result, evolve a very different emotional attitude towards love and sex. The burgeoning

SEXFACTS

OBJECT FIXATION
Boys appear to be more susceptible to sensual emotion than girls, with the result that by far the greatest number of sexual fetishists are men. For young boys sexual arousal is often accidentally associated with an object, such as a high-heeled shoe, and this association then crops up again during adulthood.

AS A GENERAL RULE, women view sex as a means of expressing their love for their partner, and are less inclined to seek "no-strings" sex than men.

of female sexuality tends to happen during the teens, in some cases even as late as the early twenties. Since less genital exploration will have been experienced, the imagination tends to play a bigger part in sexual stimulation. This is not to say that all women fantasize but rather that most women associate the stirrings of sexuality with an interesting partner. In this major sense, therefore, female sexuality differs from male.

Self-exploration and stimulation

Many women only learn to masturbate well after entering their first sexual relationship. The main reason for this is that self-stimulation is generally regarded as unusual and undesirable for women, rather than natural and pleasurable. Frequently, this attitude needs to be "unlearned". Masturbation is regarded by sexologists and psychologists as an important part of human sexual development, and the lack of masturbation in earlier years may represent a retardation of sexual development. Fortunately, it is one that can be speedily made up (see pp.70–71).

Love and sex

Men seem to find it easier than women to divorce sex from love, probably as a result of their objective sexual development. Many men would agree that sex with love is far more rewarding and enjoyable than sex for sex's sake, but many can also derive great physical and emotional pleasure from "no-strings" sex. For women, sex generally tends to be experienced as an expression of love, first and foremost. Although some women are not averse to the occasional one-night stand, most find it less satisfying than sex with someone with whom they have built up an emotional bond. However, it is important to stress that attitudes to sex and the meanings we attach to sexual encounters vary greatly from one individual to another.

FREUD'S IMPACT

THE TEACHINGS of Sigmund Freud (see p.18) had a great impact on people. He claimed that women suffered from penis envy, that clitoral orgasms were inferior to vaginal ones, and that men could only feel confident by having sex with an ethically inferior woman. However, Masters and Johnson's physiological research in the 1960s and 1970s disproved these theories, and this helped to change women's beliefs about their sexuality.

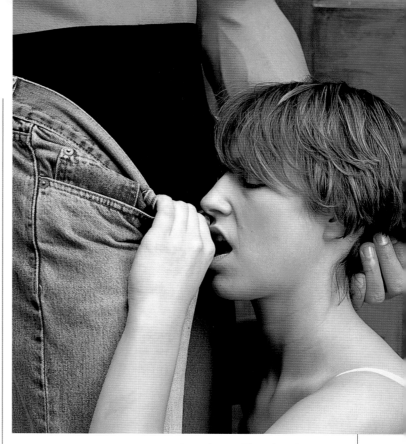

MEN ARE MORE LIKELY THAN WOMEN to seek sex without love. In extreme cases, some men can enjoy sex only with someone they barely know or may not like, yet cannot turn on to the person that they love (see p.41).

How sex differences affect relationships

When the different attitudes towards sex come together there are discrepancies, and misunderstandings can often result. Women eager for closeness may be dismayed by their man regarding the most intimate act of all as a type of mechanical release. Men, satisfied with the idea of "no-strings-attached" sensuality, may feel hampered and oppressed by a woman's need for intimacy. These differing approaches still cause problems within many male–female relationships, but fortunately attitudes are changing slowly.

Learning from each other

Today's generation of young men and women, making sexual relationships for the first time, come into a partnership with a much more realistic and "equal" view of the sexes than their forebears. Western men generally no longer believe women to be inferior, and are not perceived as "cissy" if they hug or embrace. The sexes can learn from each other – men can benefit from allowing the feminine side of their emotional approach to sex to flourish, while women can gain confidence by achieving assertiveness. Some of the most rewarding parts of long-term relationships lie in discovering each other's differences and gaining new views that will help you to better understand and appreciate the opposite sex.

INNATE SEX ROLE DIFFERENCES

EVERY INDIVIDUAL has unique qualities that are the result of his or her personality, upbringing, and culture. However, there are also certain innate qualities in men and women that are thought to be universal differences between the sexes. These divide into physical, mental, and behavioural differences.

Physical differences in the early years

There are obvious differences between the sexes, such as anatomy. But where the development of sexuality is concerned, hormones play the most important role. Until the sixth week after conception, the developing baby in the womb is female. It is at that point that a boy child's male hormones (androgens) kick in and begin the process of masculinizing the child. Those male hormones are not just responsible for the differences in anatomy, but also for the different growth of the brain, neuronal development, energy levels, and aggression. Boy babies who receive rather less of these androgens than usual have less obvious body development and, in later life, look physically immature, feel less sex drive, and may be late in starting their sex life.

Girl babies have less androgens and therefore feel the greater effect of the "female" hormones oestrogen and progesterone. Oestrogen in particular offers a feel-good effect and may be partially responsible for the "calmer" personalities that girls possess in contrast with boys.

Physical changes in adolescence

Girls develop physically earlier than boys. At the ages of eleven and twelve, most girls are taller than their male classmates and the first physical signs of womanhood begin to emerge. They also develop an emotional sexual maturity before their male classmates. When boys reach puberty,

LONG LEGS *are considered a major turn-on for men because males make a subconscious association between the childhood experience of looking up at an adult female's legs (which seem endless to a small boy) and an early flood of sexual emotion.*

some two or three years later, their bodies start to produce more testosterone – the hormone that promotes sexual development, and muscle and bone growth – and they become substantially sexually motivated. Often, teenage boys become consumed by the thought of sex.

This sex drive is reinforced by peer pressure, and young men often set out to lose their virginity at the earliest opportunity. At this stage in their lives, many young men see young women as sexual objects, desired only as a means to relieve sexual frustration and to gain admiration and respect from peers. Fortunately, this is a viewpoint that most men grow out of.

Mental differences

Studies have found that boys tend to possess more visual and spatial awareness than girls. This means that, in practice, they judge distance, direction, and even physical closeness better than women. However, 25 per cent of women share this visual/spatial ability.

Psychological surveys have proved that men are more likely to be turned on by what they see than women. Men tend to associate sexual turn-on with visual sights and objects. The theory is that this is due to a kind of mental conditioning from childhood, where an unconscious sexual emotion becomes associated with a simultaneous sight, texture, smell, or taste. For example, perhaps a man remembers experiencing an erection while sitting on a rubber mat in the bath as a child. The rubber becomes associated with the accidental sexual overtones experienced, and this impression remains into adulthood.

Many men and women may have minor fetishes of some sort, but because of their natural tendency to associate objects with sexual emotions, men are more likely to be fetishists than women (see pp.154–57).

WHEN THERE IS CONFLICT, men often react by turning away and refusing to speak about it. When this happens, a partner should gently encourage discussion of the issue, rather than reacting confrontationally in return.

Behavioural differences

According to renowned marital therapist Dr John Gottman, women are better at dealing with confrontation than men. In contrast, some men have a tendency to do something Gottman calls "stone-walling" when they are faced with certain situations. Instead of actually dealing with the issue in hand, they block off the problem, refuse to talk about it, or walk out of the room. Where a sex problem is concerned, this can be disastrous, because it is only by facing problems that solutions can be found. Virtually all of the many studies on sex difference demonstrate that men are more aggressive than women. This shows up as early as the age of two and it is seen in every culture throughout the world. Obviously, there are exceptions to these rules, and the two sexes can complement each other rather than experience conflict.

THE EMOTIONAL MENSTRUAL CYCLE

FROM PUBERTY ONWARDS, women start feeling emotions on a cyclical basis, in line with whichever hormone is in ascendance. Therefore, a woman's sex drive is directly affected by the phase her menstrual cycle is in. Although women vary considerably, many experience "highs" and "lows" at specific times:

- Week One - relaxed well-being and easy sexual desire.
- Week Two - similar to week one.
- Week Three - less interest in sex and less sense of well-being.
- Week Four - spiky emotions and pre-menstrual irritation, but prior to menses, acute sexuality.

LEARNED SEX ROLE DIFFERENCES

WHILE SOME DIFFERENCES between the sexes are innate, environmental factors such as family background, upbringing, and culture are extremely influential, and play a large part in shaping male and female sexual behaviour.

As children we learn from the adults around us that men and women are different – not just physically, but emotionally and behaviourally. We unconsciously take in that men and women bring very different roles to their loving. These learned differences later get reinforced through relationships with peers as we mature into sexual beings.

The relationship between men and women that you observe as a child will, unconsciously, contribute to the sexual being you are today. Think about the dynamics of these relationships and, whether you like it or not, you are probably also seeing the dynamics of how the sexes interrelate. For example, did your father behave in a domineering way towards your mother? Or perhaps your mother used to manipulate your father and wrap him around her little finger? The way adult couples around you behaved as sexual partners will affect the way you perceive males and females in the outside world, and they will be an important factor in the role you assign to yourself when you grow up and start to form sexual relationships yourself.

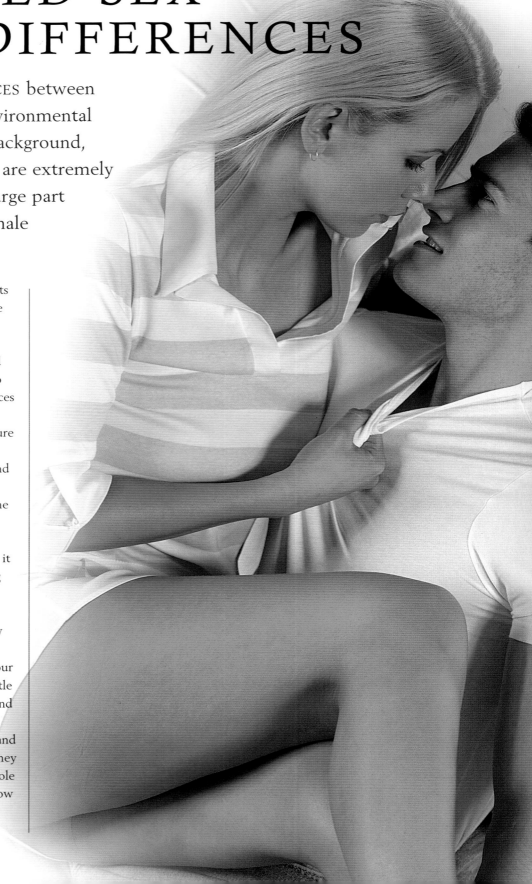

Taking the lead

Traditionally, men have been responsible for making the first social moves, such as asking a woman out on a first date, as well as the first sexual moves. Women, educated by their mother's example, traditionally took a more passive role, waiting to be asked. Today, although these passive/active roles are still in evidence, this behaviour pattern is in the process of change: women are beginning to make it clear to men how much they like them, and do occasionally ask men out and initiate sex. While many men appreciate this direct approach, there are still some who find it intimidating.

Media representation

Images from television and magazines perpetuate the idea of women as sexual objects. Women are encouraged to be beautiful, pouting, smouldering objects of desire, and are told that they need to be thin in order to be attractive to men – a particularly destructive message if your body shape is short and plump. Since few can match up to this "ideal", such images are extremely damaging to many women's self-esteem and body image, and have a very negative affect on their sexuality and relationships with men.

MANY YOUNG WOMEN today are comfortable making the first sexual move with a man, and men are frequently happy to be seduced.

Rather than allow yourself to feel inadequate, focus instead on your many positive attributes and make the most of what you have to offer (see pp.34–35).

Roles in bed

Ideally, a good sexual relationship will "grow" and develop in such a way that suits a particular couple. No one person will be responsible for initiating every move, and each partner will learn and follow from the other. This is probably true for about 50 per cent of established couples: US studies show that between 33 and 50 per cent of people are happy with their sex life within marriage. However, the remainder are not so satisfied, frequently because they follow the old, traditional pattern of behaviour in bed. This involves the woman expecting the man to "know" what to do and to "teach" her about lovemaking. It is important for both sexes to realize that even the best lover doesn't know what any one particular female is capable of in her sexual response without some guidance from the woman herself, nor

is it desirable or fair that the man should take sole responsibility for sexual success between a couple. Women need to know something about their own sexuality and to have some idea of what will please themselves as well as their man if sex is to be a rewarding and mutually pleasurable experience.

Female inhibition

Some women suffer from partial inhibition and find it hard to respond sexually. No one knows the cause of this, but it may be a result of conditioning. The women may believe that it is "bad" to feel sexual and so have unconsciously programmed themselves to cut out sexuality.

A smaller percentage of women suffer from an extreme form of inhibition (known as "global inhibition") and never feel sexy. Research suggests this is likely to be caused by a chemical imbalance, since the prescription drug phentolamine is often a successful antidote. This causes the part of the brain associated with inhibition to relax, giving sexual desire the chance to emerge.

SEX FACTS

SEX DRIVE DISCREPANCY

Men are thought to be at the height of their sex drive between 18 and 25 years old, while women often don't reach a sexual peak until their late twenties or early thirties. Only when people are in their sixties or seventies do the two patterns of sexuality converge. Some primitive cultures encourage young men to marry older women purely to combat this discrepancy. In the West, however, where youth and beauty are closely associated and generally highly prized by males, this is uncommon.

INTIMATE RELATIONSHIPS

TRUE INTIMACY IS NOT JUST about doing anything you dream about in bed and knowing it will be okay with your partner. Intimacy involves a special feeling of comfort and awareness between you and your lover – you feel closer to each other than you do to anyone else. This doesn't mean that you will never have difficult patches, but intimacy will help you deal with dilemmas.

Of course we achieve intimacy of sorts with close friends. Friends may speak freely, be physically close, spend hours together, and gain emotional satisfaction from each other's company without being sexual. The sort of intimacy we develop with friends from childhood onwards might be seen as a forerunner for that later intimacy that you anticipate with a partner. It is not just fulfilling in its own right; it serves as a kind of trial run for what will hopefully be the closest of all relationships.

Intimacy with your lover

Sexual intimacy takes a relationship that special step further. It involves knowing that you can make any sexual move and your partner will understand and accept it. Sexual intimacy is not something that you instantly and automatically acquire when you meet Mr or Ms Right. It is closely linked to the overall trust that is gradually built up in a relationship. The nature of our individual sexual intimacy is also linked to our background.

Intimacy in childhood – be it from parents, grandparents, foster parents – is very important, as it influences our later behaviour. This is because we get our ideas of intimacy from the people we have been especially close to. If you have parents who never stop kissing and cuddling, for example, then that is how you will spontaneously behave yourself.

Then of course, intimacy will be directly affected by the kind of person your partner is and what attitude he or she brings to the bedroom. If your partner is terrified of commitment and makes this clear by leading a very separate life from you, you may feel rejected and find it impossible to be as loving as you would like to be. Interestingly, if your partner is mad about you but you find this attention smothering, you may be the one to back off even though you are in love.

When intimacy goes wrong

One of the mistakes couples make is to think that a lack of interest in sex is caused by problems within the relationship. For example, the wife whose husband stops making love and is suddenly unable to communicate might be forgiven for interpreting this loss of intimacy as an indication that he is having an affair. She may assume

ENCOURAGING INTIMACY

GIVE AND RECEIVE love by kissing and cuddling, and don't assume sex is the only sure indication that you are loved. Remember that people who feel stressed or depressed stop being sexy. If outside events have affected your partner, don't assume that you are no longer loved.

ALWAYS ENCOURAGE the other person and never criticize. If you are feeling depressed but are unsure why, take a look at your partner and see if you are picking up on his or her problems. If one of you is feeling down, this mood can seep across to the other, so identify who the strong feelings belong to.

SUGGEST SOME practical options for your partner if he or she is having difficulty resolving a problem. Although we all have to take responsibility for ourselves, we can also all do with help along the way. This aspect of intimacy will always form part of a strong relationship.

that he has switched his intimacy to someone else. Yet a reality check may disclose that this husband is struggling with various problems at work and is unconsciously switching all his concentration to agonizing about the situation. Stress can use up every jot of loving attention, but a partner should not confuse this with a loss of love.

SEX FACTS

MARRIAGE AND SEX

A study carried out by the University of Chicago into American social and sexual behaviour shows that married people have sex significantly more often than single people. The study, which focused on 18 to 59 year olds, showed that 86% of married men and women have sex at least once a week, compared to 52% of single men and 44% of single women.

Intimacy can fluctuate

In a relationship, feelings of intimacy can wax and wane and this is perfectly normal. Partners are separate and different individuals, and this is something that people often forget when they have enjoyed the closeness of the first flush of love. One of the greatest lessons couples need to learn is to let the other person be different. This is surprisingly difficult to do – tolerating differences can be one of the most mature actions any human being makes. Lesson number one is not to expect your partner to feel exactly the same way as you do.

However, it is never a good idea to let something that actively worries you in your relationship continue for too long. The longer a difficulty persists, the harder it will be to put right. So even if tackling the problem only involves talking, it's worth doing. But if you are downhearted about an ongoing problem, take heart from the

fact that couples can be seriously estranged for years and then resurrect those all important emotions – love, affection, and a sex life.

Dealing with problems

There are some practical ways of sorting out loss of intimacy issues.

- Don't panic if sex suddenly becomes a no-no, but do try and find out why.
- Don't confuse sex acts with being loved. Sex is not the only activity to confer the feeling of love.
- Don't shrink from confrontation if something is seriously wrong.
- Try to talk about things. Give your partner a platform for disclosing his or her feelings.
- Be prepared to make some changes if your partner makes it clear these are necessary. But don't make so many that you feel compromised – just enough to indicate that you care enough to do something that is hard for you.

CASUAL RELATIONSHIPS

NOT EVERYONE DESIRES the depth and closeness that a serious relationship requires. Some people may prefer less serious sexual encounters, which fit well into the busy lifestyle many of us now subscribe to. In casual relationships your partner is not your number one priority – he or she may take second place to a career, or you may want to enjoy a series of relationships with other people before settling down for good.

It takes particularly strong individuals to cope with knowing that they do not come first with their lover. On the other hand, it may also be particularly needy people who opt for such casual status on the grounds that this is better than no relationship at all. There are also some individuals who live so much in the present that they value what they have got and are happy for things to remain as they are, however part-time their relationship may be. Not surprisingly, casual relationships have less likelihood of survival than more committed ones. However, relationships can and do change – your partner may wake up one morning and suddenly see that a career isn't everything and that he or she would like to spend more time with you, and married men and women regularly leave their partners to commit to a previously casual relationship.

When career is top priority

A common scenario today for both men and women is when the career comes first and there is little time left over to spend on the seriousness of maintaining a love affair. Love and sex get confined to the weekend, or to casual meetings in clubs, perhaps with someone in the same situation. Many careerists subscribe to dating organizations, which offer instant "friends" and potential sex partners on the grounds that it cuts out time-consuming groundwork.

When time is short, any relationship development has to happen fast – information is exchanged quickly, and the action is somehow concentrated. This can be fantastically exciting, and can also be poignant when you discover someone really attractive but whom you will never know any better than at that particular moment. A weekend together can possess the thrill of the new mixed in with the frustration and sometimes exquisite pain of knowing you may never experience such intensity again. What tends to happen long-term in such relationships is that eventually someone shows up who is just too good to lose. When that happens, one person often makes massive life adjustments and does his or her best to fit in around the other's career.

Extra-marital affairs

If you happen to be of a "certain age" and without a mate, there tend to be very few unmarried men or women left over as suitable partners. As a result, you may find yourself becoming involved with someone who is already married, whether you planned to or not. Very few people actively choose to be the "other" man or woman, yet there is an ever-increasing number of men and women whom this actually suits.

For all the pain involved, such as never having a partner around at the weekend, or missing the intimacy that everyday living together brings, there are also huge advantages. It means you only ever see each other at your best, and, as a result of the valuable quality time you have to yourself in between visits, you particularly appreciate your mate on the happy occasions you do get together. In addition, you get more time to see friends, you don't get consumed by family life, and the arrangement gives you more time and energy to devote to your career. Although extra-marital affairs vary in duration, the average term for

such a romance is around three years, even if in many cases they can last considerably longer. Interestingly, the divorce figures are quite high for couples who marry after such a long time semi-together.

When lust takes over

Hormones have a habit of turning you on at certain times, sometimes inappropriately and in spite of yourself. This often happens in social circumstances, where alcohol acts as a major influence and reduces your inhibitions, or with a colleague at work with whom you have been working very closely. In addition, it has been proved that traumatic encounters have a way of leading to sex. Certain shared experiences, such as sitting next to each other during a flying emergency or being stuck in a lift together, can be enough to make complete strangers fall on each other after the event and make mad passionate love. It appears that sexual desire is the natural reaction to the adrenaline aroused by these abnormal circumstances.

Whatever the circumstances of your sudden and unexpected lust, try not to feel mortified after the event, particularly if no one has been hurt in the process. Just put it down to experience and move on.

GROUND RULES

IF YOU WANT TO SURVIVE a casual relationship with your ego intact, there are a few general points that you should bear in mind:

1 Learn to live happily inside yourself without depending on one particular person. Measure yourself by how good you feel here and now, not by how the other person relates to you.

2 Take care not to crowd your partner. If he or she doesn't respond to a telephone call or e-mail, just view it as a busy time rather than a disaster.

3 Recognize the times when the other person is in particular need of attention and make plans to accommodate them whenever possible so that you might offer it.

4 Think positively about your casual relationship and concentrate on enjoying other aspects of your life, such as your family, friends, work life, and pursuing other interests.

LEARN TO LOVE YOURSELF

WE TEND TO ATTRACT the people we think we deserve. This means that if you like yourself, you're in a better position to attract someone who respects you; conversely, if you don't like yourself, you're more likely to hitch up with someone who doesn't respect you either, because you unknowingly project a poor self-image. Love yourself, and others will follow your lead.

So where does our unconscious self-image come from? Psychologist Alfred Adler (see p.18) said our beliefs are formed within, and influenced by, our immediate family. By six years of age, we have formed the basis of our entire belief system. This includes the moral values we possess and what we expect from close relationships.

The snag about forming this belief system so young is that we often end up with ideas that may be wrong or misdirected. Yet for the rest of our lives, we will be trying to adhere to them. These beliefs will influence us in the way we relate sexually: whether we are close or distant; whether we are expressive or sullen. For example,

if your parents enjoyed a love match, you will probably expect to experience the same in your own relationships. If you grew up in a family where shows of emotion were discouraged, you may find it difficult to express yourself. Or if a sibling constantly belittled you when you were young, you may grow up feeling unattractive, and it will be hard to overcome this poor self-image. Understanding your beliefs does not automatically rid you of them. But it does put you in a position to alter your behaviour so that you achieve a different result.

Self-confidence for women

In sexuality discussion groups for women, it is often found that there is a common denominator in the

characters of the women attending. This is that they are singularly lacking in self-confidence when it comes to sex, and that this is linked with a likelihood that they have never masturbated.

One of the lessons women learn by attending the group is how to masturbate (see pp.70–71), on the grounds that masturbation is an extremely pleasurable activity in its own right; it teaches women about their own sexual response, which in turn brings them confidence; and it allows women to take the newly discovered knowledge of how to reach climax into their relationships with lovers, thus offering themselves a much greater likelihood of climaxing during sexual intercourse. It may sound far-fetched to link such a physical activity to feelings of confidence, but clinical experience shows that women who learn how to climax feel better about themselves than they have done for years.

LISTING *exercises*

BELOW ARE THREE EXERCISES that will help you clarify your own personal beliefs. It is important to understand that you are NOT limited by these beliefs. Once you have recognized and understood them, you can consciously act differently, in order to change patterns of behaviour and achieve different outcomes.

Stepping stones
This exercise helps you to work out where your beliefs originate from and which member of your family might have been most responsible for influencing you.

1. List ten beliefs on separate pieces of paper and put them on the floor. These must refer to your personal life, for example, "I should remain a virgin until I get married."
2. Walk over to the belief you think you might have the most problem fulfilling.
3. Ask yourself: "Where did this belief come from? Was it from a member of my family? Is this belief relevant to me?"
4. Repeat with the other nine statements.

Sexual priorities
This exercise will help you to understand your attitudes to sex.

1. List ten points stating why sex is important to you in order of priority. The following ideas might feature on the list:

sexual release; closeness and intimacy; discovering your own sexual nature; loss of virginity; an end to masturbation.
2. Place the points in order of difficulty of achievement. Starting with the easiest, consider whether it is a realistic priority or whether it is something you are conditioned to believe. If you feel it is realistic, then see how you could consciously work towards it.
3. Examine all the subsequent priorities in the same way.

Family constellations
This exercise helps you pinpoint family influences. Imagine that you are a star and your relations are neighbouring stars.

1. Place the family members and friends who most influence you close to your star and those with less influence, farther away.
2. Think about the character traits of those you have placed close to you. Ask yourself how these people have influenced you.

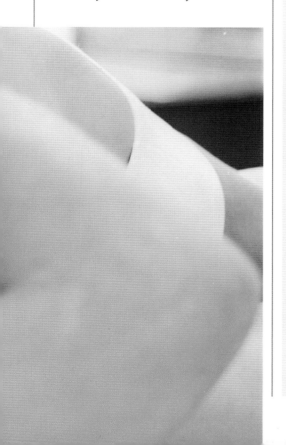

WHEN YOU ARE HAPPY with yourself and the way you look, you will naturally project a confident, relaxed self-image, and this is very attractive to others.

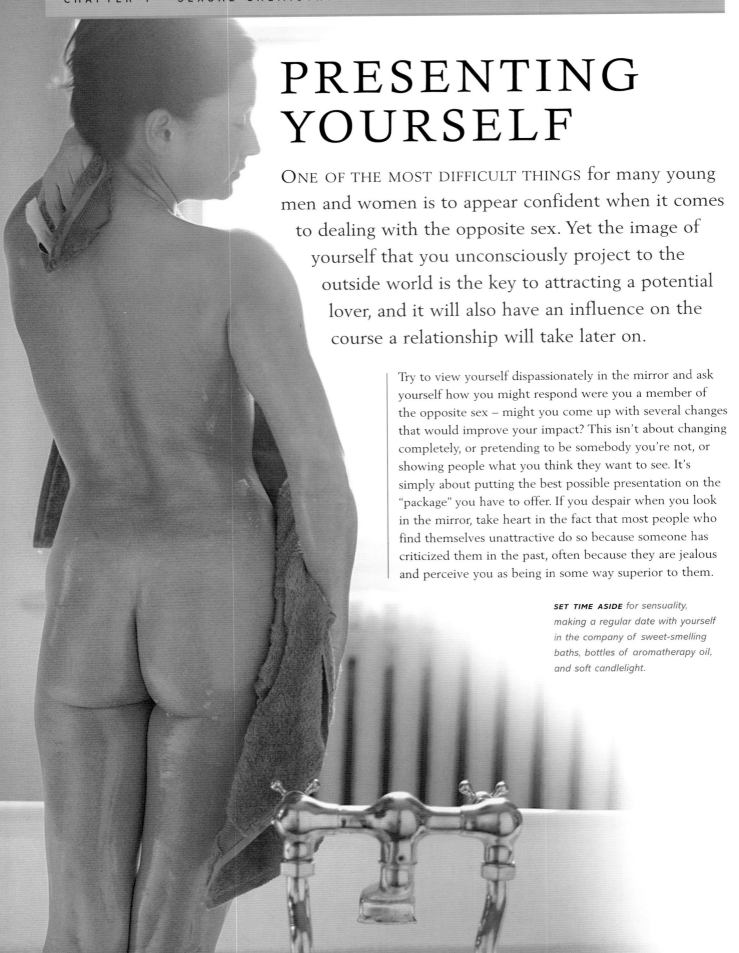

PRESENTING YOURSELF

ONE OF THE MOST DIFFICULT THINGS for many young men and women is to appear confident when it comes to dealing with the opposite sex. Yet the image of yourself that you unconsciously project to the outside world is the key to attracting a potential lover, and it will also have an influence on the course a relationship will take later on.

Try to view yourself dispassionately in the mirror and ask yourself how you might respond were you a member of the opposite sex – might you come up with several changes that would improve your impact? This isn't about changing completely, or pretending to be somebody you're not, or showing people what you think they want to see. It's simply about putting the best possible presentation on the "package" you have to offer. If you despair when you look in the mirror, take heart in the fact that most people who find themselves unattractive do so because someone has criticized them in the past, often because they are jealous and perceive you as being in some way superior to them.

SET TIME ASIDE for sensuality, making a regular date with yourself in the company of sweet-smelling baths, bottles of aromatherapy oil, and soft candlelight.

LOOK YOUR BEST

YOU WILL FEEL SEXIER if you believe you look your best. Take a look at yourself and ask what sort of changes you should make, if any. If you're planning to revamp your image, do it gradually over a period of weeks.

1 If you take care over your clothes you send out the message that you care enough about yourself to look good. Select the most flattering styles, opting for those that suit your colouring and body shape. If you usually dress in a restrained, fairly formal way, try choosing sexier styles or liven up your outfit with jazzy accessories.

2 Consider how to make the most of your facial features. Women might make an appointment with a beauty consultant to get advice on the best haircut or make-up scheme. Men with a beard or moustache may think about shaving them off or trimming them differently in order to draw attention to their cheekbones.

3 Invest in some sexy underwear: even if no one else knows about it, this can work wonders for your sense of being a sexual person.

4 Join an exercise class, or take up some form of sport. You will begin to feel far more confident and will soon see results.

Pamper yourself

If you pay a lot of sensual attention to your body you begin to feel like a sensual being, and unconsciously you will begin to communicate this to others. Men particularly may need this experience. There's something about a typically masculine upbringing that teaches sensuality is not for boys. But this is quite wrong – sensuality is for everyone.

Your body talks

We are usually unaware of the fact that during the time our mouths open and conversation flows, our bodies also send out small, almost imperceptible signals, which give the other person a very clear idea of how we are feeling. Using this body language to your advantage can make you seem more attractive, and help let a potential partner know that you are interested in him or her. You should always bear in mind that in some environments flirtatious behaviour is inappropriate, and can even be offensive. The office is an obvious example of this, but so too are lectures, public spaces, or public transport. If in doubt, always act with restraint and respect.

Send out positive signals

You may naturally be a little shy and defensive when you meet someone new. If you watch yourself closely, you'll notice that your arms and legs may be crossed, and you may even have turned sideways-on, to avoid facing the other person directly. These are barrier signals that make the other person feel unwelcome and uneasy.

To encourage a new friendship, adopt a more open stance – uncross your legs, drop your arms at your side, and stand with your shoulders back. Making your body language open and receptive gives the message that you are interested in the other person. Lean forward slightly when talking and don't be afraid to show affection with your body language once you know each other better. A hug on greeting or an arm around the shoulders are ways of projecting the warmth that you feel and will make the other person feel welcome and at ease in your company.

SEX FACTS

EYE CONTACT

Maintaining eye contact is a powerful indication of sexual attraction and can also increase sexual arousal. Research shows that when men are shown near-identical pictures of the same woman, they always choose the one in which the pupils have been widened artificially over the ones that haven't.

MEETING A NEW PARTNER

MEETING PEOPLE IS NOT ALWAYS EASY, so where can you go to find that great love of your life? Ideally we'd all prefer to be swept off our feet and know straight away we'd met "the one", but it doesn't usually happen like that. Sometimes you need to be proactive and to "plan" to meet new people by putting yourself in the right place at the right time.

We tend to make friends and lovers most easily when we're young, mainly because the majority of young people move around in a crowd. School, college, and local friendship circles are all avenues for love. However, when we're young early love affairs tend not to last too long. And by the time we're ready to move on, the cosy, compact community of young friends may well have dispersed. This means that the older we become the harder it tends to be to meet new lovers in a natural, spontaneous manner.

In addition, there are always a few incredibly shy people who long for love but who have been unable as yet to bring themselves to make the social moves necessary in order to date.

If you find yourself in a situation where you're looking for love but you don't necessarily meet enough new people – or the right types of people for you – try to think of meeting new partners and dating as a social system. You will need to make a conscious effort to think about where to meet a potential new partner – remember, this planning in advance does not in any way diminish the quality of the new relationship if and when you form one.

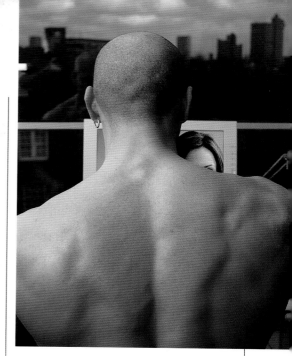

Where to meet people

Parties are frequently a good way to meet people – it's through these kinship groups that you will often meet other like-minded people. If there aren't many parties, then you could go to pubs and clubs instead. Get used to initiating conversations, but don't take it badly if someone doesn't seem interested. It may take several attempts before a person recognizes you as being "special", particularly in a noisy environment.

Where you choose to seek your meetings will obviously influence the type of people you are likely to meet. For example, if you decide to frequent the local bars and pubs then you will meet other people for whom bar or pub activities are a focus. If, on the other hand, you choose to go to the social occasions at the nearest institution of scientific learning, then you will meet mostly intellectual types. It makes sense, therefore, to spend a little time on working out just who ideally might suit you – the bar and club scene isn't for everyone, and you're more likely to find a suitable partner if you meet people with interests similar to your own.

Agencies, classifieds, and the Internet

If you don't know where to start with finding a mate, or live miles from a town or city, a dating agency would take some of the hard work out of the meeting process. Most local newspapers carry classified ads for such agencies and there is usually a variety to choose from. Do some research here so that you opt for the agency most likely to suit you.

Classified advertising columns also carry advertisements from individuals. Sometimes listed as "Lonely Hearts", these are also found in most local newspapers as well as in regional and national magazines and newspapers.

The Internet is packed with online dating agencies. To access some of these, type "matchmaker" into your search engine. A lot of sexual services will appear, but there are also

PEOPLE CAN and do meet in chat rooms on the Internet and then after a while decide to meet, sometimes leading to a serious relationship. If you are lonely this can be a real lifesaver.

relationship groups for men and women wanting to short-cut the dating process. Please be aware that the virtual person you are "dating" may turn out to be quite different from the person he or she claims to be.

Develop conversational skills

Some people find it easier than others to communicate well and to lure a mate with their deft verbal skills. Life coaches generally agree that the individual who shows interest by asking questions, listening carefully to the replies, giving feedback, and showing concern will do best at making new friends. If you are shy or a poor communicator you might need to practise your conversational skills by trying out a few simple techniques with a sympathetic friend (see p.38). Take heart in the fact that very shy people can and do learn how to navigate the reefs of dating.

To develop empathy, try to put yourself in the place of the other person during a conversation and concentrate on what they are thinking rather than what you are feeling.

DATING TIPS

IT'S OF PARAMOUNT IMPORTANCE to feel safe in both a physical and an emotional sense when dating, so bear in mind a few basic rules:

1 Be selective in your choice of hunting ground and match your target to your goal, particularly if you're looking for a mature partner and have long-term plans in mind.

2 You can only make your best impression if you feel comfortable, so plan to meet your date at a place where you feel relaxed.

3 For safety reasons, don't give your address to someone you don't know, make sure that you can get home safely at the end of the evening, and tell a friend where you are going. Alternatively, take a mate along with you to begin with.

4 Make sure that you listen as well as talk when you're on a date. Conversational skills and empathy are both important when it comes to attracting a partner. Remember to ask questions to indicate you're interested in knowing more.

5 Take things slowly and remember the golden rule: if you're not comfortable with something then don't do it.

EARLY RELATIONSHIP ISSUES

IN THE FIRST FLUSH of sexual passion, it's easy to overlook the key issues that influence a relationship. Most of us in the early stages of a relationship don't think seriously about the future because we're so busy having a glorious time in the present. But many of us are looking for Mr or Ms Right, even if we don't know it, so understanding in advance the unexpected emotional dilemmas that occur at this early stage can definitely help.

Take a look at the way the two of you communicate. Does one of you do more talking than the other? Does the other pick up the tiny clues that you drop into the conversation? Do you feel listened to? And do you honestly think you listen to your partner? These details are important because they demonstrate what joy or frustration you may meet in the future should the two of you become a serious item.

IDEAL COMMUNICATION

WHEN ONE PERSON TALKS it is vital for good communication that the other listens and shows the person who is talking that he or she is being heard. The ideal conversation goes as follows:

1 One talks and the other listens. The listener must never interrupt and must let the talker finish.

2 The listener gives feedback in the form of nodding in agreement and occasionally muttering comments to demonstrate to the talker that he or she is listening attentively.

3 When the talker appears to have finished, the listener may ask for more information and offer comments or constructive suggestions.

4 The talker answers any questions and responds to the listener's comments and feedback in a positive way.

5 Both parties must carry out any actions they have promised to undertake in the course of the discussion.

Personal space

If you have been used to independence and living on your own, it sometimes feels claustrophobic to have someone always breathing down your neck, however much you may feel for him or her. Potentially good relationships have fallen by the wayside because one person unconsciously "smothered" the other. Be aware that not everyone wants the same degree of closeness and tread accordingly. Build in days on your own, or days with other friends. And structure your life so that this happens, planning it in advance. Don't ever feel ashamed of wanting to spend time purely on your own: you are entitled to your personal privacy.

Balancing love and work

Time is always an issue in the early days of falling in love. Part of you wants to be welded to your lover's side, while the other part knows you must devote yourself to work. Finding the right balance becomes a personal struggle, a situation that can benefit from actual time-tabling. This may sound artificial but it is no different from running a straightforward diary. If you schedule in certain nights of the week or a particular day over the weekend devoted to a partner, you can feel fine about the times when you prefer to work hard. Most people find that as the relationship progresses, they want to move in together because this allows them more time together in a busy working life.

Insecurity and jealousy

Feelings of insecurity or even jealousy (an extreme form of insecurity) can be common in new relationships. The solutions are to ask for a great deal of reassurance, promises of fidelity, and then the actual experience of fidelity itself, so that you can build up feelings of trust in the other person. If you don't get such reassuring behaviour your relationship may not be worth keeping. But bear in mind that partners often experiment with others at the beginning of a relationship before truly settling down.

PATHOLOGICAL JEALOUSY

THIS IS WHERE JEALOUSY receives no cause from a partner's behaviour but the jealous person projects his or her paranoid suspicions onto a faithful lover and cannot see that there is no foundation for them. It is an obsessive disorder, based on a paranoia usually stemming from an insecure childhood, and can be treated with counselling, anti-depressants, or anti-anxiety preparations.

WHAT DO YOU WANT FROM A RELATIONSHIP?

POSSESSING WIDELY DIFFERENT EXPECTATIONS of a close relationship can act like a trip-wire. One way of understanding your expectations is to look at your own family and question if you are hoping for something similar or different. If your partner does the same you can compare notes and get an idea of where dangerous waters lie!

Monogomy

In the Western world, monogamy – literally, a relationship with one person – is the accepted form of a legitimate sexual relationship. In actual fact, we have graduated to become a society that subscribes to serial monogamy – most of us have only one partner at a time but many of us go on to change partners as we grow older.

Multiple sexual relationships

Many people consider that humans are not naturally monogamous and that monogamy puts an unnatural strain on individuals. In the US and Europe, swingers change partners for recreation at parties or at clubs (see pp.158–59). Some men and women cope with the strain of monogamy

---

HISTORYFACTS

THE MORMONS

In 1847, the US Mormon leader Brigham Young (see right) led the migration to Utah, where he founded Salt Lake City, the world capital of the Mormon Church. Mormon marriages consisting of one man and many wives still exist in the US, albeit rarely these days, since President Abraham Lincoln declared plural marriages illegal in 1862.

SEXUAL SPLITTING

SEXUAL SPLITTING IS A CONDITION in which a person is unable to make the link between love and sex and polarizes relationships, categorizing them as sexual or non-sexual.

Some people are unable to turn on to their loved partner even though they want to, yet manage to enjoy great sex with someone they may not know or like. Perhaps they learned something disturbing about love and sex in childhood and have separated the "dangerous" sexuality off from any person who gets close to them.

   Some men manage the split by turning close relationships into "pure" ones and sexual relationships into "dirty" ones, a condition known by therapists as the "Madonna and Whore syndrome". A classic example is a man who puts his wife on a pedestal and sees her as too "good" to enjoy exciting sex, but indulges in creative, exciting sex with another woman. This has nothing to do with the women's behaviour and occurs only because the man needs to view them in this way. Therapists can do much to treat splitting.

A MISTRESS OR PROSTITUTE may satisfy a man's need to have "naughty" sex without emotional attachment.

by "sexual splitting" (see above). Some muslim countries in various parts of the world still follow the practice of one man taking up to four wives. For practical purposes, this means the wives must learn to tolerate each other and subsequently the term "sister–wife" has been developed to describe the relationship between such multiple wives.

Sexual friendship

Not everyone falls in love. Some people feel passionately about preserving their own lifestyle and freedom. This doesn't mean that they can't enjoy sex or have affectionate caring friendships. Many people have sex with friends on the grounds that this is a really pleasant thing to do but does not involve any serious commitment. As long as both partners feel like this, it's a good working compromise. Problems only surface when one partner wants a lot more but has little likelihood of getting it.

Singles marriage

Certain young men and women feel very possessive indeed of their lover and certainly do not want to find out that their partner is dating someone else. Yet these same people may also have a lot of investment in maintaining their own home. A young parent, for example, may not want to experience the upheaval of moving to live with a new partner. A committed careerist may be certain that the job

comes first. These situations do not mean that such people are heartless, but they do need to juggle love, friendship, and work in a way that has never quite happened in history before. Today, we see men and women living in separate households but who are still totally committed to one another. They may even be married, but see each other on certain agreed occasions.

Relationship contracts

Not everyone wants traditional marriage, feeling it to be an outdated concept. But most people do want to know where they stand, both with a partner and the law in the event of break-up or death. Relationship contracts, drawn up between two parties stipulating various agreements and then checked by a lawyer, may go some way to prove any intentions. It's also a good idea to draw up a will at this stage. Some countries ratify pre-nuptial agreements where, in the case of the wealthy, both parties agree prior to marriage to financial and property splits in the event of a break-up. In the UK, however, all contracts between parties are nullified on marriage so any such agreement could only be made after the event.

   Some couples make mini domestic contracts where they stipulate who does the washing-up or who owns the piano. These have no standing in law but are useful because the act of drawing them up often clarifies any expectations.

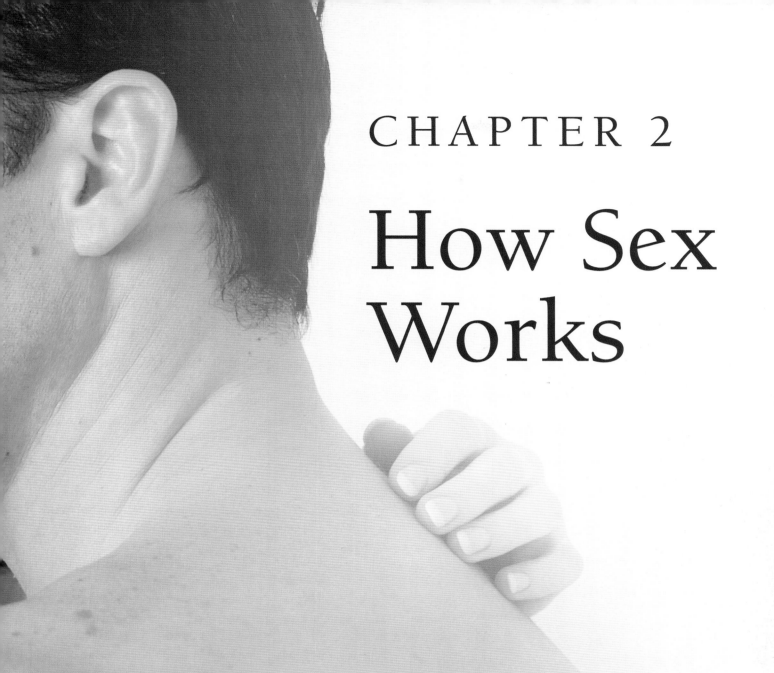

CHAPTER 2

How Sex Works

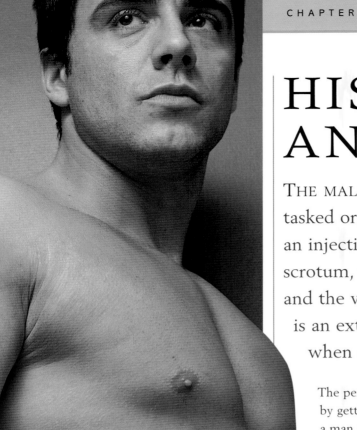

HIS SEXUAL ANATOMY

THE MALE GENITALS consist of the penis, a multi-tasked organ that enables urine excretion and provides an injection-method of creating new life, and the scrotum, which contains two testes, the epididymis, and the vas deferens. As all men will know, the penis is an extremely sensitive part of the body which, when stimulated, provides fabulous sensation.

The penis functions sexually by getting an erection. When a man thinks a sexy thought, spongy pockets of tissue in the penis fill with blood, making it strong and firm enough to be used for penetration (see p.89).

Stimulation of the erect penis usually results in orgasm, which is virtually always accompanied by ejaculation. Most men think that orgasm and ejaculation are the same thing. It may come as a surprise to hear that, in fact, these are separate processes and that some men are thought to be able to experience multiple orgasms without ejaculation taking place (see p.96).

The sperm factory

The epididymis is a kind of pocket area on the testes which holds sperm as the testes produce them. When a man becomes sexually aroused, millions of sperm are carried via the vas deferens, a fibro-muscular tube, to a storage chamber just behind the bladder (the seminal vesicle), where they wait for ejaculation. At the point of ejaculation, the sperm merge with seminal fluid (manufactured in the prostate gland) to form semen, which is expelled through the penis (via the urethra) out of the body. Nature of course intended that it should be conveyed directly into the vagina so that the human race continues. However, many of us may prefer to

---

PENILE HEALTH

ONE OF THE MOST common anxieties of boys during puberty concerns the appearance of small bumps that look like spots on their penis or foreskin. The sufferers often think that they may have mysteriously acquired a venereal disease, yet in most cases the spots are normal sebaceous glands on the genitals.

If you have any concerns regarding any aspect of penile health, consult your doctor or a genito-urinary clinic (see p.180).

THE SEMINAL FACTS

The amount of semen ejaculated varies from between 1 and 6 millilitres (0.03 and 0.2 fluid ounces), which is the equivalent of about a teaspoonful. If there is repeated ejaculation, the amount of semen that is produced diminishes each time.

prevent conception by using a barrier contraceptive to restrict the passage of sperm (see p.185).

Penile appearance

Penises vary greatly between individuals, yet many men are unhappy about the way their penis looks, which in turn can affect their confidence and sexual response. Bear in mind that the size of your penis has nothing to do with your virility or skill as a lover, and that the shape can be highly variable. However, if the penis becomes increasingly curved over a period of time you should seek medical advice, since it may indicate the onset of Peyronie's disease.

Penis-centred psychology

Males tend to feel comfortable with their sexual response from an early age, mainly because their genitals are so easily accessible. As children they get used to fondling themselves, and by the time they reach puberty, sexual excitement and release are familiar processes that have all happened independent of a partner. For this reason, men usually associate good sex with their penis. Women frequently discover their sexuality later, often with a partner, and often associate sex with a relationship.

MALE SEXUAL ANATOMY

THE INTERNAL SEX ORGANS consist of spongy tissue, which fills with blood and causes an erection, and the testicles, epididymis, vas deferens, prostate gland, seminal vesicles, and urethra, which together cause ejaculation (see pp.88–89).

HIS INTERNAL ANATOMY

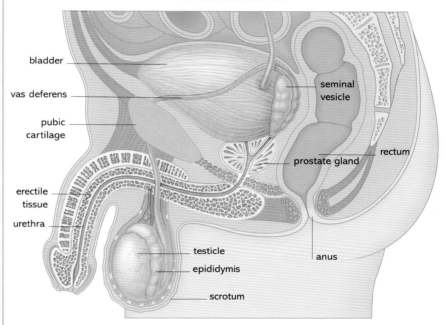

bladder
vas deferens
pubic cartilage
erectile tissue
urethra
seminal vesicle
rectum
prostate gland
testicle
epididymis
anus
scrotum

PENIS STRUCTURE

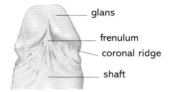

glans
frenulum
coronal ridge
shaft

PENISES can differ greatly in size, shape, and colour. However, all share a common structure. The most sensitive areas are the glans (head), the frenulum (the line along the shaft), and the coronal ridge (the area just below and around the head).

CIRCUMCISED OR UNCIRCUMCISED?

SOME MEN HAVE THEIR FORESKIN REMOVED in an operation known as circumcision, usually carried out for religious or health reasons. Many people feel that circumcision affects a man's sexual response, while others believe this to be a misconception.

THE FORESKIN on an uncircumcised penis covers and protects the glans. After the foreskin has been removed, the glans is permanently exposed.

foreskin surrounds glans

glans is exposed

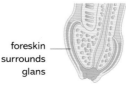

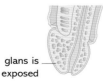

UNCIRCUMCISED

CIRCUMCISED

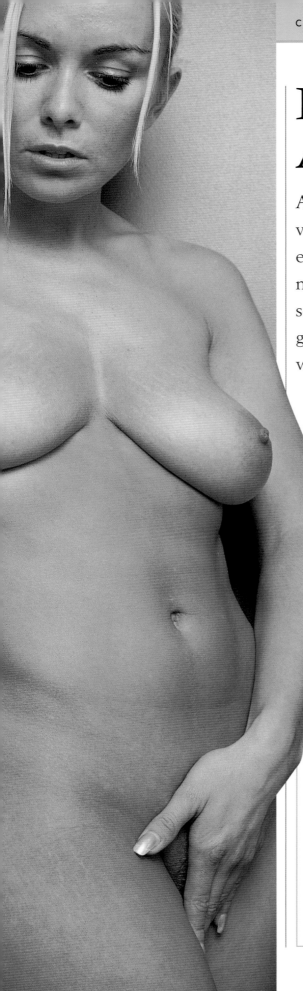

HER SEXUAL ANATOMY

A WOMAN'S GENITALS, known collectively as the vulva, consist of the clitoris, the labia, and the vaginal entrance. Although they look very different from a man's sex organs, recent research has proved what scientists have long suspected – male and female genitals work in a very similar way when aroused. The whole area is highly sensitive to physical stimulation.

The visible folds of skin known as the labia, or "lips", have several functions. Perhaps most importantly, they protect the extremely sexually sensitive clitoris, the vaginal orifice, and the urethra, all of which are hidden away beneath the folds. Another possible purpose dates back to an earlier stage of evolution, when human beings were primates – the labia probably acted as a signal that a female was sexually interested. That is because the labia grow bigger and flush red when the owner is sexually aroused. In addition, the labia also act as a pathway to guide the inexperienced male to the entrance of the vagina.

Labia shapes are highly variable. Some are long and tent-like, while others are barely discernible. The shape is generally characteristic of your body type, which tends to be influenced by genetic factors, as well as nutrition.

The ultimate erogenous zone

Situated above the vaginal entrance, the clitoris is a kind of "smart button" that provides exquisite sensation when stimulated. It acts as both a receiver and transmitter of these wonderful feelings. Stimulation of the clitoris

---

VAGINAL HEALTH

WHEN GIRLS REACH PUBERTY they begin to experience a vaginal secretion. This consists of a whitish mucus, and during ovulation it alters in consistency to resemble egg-white. Many young women don't realize that this secretion is completely normal, and are concerned that they have got a sexual health problem. Most of the time, vaginal secretions are nothing to worry about, and it is only when they radically change colour or smell very unpleasant that it may be something more serious (see pp.220–22). If in any doubt, always consult a doctor or genito-urinary clinic for advice (see p.180).

sends signals to the brain saying, "this feels terrific", and then the brain sends back signals to the clitoris and to the rest of the body's sexual zones saying, "this feels so terrific that you need to get even more sexually excited", so the stimulation works in a kind of loop. The right kind of stimulation of the clitoris (see pp.94–95) results in a high state of arousal, frequently leading to orgasm (see p.91).

Female erections

When a woman becomes aroused, her genitals alter considerably in appearance, and she experiences erections similar to the male, although not as obvious (see p.90). The spongy tissue inside the labia fills with blood, thereby making the labia swell up and become erect, the clitoris is enlarged and pulls back against the pubic bone, and the vagina expands and swells.

Does everyone possess a clitoris?

Virtually every woman has a clitoris, although some are less developed than others, and not all necessarily give the same high levels of intense sensation. There are some women who, for racial and cultural reasons, will have had their clitoris removed as children. This operation is controversial, since it carries a high risk of infection and

FEMALE SEXUAL ANATOMY

THE INTERNAL ORGANS consist of two fallopian tubes, which connect the ovaries to the uterus, and the cervix, which connects the uterus to the vagina. All of these organs play a vital role in reproduction (see pp.50–51).

HER INTERNAL ANATOMY

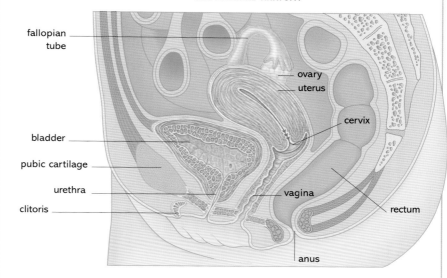

THE VULVA

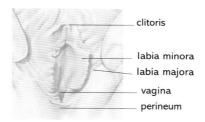

THE VULVA COMPRISES the labia majora (the large, outer folds of skin that protect the vaginal and urethral openings); the labia minora, which secrete a lubricant for the vagina; the clitoris, with its numerous nerve endings; and the vagina, which acts as a pathway to the uterus. The sensitive perineum lies between the vagina and anus.

many people consider it to be mutilation and a method of controlling a woman's sexuality.

Into the vagina

The vagina is the internal passage up to the cervix. It is through the small hole in the cervix that the sperm swim into the uterus in their race to fertilize the ovum, which is released from the ovary, in order to reproduce (see pp.50–51). The vagina is equipped with some, but not many, sensitive sexual zones – the G-spot is one example, which can lead to very powerful orgasms (see p.95).

The hymen

Most girls are born with a hymen, a thin web of skin stretched across the opening to the vagina, which nevertheless leaves enough opening for the emission of menstrual blood in later life. Traditionally, the hymen has been valued as the mark of a girl's virginity and in some cultures it continues to be so. Some westernized Muslim women, for example, seek plastic surgery to restore their hymens on engagement or shortly before the wedding. It is important to note that the hymen can spontaneously break as a result of athletic activities.

HORMONES

OUR ENERGY LEVELS and sexuality are controlled to a large extent by our hormones – chemical substances that are produced in the endocrine glands and are transported in the blood to certain parts of the body, where they may exert a dramatic change. Where sexual development and drive are concerned, men and women are affected by the main sex hormones: testosterone, oestrogen, and progesterone.

Testosterone
The hormone testosterone tends to be associated with males, although women also experience some in their chemical make-up. In men, it is secreted mainly by the testes, while in women it is produced in the ovaries and the adrenal gland.

In the sixth week of foetal development, a testosterone supply is "switched on" by a male child's XY chromosome. As a result, the foetus is bathed in the hormone, which determines that the baby will be male. In puberty, testosterone aids the growth and development of the genitals and secondary sexual characteristics, such as body hair. It is also responsible for building muscle and energy levels. It is because boys experience such a surge of testosterone in puberty that their behaviour dramatically changes. Males are probably most sexually driven around the age of 18. From then on, their testosterone levels very gradually decline. Young men with a low sex drive, little body hair, and symptoms of tiredness may be naturally low in testosterone and might benefit from a hormone supplement (see pp.202–203).

It is thought that "tomboys" probably possess high levels of the hormone, and it is often these who go on to have a high sex drive. Clinical evidence suggests that women with lower levels of testosterone tend to have less developed genitals and sometimes problems with sexual response.

FROM PUBERTY ONWARDS, most males develop a strong desire for sex, triggered by the surge of testosterone. Females also produce a certain amount of the hormone which, as in boys, fuels their libido.

EMOTIONAL AND MENTAL FACTORS

HUMAN SEX DRIVE is not only a result of physical factors, such as hormones. In addition, various emotional and mental factors come into play. When both men and women become anxious, angry, or depressed, they produce chemicals that can interfere with their sexual response:

ANXIETY CHEMICALS When anxious, men can experience a lack of control over their arousal and climax too quickly for their partner (see pp.208–209). Anxious women may find that they unconsciously "block out" sexual excitement.

ANGER CHEMICALS The surge of anger chemicals is even more complicated. Some degree of anger can actually arouse people and make sexual response very easy. However, too much anger can reduce sexual response and eventually turn it off altogether (see p.224).

DEPRESSIVE CHEMICALS One aspect of a state of depression is that levels of the hormone testosterone diminish. This reduction generally results in loss of sexual desire and sex drive, and lack of energy (see pp.204–205).

The side-effects of these emotions make it clear that mood generally affects how men and women experience sex.

If there are sexual problems within a relationship, couples are often advised to try and sort out the emotional issues such as anger, anxiety, or depression, perhaps with the help of a trained relationship counsellor or sex therapist, on the grounds that by doing so they may restore sexual response (see pp.202–203). Alternatively, numerous drug treatments for various sexual problems have been widely developed over the past ten years. It is now possible to lift sexual inhibition by taking the drug phentolamine and to curb over-excitement by the use of beta-blockers.

Oestrogen

Secreted mainly by the ovaries, oestrogen is responsible for lining the womb to prepare it for the fertilized egg. In addition, it brings women a sense of health and well-being, it feeds collagen, the elastic substance that firms the skin, and it moisturizes body tissue, particularly in the vagina, to make intercourse pleasurable. It is when oestrogen diminishes, such as during the menopause, that intercourse can become painful. Although oestrogen does not seem to be directly responsible for sexual pleasure, the lack of it can bring such discomfort that women are put off sex. A vaginal lubricant and HRT can help (see p.211).

Progesterone

This hormone, secreted by the ovaries, is responsible for shedding the lining of the womb during the menstrual cycle. It can make women feel unwell, and the synthetic version of progesterone, progestogen, which is a constituent of birth-control pills, can also make some women feel depressed and miserable. Despite the side-effects, progesterone is a vital health safeguard to prevent a cancerous build-up of the uterine lining.

The monthly cycle

A woman's menstrual cycle depends on the secretion of certain hormones at a particular time (see p.50). In the first 14 days, oestrogen increases, then around the middle of the month ovulation occurs, and for the next ten days or so progesterone builds up. Overlying this is a testosterone cycle that is at its lowest around ovulation, but at its highest in the third week. Many women feel very sexy just before their period, probably because the progesterone starts dropping and the testosterone levels are still high.

SEXFACTS

SEXUAL SPECTRUM

Scientist Alfred Kinsey (see pp.20–21) defined people's sexuality in terms of a natural spectrum, with the highly sexed at one end, the lower sexed at the other, and most people somewhere in between. His measurement definitions are controversial, since they were based on the number of sex acts experienced rather than desire or enjoyment.

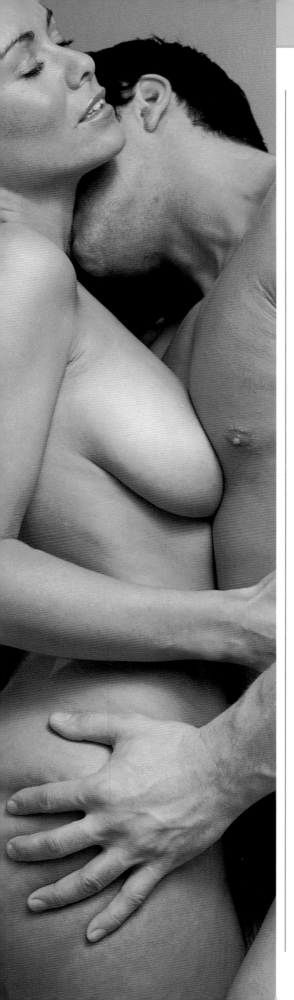

REPRODUCTION

IT IS REMARKABLE TO CONSIDER that human beings, so complex in numerous ways, originate and develop from a single fertilized cell. Before they are born, females possess all the eggs required for reproduction in their ovaries, and are unable to form any later in life. Men, on the other hand, produce sperm continually in the testicles from puberty into old age.

When a man ejaculates during sexual intercourse, up to five hundred million sperm, produced in the testicles and transported via a series of tubes, are ejaculated from the man's penis into the woman's vagina (see p.89). These travel up the genital tract, decreasing greatly in number the further they go. They wriggle their way through the uterine entrance into the fallopian tubes, where they may meet an egg, or ovum, working its

way down from the ovaries. If an ovum is present, the sperm begin to push their heads into the ovum's outer casing, attempting to penetrate it. However, only one sperm will be successful. The moment it has entered the ovum's inner cell plasma, the outer shell of the ovum hardens, and all other sperm are shut out while the egg is fertilized. Generally, the process from ejaculation to fertilization takes about one hour. Once the ovum is

THE MENSTRUAL CYCLE

THE MENSTRUAL CYCLE lasts an average of 28 days, although this can vary. A woman's period begins on Day 1 of the cycle, and usually lasts five to seven days. A follicle-stimulating hormone (FSH) causes an egg follicle to develop in the ovary, and the hormone oestrogen is responsible for lining the uterus in preparation for a fertilized egg. A surge of luteinizing hormone (LH) triggers ovulation, usually around Day 14. In the last third of the menstrual month, a rise in the hormone progesterone causes the uterine lining to thicken and then shed, resulting in the next period.

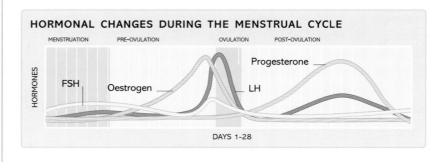

HORMONAL CHANGES DURING THE MENSTRUAL CYCLE

MENSTRUATION   PRE-OVULATION   OVULATION   POST-OVULATION

Progesterone

HORMONES

FSH   Oestrogen   LH

DAYS 1-28

fertilized, it begins to divide and multiply as it travels through the fallopian tube. It will then implant itself in the uterine lining, where it will develop into a foetus.

The baby's sex is determined by the sperm that has fertilized the ovum. If the sperm contains an "X" chromosome, a girl will result, while one containing a "Y" chromosome will produce a boy. Occasionally, more than one ovum escapes from the ovary. If the additional ovum or ova are fertilized, non-identical twins or triplets will result, each with its own placenta. Identical twins develop when a single fertilized egg divides into two equal parts, and results in the two foetuses sharing a placenta.

Maximum fertility

Women are at their most fertile after the egg is released from the ovary and before it prepares to be shed from the body in menstruation. This occurs around the 12th to the 14th day of a 28-day cycle. Menstrual cycles vary considerably in length. In order to discover when your regular ovulation time is, you might use a home ovulation test or electronic fertility monitor. Alternatively, record your body temperature (see p.184) or observe your vaginal secretions throughout the month. During the days of ovulation, the mucus is transparent and slippery, looking a little like egg-white, while at other times of the month it is usually milky and slightly sticky. For the best chances of conceiving, try to have sex around the time of ovulation.

WHAT HAPPENS DURING SEXUAL INTERCOURSE?

ALL HUMAN LIFE begins with sexual intercourse, when a single sperm ejaculated through the penis fuses with a female ovum to create another human being. If no contraception is used, the usual chances of conceiving are about 80 per cent.

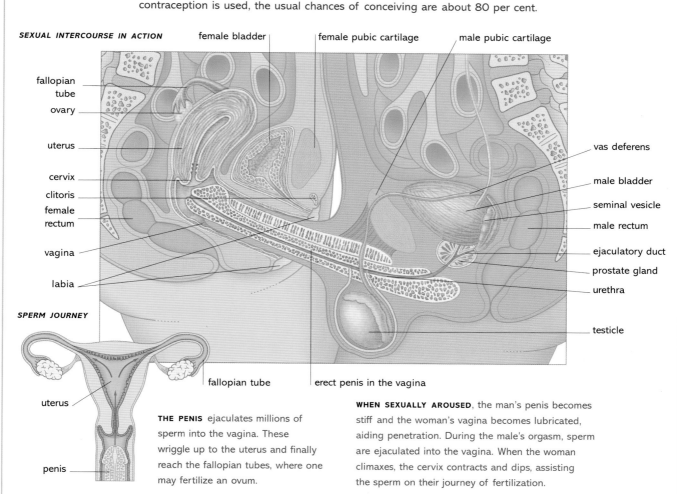

SEXUAL INTERCOURSE IN ACTION

female bladder | female pubic cartilage | male pubic cartilage

fallopian tube
ovary
uterus
cervix
clitoris
female rectum
vagina
labia

vas deferens
male bladder
seminal vesicle
male rectum
ejaculatory duct
prostate gland
urethra
testicle

fallopian tube | erect penis in the vagina

SPERM JOURNEY

uterus
penis

THE PENIS ejaculates millions of sperm into the vagina. These wriggle up to the uterus and finally reach the fallopian tubes, where one may fertilize an ovum.

WHEN SEXUALLY AROUSED, the man's penis becomes stiff and the woman's vagina becomes lubricated, aiding penetration. During the male's orgasm, sperm are ejaculated into the vagina. When the woman climaxes, the cervix contracts and dips, assisting the sperm on their journey of fertilization.

CHAPTER 3

All About Foreplay

TEASING

exploration

pleasure

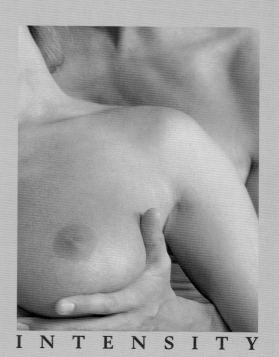

INTENSITY

arousal

SETTING THE SCENE

Many people forget that sensuality lodges within the imagination just as much as at the tips of their partner's magic fingers. Long before we enjoy any form of touch, we can arouse the senses, whet the appetite, and become excited by what we see, smell, feel, and hear. Preparing a room for massage is the same process as preparing a nest for loving – make it as sensual as possible in terms of colour, warmth, and scent.

Take a good look at the room in which you plan to carry out the massage. If it's dirty, untidy, and cold it will be a turn-off. If it's white, sparsely furnished, with a standard massage table it will seem clinical. But if it's glowing with colour and heat, it will help your partner feel warm and sensual. Massage can be a gorgeous preliminary to lovemaking, so it's important to make the room look as inviting as possible. Some of the most attractive rooms I've been massaged in possess a distinctly oriental flavour.

Sumptuous colours
A good reason for planning an "eastern" look is that oriental cloth glows with colour. And warm colours – lots of reds, purples, and pinks – look so enticing that you can almost feel the heat. One man I know actually rolls in such vibrant fabrics because he feels he must somehow "bathe" in them.

But not everyone likes very bright tints. If you're of minimalist bent, you've probably subscribed to lots of white, soft beige, or very pale autumnal hues. No matter. This is where a handful of red rose petals strewn across sparkling white bedlinen fills the head with ideas of beauty. Remember the classic shot of the young blonde girl surrounded by red rose petals in the movie *American Beauty*? It was both romantic and highly suggestive. Red rose petals also hold

A MASSAGE in front of a roaring fire is one of the most relaxing and sensuous of all experiences. The flames provide warmth as well as soft, ambient lighting.

the advantage of coming straight from the pages of the erotic classic of all times – the 4th century *Kama Sutra* (see pp.250–51) – where it recommends that young honeymooners should "throw down sweet-scented petals then crush them with the weight of your entwined bodies". It also states that the bed should be "covered with a clean white cloth ... having garlands and bunches of flowers upon it".

Atmospheric lighting

You can almost instantly achieve an intimate atmosphere with effective lighting. Candles are a great source of illumination, because candlelight pools only where it burns, so large areas of the room remain in shadow. There are many kinds of candles available, each establishing its own ambience and quality of light. Some are fragrant and permeate the atmosphere with heady scent. Here are just a few ideas you could try:

- Huge white or cream altar candles are truly ecclesiastical and may coincide with some imaginative lovemaking – you could introduce your own rites!
- Dozens of small bowls of floating rose-shaped candles placed across the floor, around the massage area, or around the bed, create a romantic atmosphere.
- Red, strawberry-scented candles evoke memories of summer and sunlight.
- If you're of gothic mind, a couple of iron candelabra, with black dripping tapers placed at the head and foot of the massage area or bed, arouse all kinds of slightly anxious expectations. Anxiety in itself can be arousing.

BURNING INCENSE STICKS *fill the room with atmosphere. A light, floral fragrance can be subtle and fresh. Alternatively, choose heavier, musky tones for a heady, more exotic ambience.*

Keeping warm

The first rule of any love massage is to keep the room warm. This is an absolute must, because if the skin gets cold it tenses unpleasantly and touch is then experienced as pain rather than pleasure. Block out any draughts, and if the day is chilly, make a roaring log fire or switch the heater on to its highest setting.

Harmonious sounds

Soothing music, such as flute music, harmonious new age sounds, and many of Mozart's inimitable pieces, infiltrates the many layers of human consciousness and puts you in an open, relaxed, and receptive mood. Loud or jarring music, great though it may be for dancing, is not good for massage because it interrupts the mood too much.

Erotic aromas and oils

There's nothing to beat the scent of a good clean room, but you could certainly enhance the sweetness of the atmosphere by investing in scented candles, incense sticks, or a good-quality room spray. You could use essential oils in an aromatherapy burner – these oils not only smell delicious but have therapeutic properties. The massage oil that you use also contributes towards the general erotic aroma. You might create your own by adding a favourite perfume or a few drops of essential oil to a base of plain almond oil. Alternatively, you might prefer to buy a pre-blended massage oil. Don't use olive oil, corn oil, or baby oil as your base. To do so means that your love session ends up smelling like somebody's dinner or baby. Not exactly sexy, I'm sure you'll agree!

SENSUOUS TEXTURES

THERE IS SOMETHING EXOTIC about throws, curtains, drapes, and cushion covers in soft cottons, shiny satins, and gold embroidery. They cost little, and by simply scattering these items over existing furniture you can totally transform a room. The materials feel sensual to touch; indeed, some can be used as massage aides:

- Try stroking a piece of soft velvet up and down your partner's naked body
- Polish his or her skin with a flimsy silk scarf
- The peacock feather may seem very 1970s, but when you feel it drawn across your expectant skin you may surprise yourself by your old-fashioned feelings!
- Find a piece of fur or a fake leopard skin throw and use that to stroke and caress your partner

SENSUAL MASSAGE

Touch doesn't only involve sensation – it conveys and evokes emotions and it is the foundation for love. It is such a primitive form of connection that the minute you are touched reassuringly, you feel better. When someone caresses your body, your ego is stroked too. And the person giving the caress feels good because he or she is also experiencing the physical and emotional contact of touch.

BEFORE STARTING A MASSAGE, *pour a small amount of oil into your hands, then rub your hands together to coat them thoroughly in oil.*

Getting comfortable

Spend some time making preparations for your massage session. The floor is the best place for a massage, because it provides a firm surface and plenty of space – beds tend to be too springy. Make the area more comfortable by laying some luxury bath towels over some rugs.

Check that your fingernails are filed smooth, because you don't want any sharp edges to catch on your partner's skin. Remove any rings from your fingers, because these can cause discomfort during a massage, and make sure your hands are warm. Float the bottle of massage oil in a bowl of hot water to warm it up. Or, if you're having a bath before the massage, let the bottle float in the water with you.

When you apply massage oil, never drop it directly on to your partner's body, because the sensation will be a shock. Instead, pour a little oil into each hand, then rub your hands together to give each palm a liberal coating.

Giving pleasure

Almost anything you do during a massage will feel wonderful provided it is done slowly. If you don't believe this, take your turn and see how great it is to have all that attention focused on you! It's easy to get swamped by massage instructions, but don't worry. Stick to circling (see facing page) and you'll find that your hand movements come naturally. Keep things slow and your movements will adapt to the kind of body you are working on. Some people have very hard bodies with a lot of tight musculature and they aren't easy to massage. Others have soft, pliable flesh that is a joy to manipulate. Ask your partner what areas he or she particularly enjoys having massaged. It is always worth remembering that what feels supremely sexy to you may leave your partner cold.

MASSAGE RULES

BEFORE YOU START a massage session, it helps if you learn a few basic rules – these guidelines should ensure that both you and your lover get the most out of the session:

1 Make sure that both you and your partner understand any guidelines either of you set out before the session.

2 Listen to and respect your partner. Don't insist on the massage session if he or she is not willing.

3 Make sure that you have total privacy for the session. Set aside a time when you know you won't be disturbed.

4 Make sure that the room is warm before you start.

5 Wash your hands in hot water before you begin so that they are warm and clean – a speck of dirt feels like a pin scraping along the body.

WARM THE BOTTLE of oil in hot water before you start.

6 Use slow massage movements. If you are giving someone full body strokes, your contact should be continuous – make sure that you have at least one hand in contact with your partner's skin at all times during the massage.

7 Be attentive to how your partner reacts to particular strokes. Respond to the reactions you receive when you are *giving* a massage, rather than just being aware of what you enjoy when you're being massaged.

8 Ask your partner for feedback. Be open with your responses when it's your turn to be massaged.

CIRCLING

There are a number of different massage strokes, but the one you really need to know is circling – not only is it easy to learn, but you can use it on every part of the body. Even if you don't learn any of the other massage techniques, you can still carry out a satisfying massage using this stroke.

How to circle

Place both hands, palms down, and move them firmly in opposing circles. You can make large, wide circles, small fairy circles, or something in between. Never circle on any bony areas. For example, you might circle with both hands on either side of the spine, but always massage away from the spine – never towards it and never directly on it. Circling can be used to link to other strokes and other parts of the body. You can circle on your partner's back, front, hands, feet, face, and head. ▼

• MASSAGE TIP •

The first few times you enjoy a massage together, compare notes afterwards. Form a mental map of each other's erogenous zones – everyone is different!

VARY THE PRESSURE

ALTERING THE PRESSURE of your stroke will help you turn an ordinary massage into a highly sensual experience. Timing is the key here because your partner needs to be prepared for arousal. For example, a fingertip massage could feel tickling and unrelaxing if you have not started the session with a firmer touch:

1 Firm pressure feels detached and medical. It's a good idea to use this at the beginning of a session because it allows your partner to feel secure and to relax.

2 Moderate pressure feels more sensual – it involves moving the hands across the skin. As the massage develops, start to use this type of pressure because your now relaxed partner will be ready to experience sensuality without panicking.

3 A fingertip (or even a fingernail) massage, which involves featherlight fingertips brushing over the surface of the skin, can be extremely exciting and erotic. But it's a good idea to do this after using the other layers of pressure first.

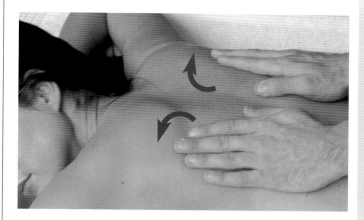

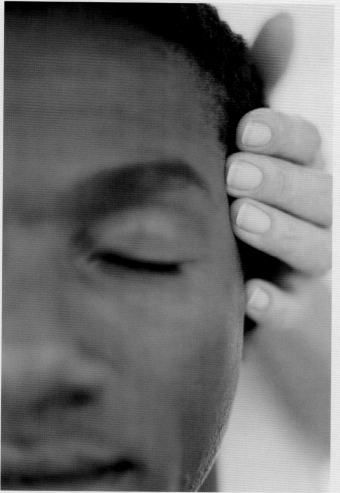

◄ Smaller circles

When you get to smaller, more delicate parts of the body, you'll need to use fingers or thumbs instead of the palms of your hand for circling. If you are massaging your partner's palms, for example, use your thumb and forefinger. For the top of the neck, use only your thumbs. When massaging the face, gently press your fingertips into the cheeks and move the flesh beneath in small circles. Don't move the fingers themselves – just rotate the cheeks.

BACK MASSAGE

Using circling strokes (see p.59), start at the neck and shoulders and then massage each arm in turn, right down to the fingertips. Next, work your way down your partner's back, over the buttocks and down each leg as far as the ankle. Don't massage the feet yet, because that is easier to do when your partner is lying face up (see p.63). Use your palms on your partner's back and your fingers and thumbs on the legs. Another useful back stroke is the glide.

All-over back stroke – the glide

> • MASSAGE TIP •
>
> Always keep your hands on either side of the spine and massage away from it – never massage directly on the spine or towards it.

1 Put your hands on the buttocks, fingers pointing towards the head, and lean your weight on your hands.

2 Let your weight gently glide your hands up your partner's body, on either side of the spine, towards the shoulders.

3 When you reach the shoulders, sweep your hands around and away from the neck, on down the arms, then return to the buttocks. Repeat the whole stroke several times.

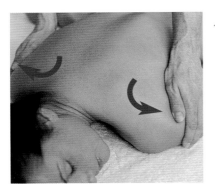

LOWER SPINE TENSION

A USEFUL MASSAGE STROKE for relieving lower spine tension is the slide. Position yourself seated across your partner's thighs and place your hands, palms down, on either side of your partner's spine, at waist level. Your hands are pointing sideways and as you lean forward, putting your weight onto your hands, allow your weight to drive your hands outwards, slipping away from the spine and over the sides of your partner's body to the ground. Next, position the hands a little below the waist and repeat. If you continue to repeat this stroke until you are leaning on the top part of the buttocks, you radically de-stress the base of the spine.

NECK MASSAGE

The top of the neck takes a lot of strain, and reflects any tension your partner may be experiencing. The tiny circling movements described below will help to relax the muscles.

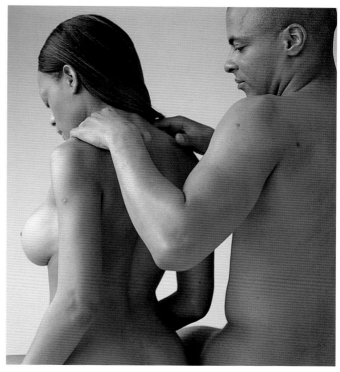

Taking the strain
Using thumbs only, knead the taut neck muscles using small circles (see p.59). Travel from the tops of the shoulders slowly up into the nape of the neck. Repeat until you feel the muscle tension slacken.

SHOULDER MASSAGE

Give the shoulders and shoulder blades a thorough "circling", using the palms of your hands (see p.59). Try doing this three times – the first time with a very firm pressure, the second with a medium pressure, and the third with a very light fingertip pressure. Once your partner is very relaxed, you could try out the shoulder blade stroke, which dispels any tension that collects in the shoulders and upper back.

The shoulder blade stroke

1 Push your partner's arm up behind his or her back as in a half nelson, taking care not to force the arm too far. You will see that this arm position has highlighted a kind of hollow space beneath the shoulder blade.

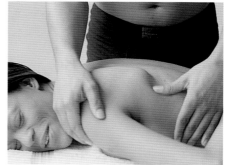

2 With your free hand, firmly press either your thumb or forefinger underneath the blade, raking it down underneath the bone, and out again. Repeat several times along the blade then do the same to the other shoulder.

FRONT MASSAGE

Lightly cover the chest and abdomen with circling strokes (see p.59), using your palms and fingers on the areas just below the rib cage and around the waist and lower abdomen. Circle around the outside of the breasts, or move the entire breast in circles. Avoid touching the genitals. After you have circled all over, you could give a full breast massage.

Breast massage

The breasts are full of nerve endings, particularly along the sides. Try to be systematic with this four-step routine.

1 Kneeling at your partner's side, slide the flat of your hand diagonally across her left breast in the direction of her right shoulder. Next, slide your hand across her right breast in the same way. Repeat these two strokes alternately, about six times.

2 Dip your fingers in massage oil and lightly trace out a spiral with one of your fingertips around one of her breasts. Start on the outside and spiral inwards until you reach the nipple, then repeat the same stroke on the other breast.

3 Using a well-oiled thumb and forefinger of each hand, gently squeeze a little skin on either side of the nipple and slide outwards as if your fingers were moving along the spokes of a wheel to its rim. Repeat, working around the nipple.

4 Gently squeeze a nipple between forefinger and thumb, sliding them up and off. For added sensation, use both hands alternately so that the action is continuous. Repeat this on the other nipple.

Abdomen kneading

After relaxing the upper body with basic circling strokes (see p.59) or the torso glide (see below), you could try abdomen kneading. Sitting to one side of your partner, use the flat of your fingers of one hand to make full circles around the outer rim of the belly in a clockwise direction. This area can take deep pressure and you can press down virtually beneath the pubic bone.

> • **MASSAGE TIP** •
>
> The chest is a much bonier area than the back and you need to beware of leaning too heavily on a partner or pressing too firmly.

TORSO GLIDE

THIS IS AN EXCELLENT STROKE to relax the upper body. Kneeling across your partner's thighs, glide your hands, palms down, fingers inwards, up from the lower abdomen and over and across the chest, stopping when you reach the neck. Then sweep your hands out and around the shoulders, returning down the arms. Repeat.

SCALP MASSAGE

There are some massages that are just as sensual as whole body routines yet they do not necessarily involve nudity. Scalp massage is one of these, and is noted in the *Kama Sutra*. It is best tried out while shampooing.

Sensual shampooing

◀ **1** Work the shampoo into your partner's scalp, using both hands. Massage it lightly with your fingertips for a few minutes, moving the hair around in tiny circles.

2 Cup your hand on top of the head and ▶ gently rotate the scalp using the flat of your hand. You will need to support your partner's head with the other hand, or alternatively against your body.

◀ **3** Holding a lock of hair between thumb and forefinger of both hands, pull the locks gently to create prickling sensations in your partner's scalp.

4 Massage the scalp again, this time using your fingertips, instead of a cupped hand, to move it around in tiny circles. Make sure that you don't snag the hair. ▼

FOOT MASSAGE

A foot massage is truly sensual. When you finish massaging the first foot, wrap it in a warm towel before beginning the next. You can do one or all of these strokes in any order.

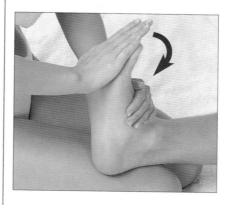

Toe bending
Using the flat of your hand, press the toes (from underneath) forwards, for a count of ten, as if you were trying to fold them up. Repeat this three times.

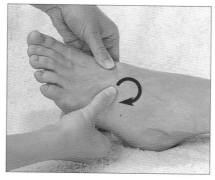

Circling
Use your thumbs to massage the top of the foot, applying moderate pressure. When you approach the ankle, circle with your fingertips and take care to avoid the ankle bone itself.

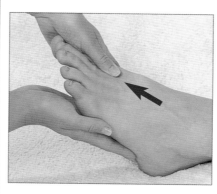

In the grooves
Pressing firmly, run the tip of one of your thumbs down the grooves located between the raised tendons on top of the foot. Work your way carefully from the ankle to the toe.

OTHER STROKES

KNUCKLING Press the knuckles of one hand hard into the sole of the foot, then cover the sole with small circling movements using the knuckles.

THUMBING Work over the whole area of the sole, making small circles with both thumbs at the same time.

EROTIC MASSAGE

These very intimate massages should only be given after the rest of the body has been massaged first. Remember that you are not necessarily aiming to bring your partner to orgasm. If that happens, it is a bonus, but if not it doesn't matter – you've still given him or her wonderful sensations.

ENERGY SWEEP

IF YOUR PARTNER is stirred up after genital massage but cannot have an orgasm, try the energy sweep. This deflects sexual tension. Hold your hands out flat with your palms down over your partner, and "brush" the energy away from the centre of his or her body and out via the arms and legs. Sweep just above the body *without touching it.*

GENITAL MASSAGE FOR MEN

After you have given your man a whole body massage, pour a little warmed oil into your hands and liberally apply it to your man's genitals ensuring that his penis, testicles, and perineum are covered. Since this is a particularly hairy area, you'll need to use enough oil to allow your hands to slide around without catching on the hairs. There are several genital massage strokes for men, among the most pleasurable are those illustrated below.

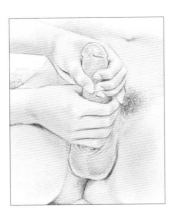

◀ The corkscrew

Put one hand on each side of the penis shaft. Slide them around in opposite directions at the same time – as if you were trying to twist the penis in half – and then slide them back again. Repeat ten times.

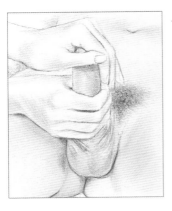

◀ The lemon squeezer

Steady the penis by grasping it around the halfway mark with one hand. Then rub the cupped palm of your other hand over and around the head of the penis, as if you were juicing a lemon.

GENITAL MASSAGE FOR WOMEN

The following massages for women can be used on their own or together with any of the others shown here.

◀ Gentle hair torture

Gently pull her pubic hair, in small tufts, working your way slowly from where her pubic hair starts and down each side of the labia. This causes exquisite pricking sensations that travel from the mons pubis straight to the clitoris.

Duck's bill

Shape the fingers of one hand into a "duck's bill", hold them above her clitoris, and pour warm (not hot) massage oil over them so that it slowly seeps through and runs onto her genitals creating a warm, flooding sensation. The oil should not enter the vagina.

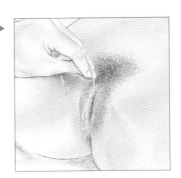

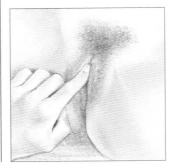

◀ Clitoral massage

Perform the following 20 times each: first, circle the head of the clitoris, then change direction. Next, rub your finger up and down one side of the clitoris then the other, then backwards and forwards just below it. Finally, rub from the clitoris to the vagina and back.

THAI SOAPSUD MASSAGE

This massage consists of total body manipulation, lubricated by soapsuds. To treat your partner to this amazing experience, you will need an inflatable airbed and a good-quality soap. Although this massage is usually given by a woman to a man, it can also be given by a man to a woman in some circumstances, although it should not be tried if the man is much heavier than the woman.

• MASSAGE TIP •

If a man is giving this massage to a woman, it usually feels safer if he slides up and down her body instead of side to side. To get extra slippery, keep applying more lather during the massage.

The Thai soapsud massage

1 Start to run a warm bath, remove your clothes, and wrap yourself in a towel. Undress your man and, when he is in the bath, begin soaping and caressing every fraction of his body.

2 Prepare the airbed and place it next to the bath. Start to layer the mattress with masses of soapy, lathery peaks until it is completely covered.

3 Ask your man to lie on his front on the airbed. Scoop soapsuds onto his body, and then remove your towel and begin to lather your own body.

4 Lie on top of him and move your body all over his, sliding up and down, from side to side, and diagonally across his back, pressing his genitals into the airbed.

5 Turn him over onto his back and cover the front of his body with more soapsuds. Begin sliding over him again, lightly brushing his genitals but avoiding his erection.

6 Now that he is aroused, tantalize him by letting your genitals touch his erection each time your body slides downwards. Start to allow his penis to penetrate your vagina, but only just.

7 Each time you slide downwards, allow more of his penis to be taken inside you, until it is fully enclosed. However, keep the focus on the whole body sensation.

8 Begin to reverse your movements by gradually lifting off his penis each time you move upwards, until you are merely brushing it. When you are both ready, start to move faster and bring him towards orgasm.

THE ART OF KISSING

Kissing is one of the most intimate, meaningful contacts that human beings can experience together. With a kiss on the lips, the senses of touch, taste, and smell are all evoked, and this combines to produce strong feelings of emotion in both the giver and receiver. Some cultures explicitly acknowledge the sanctity of this mingling of breaths – the *Kama Sutra*, for example, recognized kissing as an art, and describes the multifarious forms ranging from the tentative and the affectionate, to the sensual and passionate.

PACE YOUR KISSING

A kiss can range from a quick brush of the lips to a deep penetration with the tongue – feelings can be intensified if this type of kiss is carried out during intercourse, in a matching rhythm. The *Kama Sutra* introduces the notion that different kisses are appropriate for particular times. It makes sense to opt for innocent kissing at the start of a relationship and let your kissing build up as the relationship develops. When a kiss becomes more passionate, sensuality (and the promise of things to come) is also heightened.

Kissing the throat
Gentle, tender kisses around your partner's throat and neck can be very sensuous and loving. ▼

KISSING THE BODY

Kisses needn't just be lip to lip, of course – pay a little lip service to the whole of your lover's body. Some areas of the body are more sensitive to the softness of a kiss than others. While you are treating your partner to an all-over kissing session, don't forget to use your tongue and hands from time to time, to increase his or her pleasure. A little licking and stroking will intensify the passion of your kiss and increase your lover's pleasure.

> • KISSING TIP •
>
> The inside of the thigh is a particularly sensitive area, so try concentrating your kisses here. Breasts and nipples are also especially sensitive to loving lips.

> ## HISTORY FACTS
>
> ### THE ART OF BITING
> The ancient Indians carried kissing much further than we do in the West today. They did not stop short at open-mouthed amorousness. When passion heated up, kisses turned into something harder and sharper, transforming into the embrace of the teeth. Many of us have felt like biting a partner because we desire them so profoundly. Don't be afraid to use your teeth during an embrace. But remember, don't bite too hard!

KAMA SUTRA ON LIP CONTACT

The *Kama Sutra* lists dozens of different kisses, each expressing different emotions and producing unique sensations. By experimenting with types of kisses at particular moments, you can convey a range of feelings, from affection and adoration to lust and desire.

◀ The turned kiss

"One of them turns up the face of the other by holding the head and chin, and then kissing." This is a gentle kiss expressing feelings of tenderness.

The touching kiss ▶

"When a girl touches her lover's lip with her tongue, and having shut her eyes, places her hands on those of her lover, it is called the 'touching kiss'." Touch is introduced very gently with the tongue and hands simultaneously. The kiss is soft and tender.

◀ The clasping kiss

You or your partner "take both the lips of the other in your own ... if one of you touches the teeth, the tongue, and the palate of the other with your tongue it is called the 'fighting of the tongue'." This is what we call a French kiss.

The bent kiss ▶

"When the heads of two lovers are bent towards each other." This is a more natural angle for deep, passionate kissing.

EXPLORING THE BODY WITH YOUR MOUTH

The *Kama Sutra* states that there are at least four different types of kiss: contracted, soft, moderate, and pressed. The one you use depends on the part of the body you are kissing:

The contracted kiss

This could be interpreted as small, staccato kisses, in which the lips are applied to the skin and then pulled away quickly in a playful way. These kisses could be lavished on your partner's thighs and buttocks.

The soft kiss

These are the most tender and gentle of kisses, in which you just brush your partner's skin with your lips. Lavish these on such tinglingly sensitive areas as your partner's neck and throat.

The moderate kiss

This refers to quite general, measured kisses. A tender kiss like this along the length of the spine can be highly arousing.

The pressed kiss

A kiss like this involves placing your lips on your partner's body (for example, on the stomach), and applying gentle pressure while holding your mouth there for a moment. This is a truly loving kiss.

SELF-TOUCH FOR HIM

Most men discover their genitals as very young boys and unconsciously find out that these produce extremely pleasurable feelings when caressed. Later, they discover how to bring themselves to orgasm. But what many will not know is how parts of the body other than the genitals react to self-stimulation. The entire body is a mass of erogenous zones, and by missing out on stimulating these other areas you are effectively blocking yourself off from a complete, more enrichening experience of sensuality. Take a bath or shower before you begin your self-exploration, and ensure that you have complete, uninterrupted privacy.

SENSUAL STROKES

Coat your hands in massage oil, and run them firmly over the whole of your body, avoiding the genitals at first. Once your body is well oiled, repeat the touch, only this time very lightly. Note the stirrings of good feeling and repeat the strokes in these areas to increase sensation. Focus particularly on the abdomen, thighs, buttocks, chest, nipples, lower legs, and feet. The idea of this self-pleasuring is to bring to life nerve endings that you hadn't noticed before and to learn how to enjoy the sensations.

Nipple sensation

For many (but not all) men, the nipples are a rich source of eroticism. If you stroke, touch, tweak, or tickle the nipples, prickles of sensation flood over many other parts of the body. Some men use nipple caresses on themselves as a route to erection. ▼

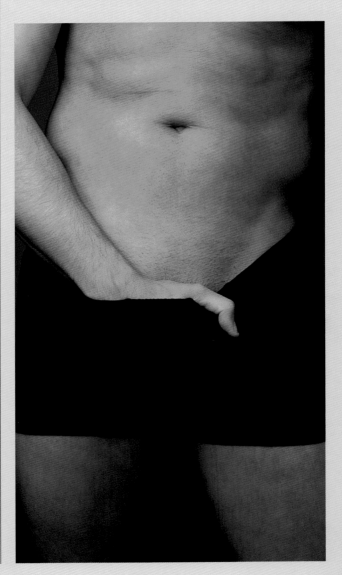

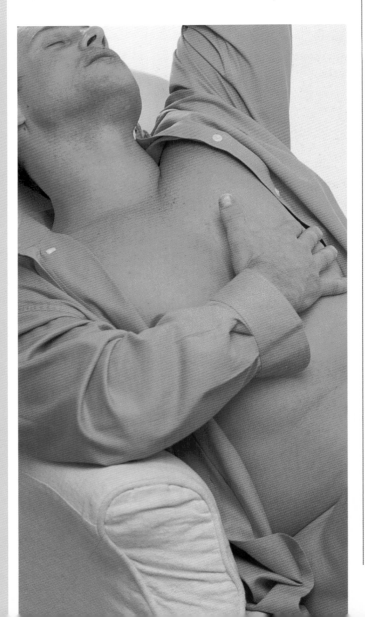

LETTING GO OF YOUR SEXUALITY

Once you have spent some time on general sensual strokes (see facing page), you are now ready to really let yourself go. Try out the lighter touches on the genitals, noting and building on the sensation. If your tendency is to be speedy, slow yourself down. The rule in massage is that the slower you are, the more sensation is provoked. Now switch your position so that you are lying face down, and carry on with the stimulation. If you have a favourite fantasy, this is the time to enjoy it. If anal touch turns you on, then relish caressing your anus. We can get stuck in masturbation patterns sometimes, so if you want to experience something different, concentrate on techniques that you wouldn't normally use. For example, you could experiment with some of the new and highly sensuous oils and gels now available, or you could try out a vibrator, anal wand, or butt plug (see pp.142–44). When you sense you are reaching the point of high arousal and you recognize you are about to climax, don't be afraid to move around. If your body feels like jerking or you want to moan, do so. Try thrusting your pelvis, and when climax eventually sweeps you up, shout and scream out loud so that all your energy is expended.

• SEX TIP •

To ensure privacy, lock the bedroom or bathroom door and unplug the phone so you will not be disturbed during your self-touch routine.

Lie back and relax
Ensure that your bedroom is kept warm so that you can relax. It helps to have a warm bath before self-touch. If you are using massage oil, first spread out a towel on the bed or floor. ▼

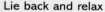

Stimulating yourself

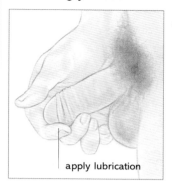

apply lubrication

1 Gently fondle your flaccid penis. If you are not circumcised, ease your penis away from the foreskin on each upward stroke. Try shaking the penis a little, or simply rubbing round or over it. You may want to use lubrication to ensure comfort, particularly if you are circumcised.

2 As your penis stiffens, slip your hand right down the shaft and then back up again. Repeat this several times. Uncircumcised men may like to do this by moving the foreskin up and down.

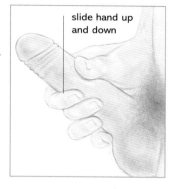

slide hand up and down

concentrate on the frenulum

3 As your erection becomes hard, focus on stimulating the head. Grasp the penis on the ridge that encircles the tip, and move the skin backwards and forwards. Sensation here can be especially dynamic, and some men like climaxing from this kind of movement alone.

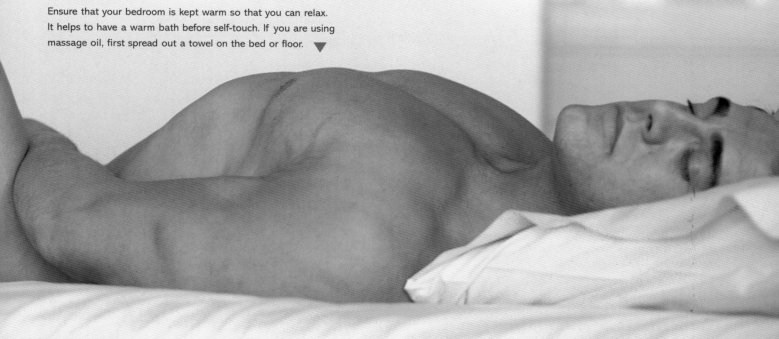

SELF-TOUCH FOR HER

Self-touch is a vital part of a woman's sexual development. Traditionally, women have expected to learn about sex (and therefore their bodies) from their partner. The trouble with this approach is that it means a woman is dependent on someone else to give her pleasure, or she misses out on this wonderful and fulfilling experience. Self-touch is also extremely important because it acts as a gateway to self-knowledge – if you want good sex with a lover, knowing your body's response brings self-confidence. Female sexuality programmes encourage participants to know the whole of their body intimately, as shown here.

LIGHT CARESSES

Start by having a long soak in a warm bath. Afterwards, in the privacy of a warm bedroom, give yourself an all-over massage using sweet-smelling oils. As you touch your body (avoid the genitals at this stage), note the erotic sensations that grow beneath your fingers. If certain areas feel more sensual than others, build on the enjoyable feelings there.

• SEX TIP •

Try touching yourself with firm strokes first, then repeat the touch with lighter strokes. Finally, use your fingertips only.

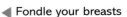
Caress your legs

Include your legs with the rest of the massage and note the areas that feel good. Surprisingly, the toes, feet, and ankles can all feel amazingly erotic.

◀ Fondle your breasts

Some women (but not all) have incredibly sensitive breasts. To find out your response, lightly oil and manipulate your breasts, making sure that you pay particular attention to the nipples and aureolae.

GENITAL PLEASURING

Once you have stroked and caressed your body thoroughly (see facing page), you are ready to move on to the genitals. Massage and stroke your labia, clitoris, and vagina in much the same way as you have done elsewhere, noting the areas that feel full of erotic sensation. Concentrate on the strokes and the areas that provide such feeling. Most women prefer a light touch on the genitals, although everyone differs in the kind of pressure they prefer. The main point to bear in mind is not to try desperately hard for orgasm. Instead, focus on the pleasure that any touch can give you in this area and enjoy it. Try and locate the area on the entrance to the vagina that gives the best sensation. If direct contact with the clitoris feels too strong, it can sometimes feel more pleasurable to caress yourself through a thin silk scarf. You might want to experiment using one of the many vibrators that are available (see pp.142–44).

Stimulating yourself

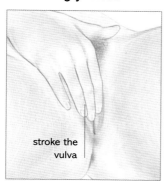

stroke the vulva

1 Start by caressing your whole body. Move on to fondling the general pubic area, letting your hands stray around the inner thighs, then gently explore the outer labia. Try out different strokes of varying pressure and see what feels best.

2 Explore the inner labia, then let your fingers stroke up and down each side of the clitoris. Note which side of the clitoris feels best. Upstrokes tend to offer more sensation, although this is not always the case.

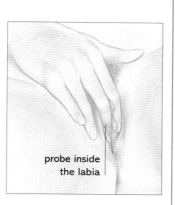

probe inside the labia

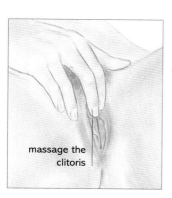

massage the clitoris

3 You can use direct touch on the clitoris in a variety of ways. You might try lightly twirling in circles with the tip of a finger, brushing from side to side, or rubbing backwards and forwards or up and down.

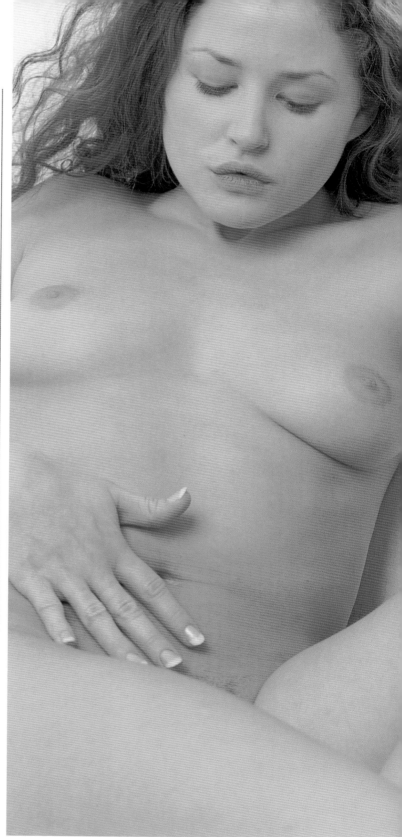

Lose yourself in touch

Revel in all the sensations you arouse beneath your fingers – you can prolong this for hours if you wish. Enjoy the experience for its own sake, and don't focus on orgasm, since this often anaesthetizes feeling. Really let yourself go – writhe around, moan, and do anything else that adds to your pleasure.

MUTUAL EXPLORATION

In the days before birth control, lovers spent months getting to know each other. Lovemaking was called "heavy petting" and it consisted of just about everything that could please the body, with one exception – sexual intercourse. The benefit of this was that it enabled couples to get to know each other's bodies in great detail long before they reached intercourse itself. You learned which of your partner's body areas responded to your touch and you discovered how to pace your lovemaking so that your partner grew more and more excited; above all, you took your time over the encounter since there was no pressure "to come". What follows is a sensual routine that encourages couples to discover each other slowly and sensually.

STROKING

Slowly stroke each other's bodies but in the first sessions omit stroking the genitals. As soon as the genitals are approached, the partner being stroked may feel pressurized to climax. And if this thought is foremost in someone's mind, he or she can start to suffer from what therapists call "performance pressure". So, to begin with, leave the genitals out. Only include them on later lovemaking sessions when you feel you know each other's bodies rather better.

◀ Exploring
Every human being differs in his or her sexual responses – bear in mind that your partner's likes and dislikes will not be the same as yours. Spend some time exploring each other's bodies.

TAKE IT EASY

Explore the notion of "delayed gratification" (see box, right). The sense that you and your lover have all the time in the world for lovemaking will undoubtedly lead to wonderful, explosive climaxes, not to mention warm, emotional feelings. The belief that it doesn't matter if you don't make sex work today (because there will be tomorrow and tomorrow and tomorrow) is liberating and reassuring. Knowing that your partner can wait for you offers an amazing sense of security and paradoxically helps to speed you up!

• SEX TIP •

Delayed gratification is the act of putting off orgasm, with the resulting effect of building up sexual tension and desire. When sexual release does eventually happen, it is longer and stronger and far more memorable (see pp.98–99).

TALK

Murmur sweet nothings to each other. Tell your partner how desirable and gorgeous you find him or her. Don't be afraid to talk about what you find pleasurable.

Confide in each other

Be candid about your feelings with your lover – this will promote trust and openness between you. ▼

ASK FOR WHAT YOU WANT

Trust and feelings of security are vital in a relationship, and these qualities give you the confidence to ask for what you want in bed. Similarly, it's important to find out what your partner wants – don't make the mistake of assuming you know this. It is also important to be able to say "no". Never let yourself get pushed into doing something sexually that you don't want to do. Feel no shame in saying you had rather wait or in admitting, "I just don't want to do that!"

ASSERTIVENESS *exercise*

BEING ABLE TO ASK FOR what they want is hard for many people – it requires a modicum of confidence. Try practising this exercise for a couple of weeks. It will help you value yourself and your decisions.

Try saying YES to three things you really want to do in a week and NO to three things you really don't want to do in a week. This could be as banal as saying, "I'm not going to eat chocolate. I'm going to say NO to chocolate" through to something as important as saying YES to finding a new flat.

EROGENOUS ZONES

THESE ARE THE PARTS OF THE HUMAN BODY that feel particularly sensual when stimulated. Every person's erogenous zones are different – what feels sensual to one may feel ticklish to another or lack sensation to a third. We all vary widely so it is a good idea to explore your partner's body in order to know what turns him or her on. The most sensitive areas are usually: the mouth, the ears, the breasts, the abdomen, the insides of the thighs, the genitals, and the feet.

THE MOUTH

THE EARS

THE BREASTS

THE THIGHS

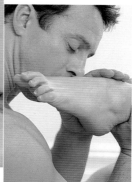
THE FEET

INCREASING SENSATION

The number of people who think that the only way to have a sex life is through penis-vagina intercourse constantly amazes sex therapists. There are so many other fabulous ways to enjoy a great time in bed, and the more researchers learn about human sexual response, the more we understand the desirability of prolonging every method of good loving. The aim of pleasuring is simply that – to give pleasure. It is not specifically to give orgasm. Indeed, the intense sensuality that is generated is sometimes so wonderful that orgasm can be an anti-climax!

SENSUOUS STROKES

One method of prolonging arousal is to continue to massage a partner once he or she is seriously aroused even though intercourse is a good alternative (see pp.58–65). Or you could focus on a highly sensitive part of the body that you might not normally think of as orgasmic, such as the neck or ears, sides of the breasts, armpits, breasts and nipples, inner thighs, and toes. Remember, the longer you stimulate your partner before intercourse, the more intense your orgasms will become. There are also specific massages for the genitals (see p.64). Try rubbing gently on and around the clitoris with a lubricated finger, or rub up and down the penis with a lubricated hand. The best time for these massages is at the end of an intimate time of caressing, laughing, and playing around. Such strokes are a fantastic continuation of the attention the rest of your body has just received.

◀ Caressing
Learn how your partner responds when different areas of his or her body are caressed. Pay loving attention to every area of the body.

SEXFACTS

TAKE IT SLOWLY
US sex researchers Masters and Johnson (see p.21) discovered that homosexual couples took far longer over rubbing and caressing than heterosexual couples. This has the effect of giving far greater sensation on climax and greater satisfaction derived from intercourse.

TONGUE BATHING

This should be done only in a luxuriously hot room. Before you begin, make sure that both you and your partner are scrupulously clean. In fact, this is a good opportunity to share a sensual bath or shower together first.

Exploring the body

1 Begin your oral exploration of your partner's body by kissing and licking his or her mouth and face. Work your way slowly around the ears and down the neck and throat to the shoulders.

• SEX TIP •

Use your tongue, lips, and breath to arouse your lover. Work near the genitals, but keep at a tantalizing distance.

---

2 When you move on to the chest, don't forget to lick and suck the breasts, areolae, and nipples. If your partner responds in a big way, don't be afraid of turning your gentle licks into extra stimulating sucks and nibbles. When you have worked your way down to the insides of the thighs, go close to (but don't actually touch) the genitals. Work down to the toes, then back up to the abdomen, and finish off kissing and licking the genitals. If your partner enjoys this, you could turn your tongue bath into an oral sex session (see pp.78–79).

SEXUAL MAPPING *exercise*

THIS SEX THERAPY EXERCISE was invented in the US. It is a method for couples to find out where each other's erogenous zones are. The object is to discover, through touching the body all over, which parts of it are sexually responsive. The person being touched is asked to rate the pleasure of his or her response.

The method
One partner sits nude in a comfortable chair, while the other stands and then kneels in front. The person doing the "mapping" strokes areas of his or her partner's skin. These areas should be up to 5cm (2 inches) in diameter and should be stroked once or twice with a finger. Work your way down the body, starting at:

- The head, including the scalp and ears
- The neck
- The face, including the lips, nose, and eyelids
- The shoulders

- The breasts or chest, including the nipples
- The arms, including the insides of the elbows
- The hands and fingers and so on, right down to the little toes.

How to score
After each stroke, the partner being stroked rates the eroticism of the touch on a plus three/minus three scale. If, for example, strokes on the forearm felt pleasant but not special they might rate as zero. If strokes on the elbow were uninteresting, they might rate as minus two, while if strokes across the nipple felt especially arousing, these might be scored as plus three.

MUTUAL MASTURBATION

Mutual masturbation is a key ingredient of lovemaking. Many women find it difficult or even impossible to climax from intercourse alone, so masturbation is an ideal way of ensuring she achieves maximum pleasure, either as a preliminary to intercourse or as a pleasurable alternative to penetration. Another great benefit is that it can be used during intercourse to enhance sensation, particularly when the position doesn't allow for sufficient stimulation of the clitoris. To prevent rapid exhaustion, make sure you are seated, lying, or kneeling in a comfortable position.

PLEASURE FOR HIM

The man should lie so as to give his partner unencumbered access to his penis. The woman should be aware that if she starts handling her man's genitals with a dry hand she may hurt him. It's easy for a dry hand to catch on pubic hair, so to prevent painful friction coat your hands liberally with massage oil or a good lubricant; alternatively, you could use your own saliva, remembering to renew it regularly. If you have anxieties that you're holding him too hard and may hurt him, ask if what you're doing feels safe. Penises can take far rougher stimulation than you might think. A good way of finding out exactly how hard a grasp your man likes is to ask him to place his hand over yours and to demonstrate his grip.

Basic masturbation

For the basic masturbation technique, grasp your man's penis at the base, then, squeezing lightly, slide your hand up it and over the coronal ridge then back down again. Continue with this sequence repeatedly, tightening your grip a little with each stroke so that the pressure on the penis increases from a light touch through to quite firm. In addition to this basic technique you could try out some variations, shown below. Genital massage (see p.64) is also pleasurable.

> **• SEX TIP •**
>
> The coronal ridge (see p.45) is usually the most sensitive part of the penis, so whatever movement you carry out when you are masturbating him, make sure that this is stimulated in some way.

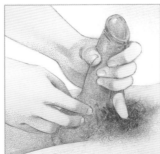

◀ Testicle stimulation

As you continue performing the basic masturbation strokes described above with one hand, use the other hand to cup, fondle, and stroke his testicles, and to caress his perineum (the area between the anus and the testicles).

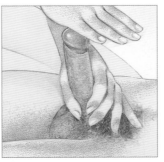

◀ Circles variation

While making the basic masturbation strokes with one hand, slide the well-lubricated palm of the other in rapid circles over the head of the penis.

PLEASURE FOR HER

Let your hand casually explore your woman's labia and clitoris, stroking over the bumps and folds as if by accident. This is an exciting preliminary, a promise of things to come if she's lucky. Next, move on to stimulating her more fully, as shown here. You may also want to try out some genital massage techniques (see p.64). Don't expect her genitals to be automatically moist. If they aren't, coat your fingers with saliva or a lubricant.

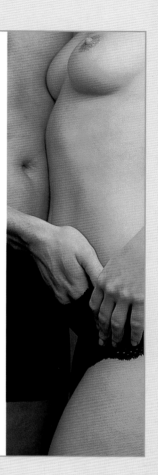

DISCOVER HER PREFERENCES

WHEN MASTURBATING your woman, ask her to tell you whether or not she likes what you are doing and perhaps get her to use her hand to guide yours and show you what she enjoys best. Steve and Vera Bodansky, authors of the book *Massive Extended Orgasm*, claim that sliding a finger up and down the left side of a woman's clitoris is the optimum move for high excitement. However, since every woman is different it would certainly be wise to do a little in-depth research yourself as well!

◀ Clitoral strokes

Begin by gently twirling a well-lubricated finger lightly on the head of the clitoris, then rub your finger on one side of the clitoris and the other several times. Rub backwards and forwards immediately beneath the clitoris, then rub very slowly up from underneath the clitoris right over the head. Rub across the head from one side to the other.

ORAL SEX

Many people enjoy the sensations and feelings of intimacy of oral sex. Fellatio is done to the man, and consists of the manipulation of the penis by mouth. The man may climax in his partner's mouth, or she may prefer to substitute a hand or tissue for the last stage of the proceedings. Cunnilingus is performed on the woman, and involves manipulation of the clitoris by the man's tongue. Don't forget – every woman's clitoral sensitivity differs; ask her occasionally for feedback. Simultaneous oral sex is known as the "69" (see p.119).

FELLATIO

Start by treating his penis like an ice-cream cone, holding it at the base and licking all over, running your tongue up and down the shaft. Then take the penis between your lips and slide your mouth gradually down to its base and back again. To vary the pleasure try out the other methods shown here.

> **• FELLATIO TIP •**
>
> If you have a small mouth and your partner has a large penis, cover your teeth with your lips when you perform fellatio, or your lover may receive a painful bite.

Taking into the mouth ▶

Take his penis into your mouth (the whole length or about halfway) and suck it vigorously. Alternatively, experiment with fellating the head only, including hand stimulation at the same time. You could move his penis around your mouth as if you were brushing the inside of your mouth with it.

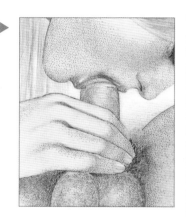

TIPS FOR MEN

SOME MEN FEEL SELF-CONSCIOUS about oral sex. A major part of this is about body odour, in particular the scent of their semen. If you have any doubts about how acceptable you may smell or taste, take a look at the following suggestions:

- Cut down on the pepper and salt – these make semen taste bitter. Instead, go for blander food such as chips and peas for a "neutral" odour. Eat cinnamon and sugar for a sweeter tang. Or if she adores all things Asian, indulge in a spicy curry beforehand.

- Some men focus anxieties on the amount of semen they produce. Be aware that it is normal to have less ejaculate when you are older or if you have had a lot of sex. Nevertheless, there is a method of boosting semen production. Try eating foods rich in zinc – these include seeds and nuts. Adequate zinc is vital for the production of testosterone, for sperm formation, and for prostate health. So knock back a large handful of pumpkin seeds every day!

◀ Kissing the tip

With his penis in your hand, kiss it gently as though you were kissing his lower lip. Next, twirl your tongue around the penis head, taking care to rub across the coronal ridge and the frenulum (see p.45) – these are usually the most sensitive spots.

Nibbling the sides ▶

Hold the end of his penis between your fingertips, then kiss and delicately nibble the sides. You could also try out the butterfly flick, which consists of flicking your tongue across and along the ridge on the underside of the penis.

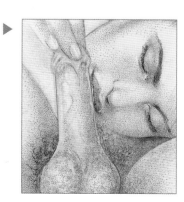

CUNNILINGUS

Position your head between and slightly below her thighs so that you can stroke your tongue upwards against the shaft of her clitoris. Experiment with your tongue tip and blade. Try stimulating one side of the clitoris and then the other, and occasionally insert your tongue into her vagina.

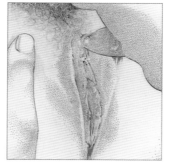

Twirling on the clitoris
Featherlight tongue-twirling on top of the clitoris itself can be sensational. So too can flicking the tip of the tongue from side to side immediately beneath it. Try covering the clitoris with your mouth gently and flicking your tongue firmly across it at the same time.

Penetrating the vagina
Run your tongue along and between her labia and insert your tongue into her vagina, moving your tongue up and down and in and out, using both shallow and deep strokes.

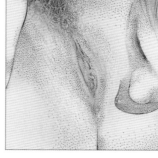

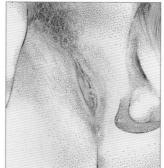

Licking the perineum
Lightly lick up and down her perineum (the area between the vagina and anus), using the tip of your tongue.

Getting in position
Position yourself so that you can stimulate the clitoris from underneath, and be very gentle because it is extremely sensitive and can bruise.

• CUNNILINGUS TIP •

The secret to good cunnilingus is to focus on the place where she most enjoys stimulation and not to move around too much.

FOOD GAMES

The jury is out when it comes to food games. One side believes that the combination of food substances and lovemaking is an exceedingly sexy juxtaposition. The other side instinctively recoils from the mess that occurs when food and bedclothes are brought into contact with each other. For those of you who are turned on by the notion of combining two of life's great sensual pleasures – eating and making love – a few of the most popular food games are described here. A word of warning: never pour any kind of food substance into the vagina, because this could encourage an infection.

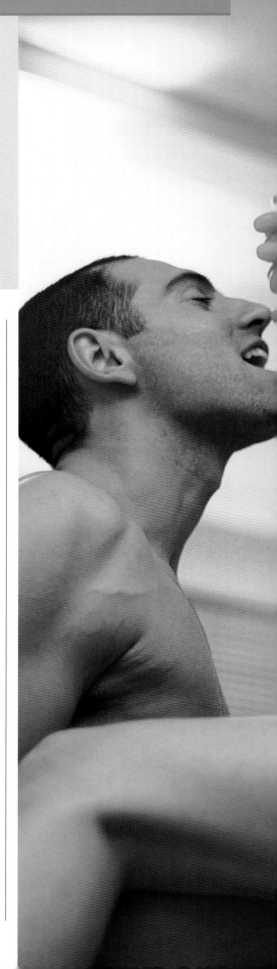

What is the appeal?

Food has been a sex aid since time immemorial. The slippery, sticky, or juicy nature of some foodstuffs – such as honey or fruit – seems to lend itself to the similarly sensual nature of the sex act. Sometimes it's not the food substance itself that's the sex trigger but the manner in which a particular food is eaten. If you eat something in such a way that suggests you would much rather be eating your partner and you do it in just such a lip-smacking, tongue-licking style, it's hardly surprising that your lover will acquire an appetite for sex.

We can only guess what our primitive ancestors may have done with their edibles, but the link between the decadent Roman sex orgies and food is well documented.

Psychological motivations

The mouth is the first source of nourishment to any human being and is therefore also the first source of sensuality. The experience of being suckled at the breast or fed by the bottle may not linger in our conscious memories as adults, but it is certainly stored somewhere deep in the unconscious. One of our unconscious

TWO ICE GAMES

THE SHOCK OF extreme cold starts adrenaline flowing, promoting feelings of anticipation and excitement. You could just rub an ice-cube all over your lover's body, or try the following:

1 Suck an ice-cube, then apply your cold mouth to your lover's nipples. Next, take a mouthful of a hot drink and reapply your hot lips to the nipples.

2 Fill a condom with crushed ice and use it to massage parts of your lover's body, such as in the creases at the top of the thighs or between the toes.

motivations during the early stages of love is to recreate the very early and primitive bonds of love and sensuality we first experienced with our mother. Sexual food games can, for some people, fulfil this unconscious need.

Another side to food games that appeals to many people is the "forbidden factor". Most children are taught to keep clean while eating, and life's natural rebels may get a kick out of combining sex and food in adulthood precisely because these are "messy" and "forbidden" activities.

Sensational games

There are numerous food games that you could try with your partner, all of which are tasty preliminaries to lovemaking. One is to decorate your lover's body, using a soft paintbrush, with stripes of honey and whipped cream. Once your partner is covered in the food, lick his or her body from the neck down to the toes. Lick around the breasts, the areolae, and the nipples, and then around the outside of the genitals. Use the honey to slide your finger between your lover's fingers and toes.

Elaborate feasts

You could adorn your lover with highly coloured food such as jams, cake decorations, syrups, and creams, and serve him or her up as "dessert", which you then "eat up". Alternatively, you could have a sexual banquet. Run your partner a hot, steamy bath, and dribble champagne over their mouth and skin, licking it off with long sweeps of the tongue. After the bath, feast on a tray of specially prepared exotic fruits. You could use the fruit in your lovemaking, crushing it against your partner's body and massaging it into his or her skin.

CHAPTER 4

The Art
of Good Sex

stimulation

PENETRATION

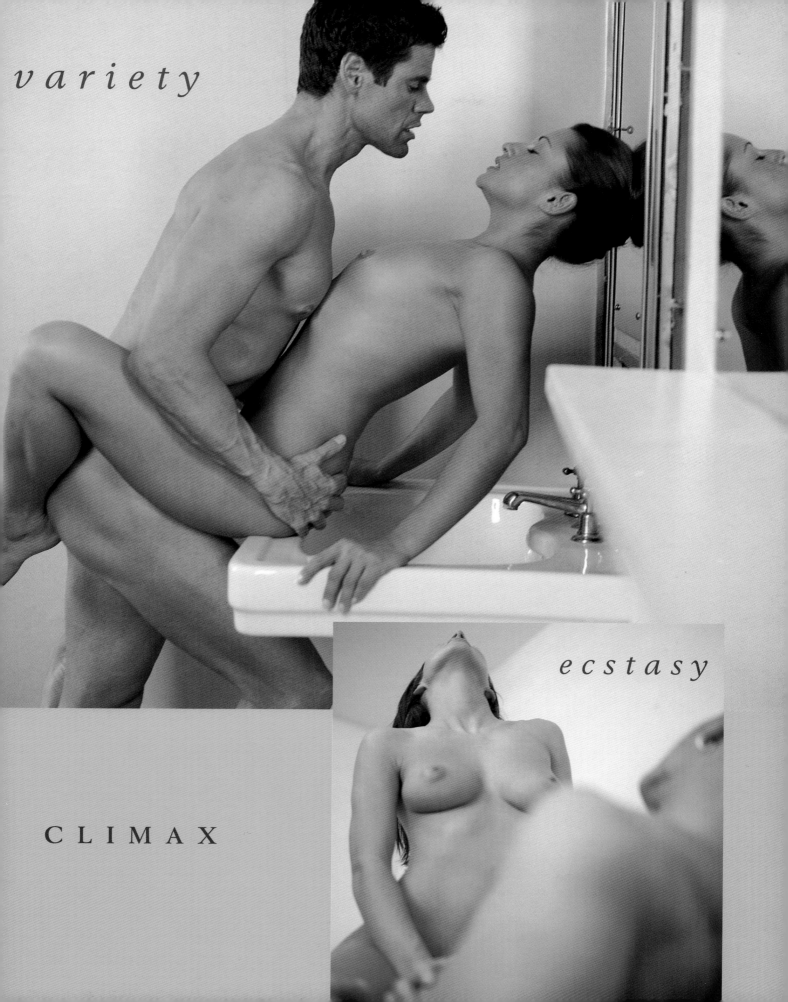

SEXUAL RESPONSE IN BOTH SEXES

Men and women's physiological experience of sexual arousal is remarkably similar. Each undergoes at least three stages of response. These consist of desire, arousal, and orgasm, after which the body returns to its previous unstimulated state (this is known as "resolution").

DESIRE

The preliminary stage of sexual response in both sexes is desire. This is when the idea of sex first comes into your head, and is usually triggered by a sexy thought or touch. In theory, it is not about the turn-on of the body although, particularly with men, the two stages (desire and arousal) can occur almost concurrently. Males are usually more turned on by a visual stimulus than females, whereas in women it is often the idea of a man – the whole person – that creates female desire.

AROUSAL

The next stage of the response cycle is arousal, where the body undergoes a series of visible changes as excitement builds. Many of these changes are common to both sexes – the blood rushes to the genitals, the body perspires, the nipples harden, and the heart rate, blood pressure, breathing rate, and muscle tension increase. The physical changes make the body extra-sensitive to touch and stimulation, increasing the participants' pleasure further.

Physiological changes during arousal

— Men
— Women

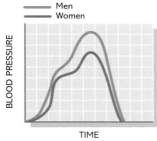

BLOOD PRESSURE / TIME

◀ **Blood pressure**
As sexual excitement builds, blood pressure rises by about one-third, reaching even higher at orgasm. This rise in blood pressure is slightly greater in men than in women.

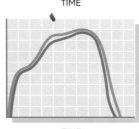

BEATS PER MINUTE / TIME

◀ **Heart rate**
Both sexes have a normal heart rate of about 80 beats per minute (bpm). In the plateau phase, this more than doubles. At orgasm, a woman's bpm can reach 175 and a man's 180.

BREATHS PER MINUTE / TIME

◀ **Breathing pattern**
When excited, men and women breathe much more loudly and quickly. At the point of orgasm, they are taking as many as 40 breaths per minute, twice the normal number.

◀ Reaching orgasm

The experience of orgasm is one of extreme sensual pleasure in the genital region. Many women can climax in other areas too.

ORGASM

When sensations become increasingly intense, both partners experience a peak of pleasure called orgasm. Orgasm is similar for the sexes, containing exactly the same timing of orgasmic contractions for men and for women (0.8 second intervals). With men, orgasm is almost inevitably accompanied by the ejaculation of seminal fluid, although this is not always the case (see p.96). The majority of men associate climax with their genital area, and only rarely experience orgasm elsewhere. Women, however, appear to be capable of experiencing orgasm in many different sites of the body in addition to the genitals, including in some cases the entire body. Orgasms for both sexes may be long and strong, short and weak, sometimes a mere flutter, other times so drawn out that they last for almost a minute. What's more, all of these variations may be experienced by one individual during a lifetime.

RESOLUTION

After orgasm, the body returns to its original resting state. The body tension is released, the blood flow drains from the genitals, the heart rate, blood pressure, and sex flush subside, and the breathing returns to normal. This process is usually considerably quicker for men than women, who can often remain aroused for some time after orgasm, and with continued stimulation can experience climax for a second or a third time or more (see p.97).

TIMING OF SEXUAL RESPONSE

ALTHOUGH MEN AND WOMEN experience sexual excitement in similar ways, there are also considerable differences, particularly in the timing of the key stages of sexual response. Men tend to become aroused very quickly, and this stage is then followed by a relatively long plateau phase before orgasm. Women generally take longer to become fully aroused, and require a lot more stimulation than men to reach the same point. However, their plateau stage, between arousal and orgasm, is shorter than in men.

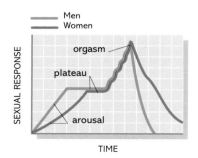

— Men
— Women

SEXUAL RESPONSE

orgasm

plateau

arousal

TIME

MEN TEND to reach the plateau phase within only a few minutes, while sometimes women need about 15–30 minutes. For this reason, a man needs to wait until his partner has "caught up".

HIS SEXUAL RESPONSE

The sexual response cycle starts off with feelings of desire. This is frequently triggered by a visual stimulus – for example, the glimpse of a woman's thigh as she puts on her stockings, or her breasts as she fastens her bra. Alternatively, a sexy thought or a light touch can put ideas into a man's head. Sexual interest will then register in his brain, which will in turn transmit signals to his genitals. The next stage is arousal, when fairly dramatic physiological changes start to take place, then finally orgasm.

SEXFACTS

MALE AROUSAL
Men generally become sexually aroused within 10–30 seconds of initial stimulation, although this timing varies according to the individual.

BECOMING AROUSED

Once the brain has registered sexual interest, it sends a message to the penis. In most cases, the man has an erection within seconds. When stimulated, the erect penis then sends further sensual feeling back to the brain and to other areas of the body, causing further excitement.

External signs of arousal

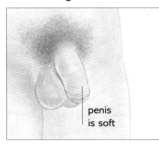

penis is soft

1 Before the brain registers desire, the penis hangs down in its flaccid state. (The genitals return to this state shortly after orgasm, at the stage sometimes known as "resolution").

2 During arousal, large amounts of blood rush to the spongy tissues of the penis, making it large and stiff so that it stands out from the body. The glans swells with blood.

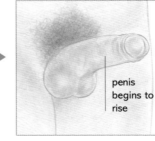

penis begins to rise

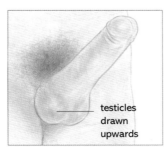

testicles drawn upwards

3 The scrotum thickens and the testicles are drawn up to the body. As more blood flows into the penis, the glans swells further and becomes a dark red or purplish colour.

All-over body changes during arousal

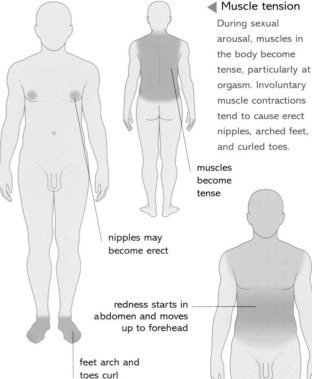

◀ **Muscle tension**
During sexual arousal, muscles in the body become tense, particularly at orgasm. Involuntary muscle contractions tend to cause erect nipples, arched feet, and curled toes.

muscles become tense

nipples may become erect

redness starts in abdomen and moves up to forehead

feet arch and toes curl

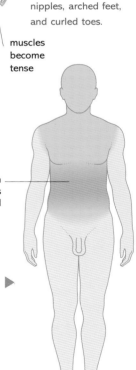

Sex flush

During the most intense phase of sexual arousal, about 25 per cent of men show a reddening of the skin. This is known as the "sex flush", and it begins on the stomach and then spreads to cover the chest, neck, and face. Many men also perspire, particularly on the hands and feet but sometimes all over.

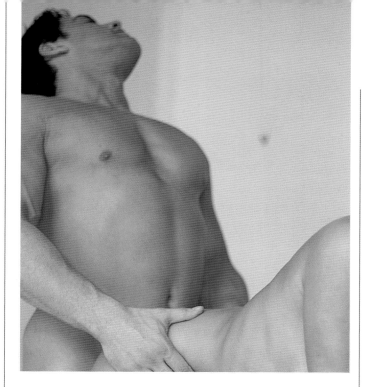

What happens during orgasm

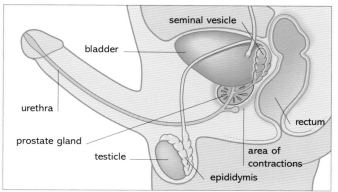

1 The sperm are produced in the testicles and stored in the epididymis. Ejaculation begins with a series of contractions in the seminal vesicle, prostate gland, and rectum.

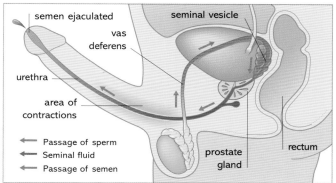

2 The sperm travels up via the vas deferens to the seminal vesicle. At the point of ejaculation, the contractions pump the sperm and seminal fluid (produced in the prostate gland) into the urethra, where they combine to make semen. Contractions at the base of the penis force semen along to the urethral opening, where it is ejaculated.

REACHING ORGASM

At a high point, the tension and sensual feeling build up so intensely that orgasm is triggered, consisting of penile contractions (at approximately 0.8 second intervals) and usually resulting in ejaculation of seminal fluid. At the moment of orgasm, breathing is twice as fast as it would be normally. The heartbeat is more than double its usual rate, and blood pressure is increased by one-third (see p.86). Most men can sense when they are about to climax – they feel a forceful, and often inevitable, need to ejaculate (this is often known as the "point of no return"). The rhythmic contractions at the base of the penis propel sperm and seminal fluid (combined to make semen) up the urethral tube and out of the penis tip.

AFTER ORGASM

Once orgasm occurs, a man goes into a refractory period where all the physical signs of sexual arousal drain from the body and he returns to his former relaxed, unstimulated state. The penis becomes limp. His heart rate, blood pressure, and sex flush subside, his breathing returns to normal, and the muscle tension is resolved. Unlike women, few men can repeat sexual intercourse immediately after orgasm, although multiple orgasms are possible in some men (see p.96).

HER SEXUAL RESPONSE

As with men, desire is the first stage of the female response cycle. A sexy thought enters a woman's brain, often triggered by touch, and the brain then transmits signals to her genitals. For women, touch and desire tend to be interrelated, and women are less likely to be turned on by a visual stimulus than men. Once stimulation begins and excitement builds, the woman starts to become aroused (this is a slower process than in men). Numerous changes start to take place in the body as it prepares for orgasm.

SEXFACTS

FEMALE AROUSAL

The time it takes for a woman to reach a state of extreme arousal can vary from a couple of minutes to three-quarters of an hour.

BECOMING AROUSED

Arousal in women usually begins with the initial physical stimulation. Once a woman starts to get turned on (and just a passionate kiss can get the ball rolling), her breasts swell slightly and her nipples harden and, like her male partner, her muscles tense, her heart rate and blood pressure increase, and her breathing rate speeds up (see p.86). In preparation for intercourse, many changes occur in the genitals: the vagina becomes lubricated, in order to enable the penis to enter smoothly, then lengthens and swells with blood – this is similar to the male erection, although it is not as noticeable. In addition, the shape of the vagina alters slightly – this is known as "tenting", and occurs when the vaginal passage creates a kind of capped tent shape. The labia also swell slightly as the sexual tension and excitement build. In fact, there is so much swelling of tissue around the clitoris that the clitoris seems to "disappear" because it gets almost hidden. At this stage of extreme arousal, the tissues around the nipples swell with fluid so that nipple erection seems to disappear.

External signs of arousal

1 Prior to arousal, the clitoris, labia, and vagina are pink in colour and in a relaxed state. (After orgasm, it can take some time for the genitals to return to their normal shape and colour.)

pale pink vulva

2 When aroused, the vagina becomes lubricated, expands and swells with blood, and lengthens. The labia swell to three times their original thickness and move away from the vaginal opening.

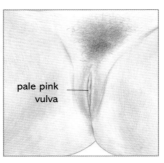

vagina expands and swells

3 When stimulated, the clitoris becomes enlarged and pulls back against the pubic bone. The clitoris may be difficult to see owing to the swelling of the surrounding tissues. The vagina and labia change in coloration from pink to a deep red or darker, purplish shade.

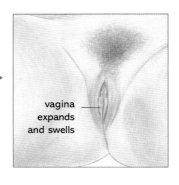

darker coloration of vagina

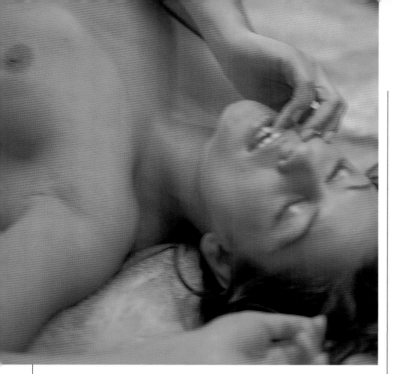

REACHING ORGASM

Once tension and sensual feeling have built up sufficiently, orgasm is triggered. Contractions may be experienced in the vagina, clitoris, and uterus, as well as other body sites. Some women experience extra "wetness" during climax. Most women, unlike men, are capable of holding off orgasm until they choose to experience one, and some can experience climax for a second or third time (see p.97). A minority of women never experience orgasm, although this can sometimes be remedied by sex therapy.

What happens during orgasm

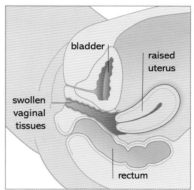

1 During a high state of arousal, the vagina expands and tissue in the outer third of the vagina swells to form the orgasmic platform, which grips the penis during intercourse. The uterus rises and the clitoris retracts under its hood.

bladder

raised uterus

swollen vaginal tissues

rectum

2 During orgasm, the cervix, uterus, and outer third of the vagina contract regularly. There are usually three to five (up to a maximum of 15) intensely pleasurable contractions at about 0.8 second intervals, although this varies.

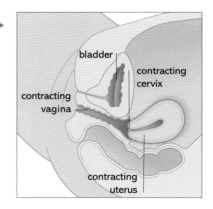

bladder

contracting cervix

contracting vagina

contracting uterus

AFTER ORGASM

Women differ from men in that instead of subsiding rapidly back into an unstimulated state, some women continue to remain sexually aroused and can be stimulated again to experience further orgasms. Eventually though, the body relaxes and returns to its former resting state – the blood flow drains from the genitals, the heart rate and blood pressure subside, and breathing returns to normal. The sex flush lingers for a while but eventually disappears.

All-over body changes during arousal

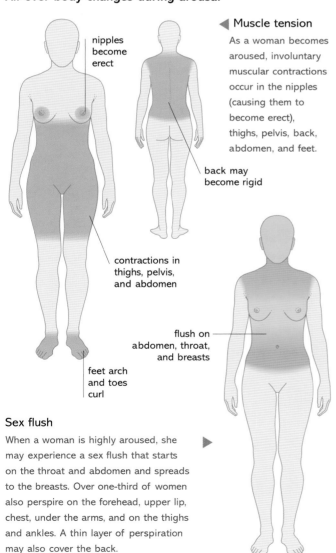

nipples become erect

◄ Muscle tension

As a woman becomes aroused, involuntary muscular contractions occur in the nipples (causing them to become erect), thighs, pelvis, back, abdomen, and feet.

back may become rigid

contractions in thighs, pelvis, and abdomen

flush on abdomen, throat, and breasts

feet arch and toes curl

Sex flush

When a woman is highly aroused, she may experience a sex flush that starts on the throat and abdomen and spreads to the breasts. Over one-third of women also perspire on the forehead, upper lip, chest, under the arms, and on the thighs and ankles. A thin layer of perspiration may also cover the back.

ORGASM TECHNIQUES FOR MEN

There's been so much written about sex techniques for women that men tend to get overlooked. Perhaps this is because they are lucky enough to become familiar with their genitals and sexual response pattern much earlier than most women. Nevertheless, male experiences of orgasm are just as individual as those of women and just as varied.

A man's orgasm depends almost entirely on having his penis stimulated, manually, orally, or as a result of intercourse. Although the actual mechanics of orgasm are likely to be the same for each male, the subjective experience is not. During climax men may lie utterly still, they may shudder slightly, or their entire body might convulse. There is an historic sex education film of a male ballet dancer masturbating, which shows him virtually dancing around the room before and during his climax. How men experience orgasm during intercourse may reflect how they have discovered sexuality as young men.

Orgasmic expectations

Although orgasm is virtually ensured for men in a way it is not for women, the sense of satisfaction from that same orgasm varies greatly. The man who yearns for a longer, stronger, and more intense experience may either have a lower sexual drive than most men or could be so anxious about his sexuality that he has physically exhausted himself with excessive sexual intercourse or masturbation. Alternatively, he may simply have unrealistic expectations of how amazing orgasm should be.

Age and experience

Most young men experience little difficulty with climax, except possibly that it happens too fast (see pp.208–209). Generally, the younger you are, the easier, stronger, and more copious in terms of ejaculation the orgasm will be. Men are believed to be at their sexual peak at around the age of 18. Ten years later, at the age of 28, that orgasmic experience will have already changed, and will continue to do so as the man ages. Although the orgasmic experience will still continue to feel intensely pleasurable, it will not be as long or as strong as in the early years. Nor will it be desired so often. For some men who identify closely with their sexual response, this can sometimes be distressing. However, we need to recognize that this is a perfectly natural part of the aging process, and that by keeping healthy and fit we can extend our sexual life.

THE WAY A MAN experiences orgasm differs between individuals. Some men are totally silent as they climax, while others call out or groan. As men age, the intensity of orgasm tends to diminish.

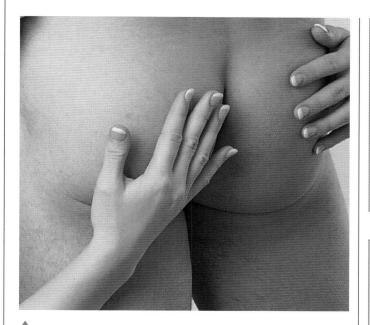

▲
Work up to it slowly
Try to take stimulation slowly. A man becomes aroused more quickly than a woman, so if his climax comes too soon she will miss out.

STIMULATE THE PROSTATE

This tends to be the man's forgotten sex organ, mainly because it is hidden at the top of the anal passage. Yet stimulation of the prostate alone, through massage, can bring a man to orgasm. There are now some excellent anal vibrators designed for this task (see p.144).

Stimulating his prostate

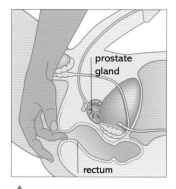

prostate gland

rectum

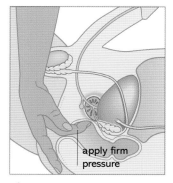

apply firm pressure

▲
1 The prostate gland encircles the urethra at the exit from the bladder. To reach it, insert a well-lubricated finger into the anus and press against its front wall (the side nearest the penis).

▲
2 You will feel the prostate gland as a firm, walnut-sized mass. Press it in a sustained, regular rhythm to give maximum pleasure. Always wash your hands immediately afterwards.

THE PULSAR

THE PULSAR IS A TECHNIQUE that enhances the sensation of orgasm, and should be done during ejaculation. Clasp your two hands around the head of your man's penis. Squeeze gently, hold for a second then let go. Pause. Then do it again. The trick is to imitate the rhythm of the pulse. Try to time your pulsations to go with his contractions.

10 TIPS TO IMPROVE ORGASM

ORGASMS PROVIDE fantastic sensations. Here are a few tips that will make them even better:

1 Delay climax – the more drawn out the build-up to sex, the more sexual tension there is to release at the time of orgasm, leading to a deeper climax. There are a number of delaying techniques you can try (see p.99).

2 Do exercises to develop muscle control so that you can time your climaxes better. These will also increase your chances of experiencing multiple orgasms (see p.96).

3 Include the prostate gland in your stimulation, either before or during intercourse (see left).

4 Stroke and caress the perineum and testicles sensitively – they are highly erogenous zones.

5 Use your imagination: think sexy thoughts, remember sexy sights, and go to places in your mind where you wouldn't dream of going in real life.

6 Abstain from alcohol, tobacco, and drugs. These can all dull sexual sensation and performance (see pp.218–19).

7 Improve penile muscle tone through exercises such as pelvic-floor exercises (see p.175).

8 Use first-class sex lubrication. A lubricated penis instantly becomes more sensitive and receives more pleasurable feeling than a dry one.

9 Experiment with the pulsar technique (see above), which feels fantastic during ejaculation.

10 Try climaxing in only one out of three lovemaking sessions – the belief is that in this way you can build up an explosive orgasm and intense sensation.

ORGASM TECHNIQUES FOR WOMEN

Most informed young men today know that the movement of penile thrusting alone may well not bring their loved-one to the heights of ecstasy. So what are the main methods of her enjoying orgasm? A woman's climax depends primarily on the amount of stimulation her clitoris receives – her clitoris being the main organ of sensation (see pp.46–47).

◀ **Guiding him**
Every woman's sexual response is different, so it's important that the woman guides her partner and communicates how and where she likes to be touched.

Extra stimulation
Some women require manual stimulation in order to continue to climax during intercourse. Here, the man reaches his hand around and stimulates her clitoris, timing the touch to his thrusts. ▼

INTERCOURSE PLUS MASTURBATION

Intercourse alone isn't usually the best way for a woman to enjoy an orgasm. This is because the clitoris doesn't get enough direct stimulation from the penis. It appears to be a design fault in the human female that the clitoris is situated so high on the genitals it tends to get missed by the thrust of lovemaking. Of the women who do manage to climax during intercourse, we now know that the in–out movement of the penis exerts a mild downward pull of the clitoral hood, which is attached to the labia, on the sensitive clitoris. For some women this slight stimulation is enough. But for most, it is not. Indeed, some women never experience orgasm from intercourse alone.

The majority of women want and enjoy intercourse but need that something extra to make it finally culminate in a climax. The most straightforward way is to give your lover a lot of stimulation by hand so that she is extremely aroused by the time you get to intercourse (see p.77). For some women, this is enough to get them up and over into orgasm. Others need the manual stimulation continued even during intercourse. This stimulation can be done either by him or by her and is extremely effective.

During the first six months of a new sexual relationship, a couple are likely to experiment with many different sex positions, partly to discover what feels best for this particular couple combination. Experimenting with sex from the rear (see pp.108–109), for example, is one sex position couples regularly try out but it can sometimes prove very disappointing for the woman because she doesn't have an orgasm this way. The reason for this is that her clitoris gets no stimulation at all from this position. However, there is an easy answer to this – the man can reach his fingers around and masturbate her at the same time. It can feel exciting, erotic, and very arousing.

THE JOY OF VIBRATORS

There are some men and women for whom the combination of masturbation and intercourse either feels uncomfortable or still does not offer enough stimulation. This is where vibrators come to the rescue (see pp.142–43). Vibrators are not just for novelty value; for some women they are essential, and can make the difference between experiencing orgasm and never doing so. Vibrators today have travelled a long way from the pink plastic, penis-shaped models. You can purchase them in bright jelly colours, in a variety of shapes and sizes, and with a number of special and very pleasing attributes.

SEX FOR ONE

MOST WOMEN LOVE the closeness and fullness they experience during face-to-face intercourse. However, they may not necessarily get intense climaxes this way. Self-touch (see pp.70–71) generally offers much longer, stronger, more drawn-out orgasmic experiences. It's a good idea to experience self-stimulation so that you learn your own orgasmic patterns as well as your own erogenous zones. If you know what gives you an orgasm, you can take this information into your relationship and help your man find his way.

THE G-SPOT

The G-spot is a small area on the front wall of the vagina, although it doesn't appear to be present in all women. When pressed, it is believed to trigger orgasm. It is named after gynaecologist Ernst Grafenburg, who first described it, relating it to the point where the urethra runs closest to the top of the vaginal wall. Others think it to be the vestiges of what would have been the prostate gland if the foetus had developed into a boy. Indeed, some women who appear to have G-spot orgasm appear to ejaculate a thin arc of fluid, which has proved to be similar to seminal fluid, when climaxing. The latest theory is that the G-spot is the root of the clitoris – hence its sensitivity.

How to find your G-spot
Place your finger inside your vagina and try to reach the far end (this can be very difficult). Reach with the finger towards your abdomen. The G-spot feels like a small bump swelling out of the front wall of the vagina.

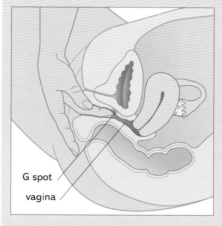

G spot

vagina

◀ **How to stimulate the G-spot**
Exert a steady pressure with your finger on the spot, pushing for a count of ten, then let go, then press again. It is pressure rather than light stroking that brings on the erotic sensation and can trigger climax.

MULTIPLE ORGASMS

Women have long been known to be capable of multiple orgasms. In the 1940s, the *Kinsey Report* revealed that 14 per cent of women interviewed experienced multiple climaxes, and Masters and Johnson's scientific laboratory research in the 1950s confirmed that this was certainly possible. It is now believed that some men may be capable of more than one orgasm in a session.

MULTIPLE ORGASMS FOR MEN

Laboratory research carried out by American sex researchers Hartman and Fithian in the 1970s indicated that men may be capable of experiencing multiple orgasms, and that their orgasms may or may not involve ejaculation. Since male climax is so associated with ejaculation, no one can say for certain whether the multi-orgasmic males observed were actually climaxing or if they were simply experiencing peaks of excitement. Whatever the case, they were clearly undergoing an extremely intense, prolonged sexual experience – their breathing quickened, their heart rate increased, and their muscle tension intensified. One of

the subjects appeared to have seven distinct orgasms in ten minutes. The men managed their multiple climaxes by self-control and training: they tensed their thighs and squeezed their pelvic-floor muscles (see p.175), thus blocking off their ejaculations by closing their urethral tubes with muscle action.

Multiple orgasm exercises

To build up muscle tension in the pelvic area, alternately flex and relax your lower abdomen, pelvic-floor muscles, and thighs. ▼

MULTIPLE ORGASM TRAINING FOR MEN

THERE ARE VARIOUS WAYS you can develop the right degree of muscle control to achieve multiple orgasms, although it does take time and patience:

1. Learn testicle control. Standing with your feet apart, pull up your testicle muscles towards your lower abdomen. Repeat as often as possible every day, but stop if your testicles begin to hurt.

2. Give yourself an erection and train yourself to keep it hard for as long as possible.

3. Climax is triggered by a kind of tension in the pelvic area called "myotonia". To build this up, alternately flex and relax your thighs and lower abdomen for as long as possible: five minutes is the aim, but stop if you get cramp.

4. Excite yourself slowly, building up to a high pitch of arousal over a long time. When you feel about to reach orgasm, clench your pelvic-floor muscles (see p.175). If you feel this isn't going to work, try the Beautrais manoeuvre (see p.99), in which you pull down on your testicles, or the squeeze technique (see p.208), which involves squeezing the penis.

MULTIPLE ORGASMS FOR WOMEN

Not all women experience multiple orgasms, but a lot more can manage it than their male counterparts. Multiple climaxes can be experienced in various ways, but they tend to consist of a series of separate orgasms occurring within a short time, sometimes with only a few seconds between, occasionally longer. Some women experience them as a series of gentle peaks of excitement that feel connected, while others have one strong climax after another.

No one yet knows why some women should be able to have multiple climaxes and not others, although carrying on with stimulation is essential. One theory is that the more testosterone you have, the more likely you are to climax easily and often.

How to experience multiple orgasms

To experience multiple orgasms a woman must always have continued stimulation after her initial climax – it is vital to maintain a high degree of arousal. Her partner needs either to continue intercourse, or to press on with manual

• SEX TIP •

Don't see it as a personal failure if you don't achieve multiple orgasms. Nearly all men and many women never experience them, and this is perfectly normal.

SEXFACTS

TAKING MEDICATION

Certain medications, such as the contraceptive pill, can lessen sexual response. If you have taken the Pill all your sexual life, it might be more difficult to determine if you can have multiple climaxes.

stimulation, instead of stopping because he thinks her climax is over. If you are experimenting on yourself, instead of removing your fingers from your clitoris because it feels so sensitive after orgasm, carry on with the stimulation. You could also use a vibrator to experiment with prolonging stimulation after the first climax.

Maintaining excitement

After your first orgasm, keep up the stimulation. At the very least you may discover that your orgasm can continue for far longer than you anticipated. At best, it may turn into more than one. ▼

CONTROLLING ORGASMS

Timing tends to be a crucial element of good sex, because it is frequently the key to whether or not both partners experience orgasm. With the right element of control, a couple can prolong the sexual experience and can vary the type of orgasm they wish to experience, for example a simultaneous orgasm, when both partners climax at the same time; a sequential one, when one partner's orgasm follows the other; or even multiple orgasms, where the woman (and occasionally man) have several climaxes in quick succession (see pp.96–97).

TYPES OF ORGASMS

Prior to all the ground-breaking sexual research of the 1960s and 1970s, the belief was that the "correct" way to experience orgasm was at the same time as your partner. Indeed, having an orgasm at the same moment as your lover can feel extremely intimate. However, many people prefer a sequential orgasm to a simultaneous one since this allows you to enjoy the intensity of your own experience rather than being distracted by thinking of your partner's enjoyment at such a crucial point.

Since most men cannot continue intercourse after ejaculation, and because most women tend to need more stimulation than their man, the best way to experience simultaneous orgasm is to excite your woman first until she reaches a point of arousal that appears to match your own. Let go of your own climax only when she is clearly almost at the point of climax too.

◀ **Bring her to climax**
To give your woman maximum pleasure, concentrate on stimulating her and hold back your own orgasm. When she is ready, either bring her to orgasm first, or time it so that you climax together.

• **SEX TIP** •

Women – to encourage orgasm or to enhance the experience, try thinking of scenes from a sexy story or fantasy, or an erotic film.

◀ **Beautrais manoeuvre**
To prolong intercourse, when you feel that you're on the brink of orgasm, grasp your testicles and pull down very firmly. This has the effect of blocking the urethral passage and so prevents ejaculation.

DELAYING ORGASM FOR MEN

In order to ensure that your woman reaches orgasm, or that the two of you manage a simultaneous climax if that is what is desired, you need to have complete control of your penis to get the timing right. This can be difficult for many men, particularly those who suffer from premature ejaculation (see pp.208–209). It is particularly important for these men to slow themselves down, or their partners may never get the chance to reach orgasm.

Fortunately, orgasm control can be learned. You could try and improve your muscle control by doing exercises (see p.96). Alternatively, the best methods of controlling climax are the Beautrais manoeuvre (see above), or the squeeze technique, which involves squeezing the ridge around the head of the penis firmly between the thumb and forefingers at the point of no return (see p.208).

DELAYING ORGASM FOR WOMEN

One of the sex differences between men and women is that if you stop stimulating a man, he remains sexually excited. If you stop stimulating a woman, her arousal fades so rapidly that it takes quite a while to bring her back to the same peak of excitement. So if you are one of those rare women who climaxes too soon, try stopping the stimulation for a short time and giving your man oral sex or manual stimulation for a while. It should slow you down without materially affecting your partner.

• SEX TIP •

Tantric sex (see pp.120–21) aims at slowing down and intensifying the orgasmic experience, and side-by-side positions (see pp.110–11) can also be slow and sensual and so likely to prolong intercourse and delay orgasm.

MAN-ON-TOP POSITIONS

Sexual positions in which the man is on top have long been favoured by couples in the Western world. This is possibly because they are the most comfortable and conserving of energy; in addition, they are among the positions in which the woman is most likely to climax. They are also very romantic: they provide close, face-to-face contact, and offer you the opportunity to kiss, caress, and murmur into your lover's ear while watching his or her reaction. The missionary position is by far the most common sex position in European and American cultures. In 1948, sex researcher Alfred Kinsey (see pp.20–21) discovered that 70 per cent of Americans had never had sex any other way.

POINTS TO REMEMBER

THE MOST IMPORTANT MESSAGE about sexual intercourse is not to take it all too seriously. Good sex is really about having fun. So the points that follow here are not about technique – they are just general reminders that sexual intercourse is play rather than work:

1 Sexual intercourse isn't a race. There's no hurry to "complete the job", and you can take your time. Make sure that you allow plenty of time for foreplay, and make your thrusting movements as slow as you want. Most people find that they like starting off slow, but that as they get more aroused, the action spontaneously speeds up.

2 Have breaks if you want them. Some of the best sex sessions are those where you talk, laugh, and fool around, without feeling you have to "get on with it". There's no rule that specifies once you have begun thrusting you must continue to thrust until the bitter end. Remember, your partner may get enormously stimulated by talking and laughing during sex, because that actually heightens his or her pleasure.

3 A partner usually likes to get some kind of indication that he or she is having an impact, so don't forget the importance of moaning, sighing, kissing, and saying "I love you". Sex communication doesn't just depend on your own temperament, it also depends on the kind of communication "fit" that the two of you create in the early days of the relationship, so share your feelings with your partner early on.

THE BASIC MISSIONARY POSITION

Legend has it that this position was so named by South Sea islanders, who spied on their local European missionaries making love. They were amused to see that the man was always on top, and found the missionaries' movements unvarying and limited. Accustomed to a more outdoor, physical life, the natives were naturally more athletic and able to sustain more energetic forms of intercourse. However, there is much to be said for this position, being both relaxing and intimate. In the basic missionary, the woman opens her legs, with her knees bent, and the man or woman guides his penis into her vagina. The beauty of the missionary is that it allows the man to support himself on both knees and one arm, thus preventing his partner from being crushed and freeing up the second arm for amicable activity. There are many variations on the basic missionary.

> • SEX TIP •
>
> The missionary position does not necessarily bring a woman to climax, so give her lots of clitoral stimulation before you penetrate. Some women like finger stimulation at the same time as face-to-face intercourse.

Close body contact

One variation on the missionary is for the woman to put her legs straight out in front and closed together once intercourse has begun. This offers an intense method of holding the labia bunched firmly against the penis so that they gain maximum stimulation. ▼

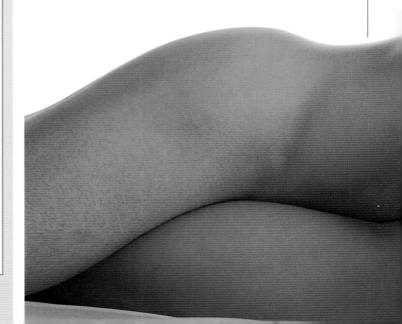

Legs entwined

If the woman wraps her legs around her lover's body she is able to take a more active role in lovemaking by helping to control the tempo and depth of his thrusts.

Relaxed and intimate

In this variation the woman keeps her legs open but lays them out flat on the bed. This is a particularly relaxing pose for the woman, and enables the couple to focus on intimacy, gentle stroking, and face-to-face contact rather than frenetic sexual activity.

VARYING THE WEIGHT

Many men and women are excited by the idea of crushing or being crushed by their partner's body. There's a sensuality to the hardness and the closeness that extreme body contact provides. However, if the man on top is considerably heavier than his female partner, it may be necessary to vary the sex position to prevent her from being injured. This doesn't necessarily mean changing position entirely. He could still stay on top, but could lift himself up occasionally on his arms so that his full weight is not bearing down on his partner.

▲
Intimate wraparound
This position, where the couple lie very close and tightly against one another, shows tenderness and passion.

Supporting his weight
Here, the couple take a break from extreme closeness. He takes the weight off her by raising himself up on his arms, while she shows her tenderness by stroking his neck and head. ▼

• SEX TIP •

Women – once your man has raised himself up on his arms you may miss the intimacy of body contact. To get closer to him, raise your hips up high so that your pelvis presses up against his.

ELEVATING HER LEGS

Sexual intercourse often creates some very primitive feelings in couples, particularly the desire to get as close as possible to another individual. It's very likely that this extreme need for closeness is an unconscious desire to get back into the womb again. One way of feeling particularly close is for the woman to lift her legs up high so that her partner has little to block his penetrating action. This allows him deep inside her body and offers him total sensation to the penis. Remember, she may need some additional manual stimulation.

◄ **She eases the way**
The missionary position is wonderfully changeable. You can begin with the basic position, with her feet flat on the bed or floor, and as you sensually slide together, she can slowly lift up her legs to create different sensations.

Supporting her legs ▶
It can feel insecure for a woman to have her legs waving in the air, so her partner might help out by wedging his arm behind her raised knee. This allows her to rest her leg in the crook of his arm instead of straining to keep it aloft on her own.

◄ **Maximum closeness**
The man now relaxes, letting his weight down onto his elbows. This has the advantage of placing his chest pleasingly along her body, giving an intense feeling of closeness. In addition, the couple's faces are close enough together to enable passionate kissing.

Deep penetration ▶
If the woman pulls her knees up and back she can greatly increase the depth of penetration. Take such powerful strokes very gently – some women have an over-sensitive cervix at the end of the vagina, and slamming into it can shock and bruise rather than delight.

WOMAN-ON-TOP POSITIONS

There are many advantages to woman-on-top positions. They allow the woman to be an active participant and to retain a sense of control, enabling her to set the tempo, movement, and depth of penetration. In addition, she can arrange the angle of thrusting so that her clitoris is in the direct line of fire and achieves optimum pleasure. The woman may initiate sex by sliding on top of the erect penis she has just coaxed into life; alternatively, the man starts off on top and then the couple roll over, reversing their positions.

SITTING ASTRIDE

In Western cultures, the position in which the woman sits astride the man while facing him is probably second in popularity to the missionary position. A 1974 survey showed that nearly three-quarters of all married couples used this sexual position, at least occasionally. This figure had increased since the 1953 *Kinsey Report*, when only one-third of couples had said they used this position.

◀ **Sitting upright**
Lovemaking while sitting in an upright position enables the woman to control her degree of stimulation.

◀ **Leaning forwards**
The forward angle of the woman's body means that her clitoris is able to come into contact with her partner's body. Since the woman is in charge of her own movement, this position is great for increasing her satisfaction.

Leaning backwards ▶
In this position, the woman can lean back, with her hands supporting the weight of her body, while continuing to move. This is a good way to slow the pace of a more thrusting sexual position.

BACK TO FRONT

If you only think of sexual intercourse as a way to achieve the ultimate goal of orgasm, you're missing out on most of the fun! Some of the best sex takes place when two people are both just enjoying each other's bodies and experimenting with new sensations. Couples fool around with all kinds of unlikely sex positions for the sheer pleasure of it, not for the specific aim of achieving orgasm.

Back-to-front sex is often a stepping stone on the way to other more arousing sexual positions. In the Eastern classic, *The Ananga Ranga*, Kama's Wheel is a woman-on-top position where the woman effectively moves full circle around the man's penis, just for the fun of being athletic and experimenting with the new.

Lift and support

As she rises and falls, support her with your raised knees and your hands to help aid her movement.

• SEX TIP •

Increase the force of your orgasm by putting it off for a while. The longer you encourage arousal, the greater the climax you will achieve.

Lying on top

Be careful to avoid sudden movements in this head-to-toe position because the unusual angle of intercourse might cause the penis to slip and catch, which can be painful. But he'll love being able to watch you move on him.

Sitting on top

While sitting on top and facing away from your partner, you can use the strength of your thigh muscles to help you push up and down on your man's penis.

SITTING POSITIONS

One of the secrets of female orgasms is that women often respond best to a steady pressure or rhythm instead of the more forceful thrust of intercourse. The bonus of woman-on-top sitting positions is that she can direct the sex – she's in charge. According to the level of sensation she's experiencing, she can speed up or slow down, move towards orgasm, or hold off from climaxing until she's ready.

Squeezing the thighs

A gentle way to achieve pleasure is for the woman to sit astride her man, rhythmically squeezing and letting go with her thighs. This pleasures his penis while stimulating her clitoris. ▼

• SEX TIP •

During penetration, position the clitoris against the base of the penis. Rub softly side to side, and round and round, so that the clitoris is stimulated by the pressure.

LYING ON TOP

Erotic and powerful as the woman-on-top strokes may be, they can also become physically tiring for the woman and difficult to maintain. However, there's a lot to be said for resting on top of your partner and enjoying the long naked sensation of each other's bodies. To keep his erection going, rock gently from side to side. Continue lovemaking slowly and gently until you are ready to swivel back upright.

Intimate contact ▶
Lying along the length of your partner's body, face to face, while kissing and whispering to each other creates intimacy and increases arousal.

MAXIMIZING PLEASURE

Caressing, stroking, and using massage can all be erotic when used on their own. They can also enhance the experience of intercourse if you can carry them out in addition to, and during, lovemaking. A good lover continues to stroke and caress his or her partner, and includes a loving touch to the genitals even during the thrust of intercourse.

◀ Stimulating him
To increase sensation for him during intercourse, reach down in front of you with your hand and grasp the base of his penis firmly. As you make love, grip and simultaneously move your hand.

Self-stimulation ▶
For her to achieve more sensation during penetration, she could try stroking her clitoris. Time the strokes with the thrusts of intercourse.

A little extra for him ▶
The area between the anus and penis is full of nerve endings. Reach behind you, down between his legs, and cup and stroke his testicles from underneath.

POINTS TO REMEMBER

IN SEX, THERE IS NO CONTEST and there is no race. The best sex is timeless and, in order to make it feel so, it's worth remembering a couple of points:

1 Try and arrange to have sex at a time of day when you're not tired. If you have more energy, there won't be so much hurry to finish — you can enjoy leisurely lovemaking.

2 Make sure your sex session is open-ended, so that you can really become absorbed in what you're doing.

REAR-ENTRY POSITIONS

Sex from the rear feels exciting because it contains a taste of the forbidden and it ties neatly into games of submission (pp.138–41). Both sexes find it extremely erotic – many women adore it because it makes them feel helpless; men tend to love it because the sensation of thrusting immediately below the buttocks is a turn-on. Some women can climax from sex in this position, while others manage it with some help from their partner's hands.

▲
Lifting a leg
If the woman lifts her leg from the knee, it stretches her vagina slightly, opening it more widely. This increases the chances of clitoral arousal.

Using a cushion
To avoid bruising her ribs, slip a cushion underneath her chest. This can also help improve the angle of penetration. ▶

Face down
If you're a man on top, avoid resting your whole weight on your partner's body. Support some weight on your elbows. ▼

LYING DOWN

This is an especially affectionate love position because your entire body is spread out along your partner's body, your head is next to his or hers, and you can kiss and whisper to each other during intercourse. The male pelvis rests at the rear of her buttocks and pivots from that angle, which means it is an easy and unstressful position for leisurely, rhythmic, and sensuous sex.

However, this is not a position that is likely to greatly excite your woman. By virtue of the male weight lying on top of her, she cannot really move that freely. This means that she is unlikely to gain any clitoral pleasure. Nor is it easy to stimulate her from underneath with your hand, since the weight of both of your bodies tends to prevent you from moving your hands easily.

Having said that, this position is great for those times when she feels like taking a more passive role, or as follow-up sex, when she has already climaxed but wants to continue enjoying the intimacy of lovemaking.

KNEELING

Probably the most comfortable of all the rear-entry positions is the one in which the woman kneels on the floor with her upper half resting on the bed and the man kneeling behind her. However, this position can prove unsatisfying for the woman. And with her thighs resting up against the side of the bed, it can be difficult for the man to reach her clitoris and stimulate her with his hands and fingers. The alternative position, doggy style on the bed, gives the man considerably more mobility and more opportunity to stimulate her genitals.

> • SEX TIP •
>
> Women – if you don't get enough stimulation from doggy-style sex, reach down and stroke yourself during sex.

Doggy style

In this position, she can use her arms to steady herself against his thrusting, yet she can raise herself up easily for closer, more intimate contact. He has easy access to her clitoris and plenty of manoeuvrability. ▼

STANDING UP

Some of the more unusual sex positions recommended in the *Kama Sutra* involve rear-entry sex where both parties are standing up. The Elephant is the classic pose. This is where the woman stretches down and touches the ground with her hands while her partner stands, penetrates, and thrusts from behind.

In order for this technique to work, the man must hold his partner firmly with both hands around the hips and pull and let go rhythmically, since she will be unable to make any real movements of her own. As well as being fun, this position can be used as an exercise in balance.

▲
The elephant

This position can be an erotic adventure for him, but it's likely to send the blood rushing to her head, so don't pursue it for too long.

SIDE-BY-SIDE POSITIONS

Lovemaking side by side is highly pleasurable and relaxing, and really comes into its own when one or both partners are physically frail or injured, because it puts less strain on the body than other positions. It's also a great boon for pregnant women (see pp.192–93), because the mattress can support the weight of a heavy abdomen.

FACE TO FACE

Couples adore kissing, snuggling up, and murmuring loving words to each other. Doing this face to face is always more intimate and meaningful than back to back. It is attractively casual to just hold each other, quietly talking. Some couples doze off together in this position and wake to find themselves tightly and sexily clasped – a good starting point for making love.

As with most side-by-side positions, the face-to-face position is lazily sensual, intimate, and extremely restful, giving lovers a break if they find sex tiring. It is also recommended as a good way of prolonging intercourse and slowing down orgasm.

◀ Legs intertwined

One of the sexiest sensations in bed is of stretching out and casually winding your legs around those of your partner. The legs, particularly the inner thighs, are full of sensitive nerve endings.

Both legs wrapped around him

One way the woman can assist her mobility is to wrap her legs around her partner's buttocks so that she can thrust against the weight of his body. ▼

FINGER-TIPPING

THIS IS A FAVOURITE sex therapy exercise, originally devised to enhance intimacy between couples (see also Sensate focus therapy, p.203, and Rediscovering intimacy, p.226). It consists of the couple lying in the spoons position, then each partner takes it in turns to spend 15 minutes lightly stroking and caressing their partner's whole body with fingertips only. The end result is for both partners to feel spoiled and loved. Ideally, they will also feel sexually charged.

FROM BEHIND

It is probably our primitive instincts that make us become sexual at the sight and sensation of a mate's buttocks. Among primates, the anal region gives a focal sexual signal, and humans are almost certainly no different from their monkey cousins. It's a good reason why cuddling in the spoons position brings on a regular reaction – that of becoming turned on. The great advantage of doing this while lying down is that it conserves energy.

Spoons position
When the man cuddles up closely to the woman's buttocks from behind it is usually a great turn-on for both partners and can lead easily to intercourse from the rear (see pp.108–109). ▼

THE SEXUAL DANCE

At its best, sexual intercourse can resemble a wonderful series of flowing movements. There are rare but blissful occasions where physical sensation is so heightened that every action, movement, and stroke feels as though you're floating. This is the result of every nerve cell in the body being so stimulated, both by touch and by suggestion (the brain is a very sexy organ indeed), that movements can glide from one to another effortlessly, and every single action feels sensational. The real skill is to remain within that floating sensuality for as long as possible and to avoid breaking the spell with sudden or jerky movements.

◀ **Turning and twining**
The erotic dance may involve twisting around each other's bodies, an activity that stimulates nerve endings in the skin.

▲
Clasping and stroking
During the best sex, any touch can bring on delicate prickles of exquisite sensuality. The stroking may be combined with moving through several sex positions, each creating more arousal.

KNEELING POSITIONS

The best sex comes spontaneously, when you and your partner pick up on each other's emotions and desires and start to create a cycle of increasing arousal. Good sex becomes like a wonderful dance, with one partner following where the other leads. Try leading your partner into experimenting with some different techniques, such as these kneeling positions.

THE NOVELTY FACTOR

MANY PEOPLE TEND to follow a sexual pattern or routine with a partner – favouring positions or techniques that they have both become comfortable with. However, most of us enjoy and respond well to novelty. To spice up your love life, experiment with a few alternative positions once in a while. Try sex while kneeling in a variety of ways – it can add a new angle to your lovemaking.

CLOSE CARESSES

Any sex act that starts off by simply getting into a kneeling position is unlikely to be a great success. Embracing and kissing your partner while you're both upright feels wonderful. Then, try kneeling down together. One partner could kneel behind the other – the man could press himself against his partner's back, while caressing her with his hands.

DEEP PENETRATION

One of the best ways to achieve deep penetration is for the woman to lie on the bed and the man to kneel up against her while she lifts her legs and places them against his shoulders. This allows him to thrust deep inside her so that he feels completely contained and she feels vulnerable and possessed. Men are especially aroused by female legs and the beauty of this position is that her legs are in full view. They can also be draped or clasped around him.

Passionate thrusting

In this position, the man is able to thrust deep inside his partner. However, the woman may find that her clitoris is not stimulated because her movement is restricted. ▼

◀ **Caressing her**
Women adore being stroked and caressed all over, and this includes the genitals. Kneel behind her and caress her with a wandering hand.

• SEX TIP •

To add variety to your lovemaking, start off caressing each other while you're both standing. Move into a kneeling position, and follow this with sex from the rear.

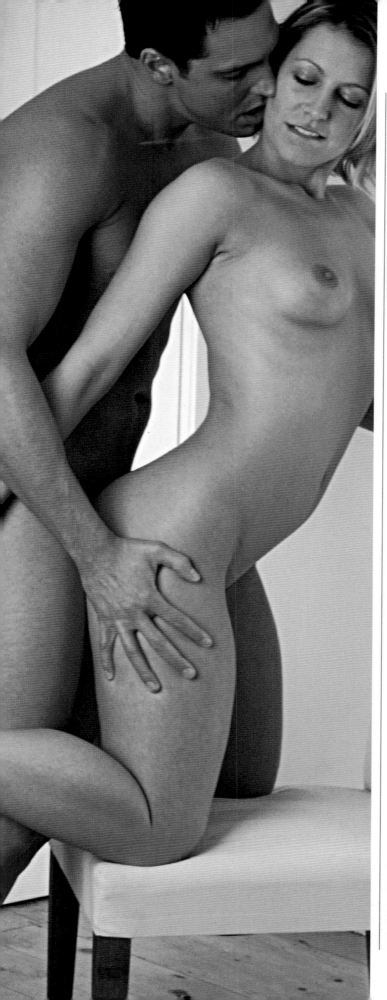

BEING SPONTANEOUS

Some of the best kneeling positions are enjoyed when you are having sex in a room other than the bedroom. The sensation of being nude in the living room or kitchen can feel deliciously forbidden, and so a degree of discomfort can be forgotten in the throes of passion. In the back of the mind, there may always be the additional thought of being discovered, adding a special "frisson" to lovemaking.

Experiment with using props for your lovemaking, too. A chair, for example, or the edge of a sofa, can prove useful props to intercourse in kneeling positions. Sex on the edge of a kitchen table may not be entirely satisfactory because kitchen tables are hard and lovers don't respond well to discomfort, but often it is the idea of what you are doing and where you are doing it that raises the eroticism and arousal levels.

◄ Keeping your balance

When you're having rear-entry sex in a kneeling position, hold on to the back of the chair to help keep your balance.

On the edge

With your partner lying on a sofa, kneel on the floor next to her so that you can get the perfect height and angle for penetration. ▼

SITTING POSITIONS

Sitting positions don't always give as much sensation as the more traditional man-on-top or woman-on-top positions (see pp.100–107), but there is something outrageously casual about seated sex that can be extremely erotic as well as great fun. You could enjoy these positions when clothed, or you could just hint at them when dressed to turn your partner on. Be aware that sitting positions can be very tiring, so don't be surprised if, halfway through something wonderful, your woman needs to have a change.

COMFORT FIRST

There are some sitting positions that are best made with a lot of back support, such as an armchair or a deeply cushioned sofa. Although it is usually the partner on top who is the more active, in some sitting positions it may be difficult to undertake certain movements without help. If she is on top she can control the angle of the thrusts (she may lean back for example), while he can move energetically and assist her movement with his hands. This has the bonus of making her feel arousingly manipulated.

◀ **Easy access**

In this position the man can reach out easily to kiss or caress his partner's breasts, buttocks, waist, and hips while helping to control the speed of penetration.

• **SEX TIP** •

Sex in the sitting position is ideal for impromptu sessions when time is short. It may not cause the most fantastic sensations but its eroticism lies in its novelty value and it can be a fun preliminary.

◀ **Arching back**

While she is leaning back in dramatic fashion, making herself supremely open and vulnerable to his thrusting, he supports her body and helps to control the speed of motion.

FACING AWAY

For those couples who don't always want sex to be the height of passion with every facial flicker observed, rear-entry sex while seated offers a lazily sensual alternative. The woman sits astride the man, facing away, and takes control of the action. Her thigh muscles enable her to rise and fall and set the tempo of the thrusts. He benefits from seeing her buttocks move rhythmically, which is a powerful, primitive turn-on; indeed, the visual experience can be enough to trigger climax.

Stimulation for her

When the woman faces away from her partner, kneeling, she can control the pace and can use her free hands to stimulate herself from the front. ▼

> **• SEX TIP •**
>
> For rear-entry seated positions, sex therapists recommend lying back on a pile of cushions propped up against a wall. This is to provide solid support as well as comfort.

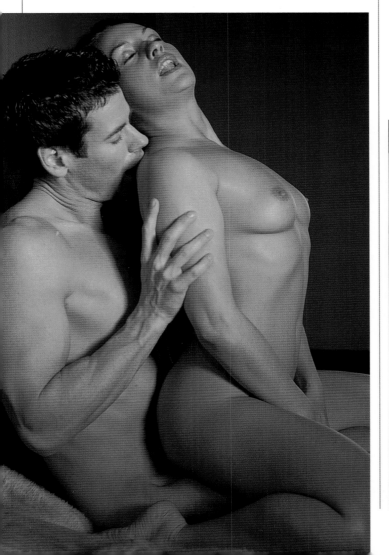

FACE TO FACE

Any face-to-face position feels supremely intimate and erotic, especially while seated, when you are squeezed up against your lover's body. A relaxed version of the face-to-face position is where the woman leans back on her arms and moves her pelvis rhythmically (this position, known as "Hector's Horse", was recorded in antique sex books).

Woman in control ▶

The woman controls the pace of lovemaking here, using her feet to provide leverage for her thrusts. The man remains fairly still and supports her body as she moves.

Equal partners

The face-to-face contact and proximity of this couple's bodies generate a feeling of intimacy. Both partners control the gentle rhythm and neither is dominant. ▼

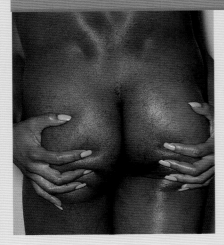

UPRIGHT POSITIONS

Some of the most fantastic spontaneous sex takes place while you and your partner are both standing upright. There is nothing quite like falling on each other in such a rush of passion that you don't even bother to get undressed or go to bed – you just do it, urgently and possessively right on the spot. And upright sex also comes into its own when you are suddenly seized with desire for each other but just happen to be in the great outdoors. There are plenty of delicious upright positions you could try wherever you are.

STANDING UPRIGHT

Every slight deviation of standing sex provides specific sensation and special eroticism. As he thrusts, it helps if she can lift at least one leg upwards – this helps to open her vagina a little more and to envelop him even further. If the woman wants to take both her legs off the ground, she might sit on a table or otherwise be supported by her man from underneath. Holding up your female partner during intercourse is a Herculean labour of love, and probably not one many men will manage for very long. In the days of the *Kama Sutra*, women were sometimes pictured clinging to their standing lovers with their arms and legs. You may be surprised by the strength that passion can temporarily give you – but don't overestimate it!

Legs entwined ▶
It's an instinctive urge to want to get as close as possible to your man during intercourse. Wrapping your crossed legs around him tightens the leg muscles, draws him closer to you, and energizes your pelvis.

◀ Belly to belly
Just holding each other face to face and belly to belly when you are having sex is very sensual – especially if you are both naked.

USING PROPS

Human beings are artistic as well as inventive. By using props such as chairs or even washbasins, not only can you get yourselves into some wonderfully sensual positions, you can create imaginary erotic stories, too. Why might she be asked to raise her leg as he slips into her from the rear? What kind of a romance takes place in the bathroom over a washbasin? Let your imaginations run wild.

A quick wash and brush up

A washbasin is often at the ideal height for upright sex, but make sure it's secure.

A leg lifted

If he slides his woman's leg onto a chair, she will feel erotically manipulated.

Wheelbarrow in the air

This position is an exciting and athletic experience, but it's not for the frail, and definitely not for women with bad backs. Don't hold it for more than a few thrusts because it might cause a back injury.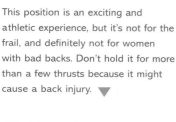

> • **SEX TIP** •
>
> Try telling her an erotic story when you use furniture as a sexual prop. She'll turn on to the fantasy.

SEX TRICKS

There are many things you can do to turn a mildly interesting sexual encounter into a deeply satisfactory one. Surprise and spontaneity in the form of unexpected sexy kisses in public, or unusual sex positions, can be extremely exciting. Tender talk is also a great aphrodisiac. Tell your partner as you make love how attractive you find him or her, and how much their smell or taste turns you on.

SEXY SCENT

BOTH MEN AND WOMEN SECRETE pheromones, which are natural scent chemicals that serve to attract a mate. Pheromones travel through the air and are drawn into our systems via our sense of smell. To make the most out of your natural chemicals, don't wash as much as usual and don't wear heavy perfume.

INCREASING FRICTION

A certain amount of friction is essential for sexual stimulation. Some sexual positions offer particularly close, intense contact – the grind, for example, involves the man pushing and circling inside the vagina without actually moving in and out, while the seizure technique involves the man holding back the top of his partner's pubic mound to expose the clitoris while he penetrates so that he is holding it against his penis.

Steady pressure
Deep, prolonged pressure is sometimes preferable to rhythmic thrusting, particularly for G-spot stimulation (see p.95). For added sensation, rub her clitoris at the same time. ▼

MASSAGE DURING SEX

One of the least exciting ways to have intercourse is to focus solely on the pounding of the penis, thereby leaving out all the other erogenous zones. The result of such single-minded thrusting is that the rest of the body ends up screaming for attention. The skin is highly sensitive, and letting your hands wander over your partner's body during intimate moments is arousing as well as loving. Below is a technique that combines massage with intercourse:

Three-handed massage

◀ 1 Rub sweet-smelling massage oil all over your body, oil your partner's body, then give him or her a sensuous back massage (see p.60).

2 Turn your partner onto his or her back, and massage the chest or breasts and abdomen (see p.62). When both of you are ready, let the penis penetrate the vagina while all the time continuing with the upper-body massage. ▶

▲
The "69" position
Simultaneous oral sex, known as the "69", is intensely intimate and requires a large degree of trust. As a result, it can be deeply satisfying to both partners. Before you begin, have a bath or shower together to make sure you are both clean and relaxed.

USING YOUR TONGUE

Many people aim for intercourse and often overlook the pleasures of oral intimacy. Yet skilful manipulation of the mouth and tongue on the genitals can be sensational. The "69" position describes where you snuggle up to each other head to genitals and give each other oral sex at the same time. It is so named because of the artistic shape created by the two bodies. If you find oral sex exciting, this is a must. However, some people prefer receiving fellatio or cunnilingus separately (see pp.78–79), on the grounds that if they focus entirely on themselves rather than on their partner their sexual sensation will be more intense; equally, if they are performing oral sex on their partner, they can concentrate solely on giving optimum pleasure. If you are unsure about oral sex, it is a good idea to experiment with tongue-bathing first (see p.75).

SEXUAL TIMEKEEPING

ACHIEVING ORGASM is largely a matter of timing and self-control. There are various ways that you and your partner can influence your climaxes:

- Practise peaking – this is a method of stopping then starting stimulation so that you reach mini-peaks of climax but go no further. Men and women can have many peaks in this manner before finally letting go for the big one.
- If you are aiming for simultaneous orgasm, give her plenty of foreplay and learn to let go only when you recognize what the beginning of her orgasm looks like. You may need to practise orgasm control (see pp.98–99). If you don't manage to achieve this, don't worry: most people prefer to concentrate on their orgasms separately.
- If you want to find out whether your woman is the multi-orgasmic sort (see p.97), don't give up on the stimulation when she has first climaxed. Women find it very hard to regain sexual sensation if stimulation stops. Assess her physical reaction: if she is reluctant to be touched, you can guess she won't orgasm again. If she groans with pleasure and is seriously responsive, keep on with the good work. Some men can also experience multiple orgasms (see p.96).

TANTRIC SEX

This spiritual approach to sex aims to enrich the mind and soul as well as provide extreme sensual pleasure. Although tantric touch may feel the same as other forms of touch, there is a different emphasis on how it is given and received. A priority of tantric sex is to prolong sexual arousal. It takes the form of extensive stroking sessions followed by very slow intercourse.

TANTRIC STROKING

Tantric stroking, a necessary preliminary to tantric intercourse, is very similar to Masters and Johnson's sensate focus therapy (see p.203). Both approaches emphasize the "touch for pleasure's sake" principle, stressing the importance of giving and receiving pleasure in a particular way. There are two sensations to be appreciated when carrying out the exercise below. The first is your own – what you feel when you touch your partner. The second is to imagine what your partner feels when touched by you. Try not to speak throughout the exercises.

Tantric strokes

1 Lightly stroke each other, first with a circling action and then up and down. Avoid the breasts and the genitals. Stroke slowly for about 15 minutes, take a break, then repeat the stroking for another 15 minutes. Later in the evening, repeat the stroking for 30 minutes.

2 Lie quietly together closely in the spoons position, but without stimulating each other (if this is too tempting, lie facing each other with foreheads together but bodies not quite touching).

3 The next day, move on to stroking each other's chest. Make light, circular movements on the chest or breast, first with hands moving towards each other, then with the action of the hands reversed.

4 Next, move on to the genitals. Slowly draw your hands or fingers up from underneath each other's genitals, using very light strokes and working along the length of the penis or up the height of the vulva. Also include the testicles, perineum, vagina, labia, and clitoris.

5 After an hour of genital stroking, take a five-minute break. Then lie motionless, with the woman on top and the man's penis inside her vagina, until his erection subsides.

TANTRIC INTERCOURSE

Only once you've completed the tantric strokes do you move on to intercourse – the key is to take your time (orgasm should be put off for at least 20 minutes to half an hour). The penis should penetrate the vagina by only a few centimetres or so, stay there for a full minute, then withdraw and rest in the clitoral hood for a further minute before sliding back in. Continue with the penetration followed by a full minute's rest in between, but for the next few strokes let the penis rest outside the vulva, then on subsequent strokes just inside it. Try to imagine all the sensation your partner is experiencing as your own. Let the boundaries between you dissolve in this manner.

There are various positions that prolong intercouse or increase the pleasure of orgasm. Side-by-side positions tend to prolong intercourse (see pp.110–11), and the missionary position is also useful because the man can control an impending orgasm by pulling his testicles downwards (see p.99). Rear-entry positions (see pp.108–109) can be excellent for enhancing orgasm. The man can easily reach the woman's clitoris to stimulate her, and when she climaxes, his proximity to her anal muscles means that his penis will be affected by the strength of her contractions.

THREE-DAY EVENT

THIS TANTRIC THREE-DAY EVENT is suitable for trying out over a long, leisurely weekend:

1 Spend the first day walking in the country, slowing down and (hopefully) feeling more peaceful. Use the lazy time spent together to renew feelings of intimacy. On the first evening, carry out the tantric strokes shown on the facing page, but only go as far as step 2.

2 The next morning, repeat the tantric strokes up to step 2, then stop again. In the afternoon, take another slow walk. In the evening, go back to the tantric strokes, only this time include steps 3, 4, and 5. Sleep on these strokes and refrain from having sexual intercourse.

3 The following day, repeat stages 1 to 4, and this time go on, after at least an hour of stroking and stimulation, to have intercourse. Don't instantly go for orgasm but prolong the intercourse (see above). Finally, when you feel the time is right, allow yourselves to climax. (NB: You may choose to prolong intercourse by breaking for lunch or having a sleep then returning to intercourse later in the day.)

THE TAO OF SEX

Thousands of years ago, Tao philosophers argued that the human body had its own energy flow that could be both used up and recharged, a belief that is still held by many today. They believed that by applying stimulation to specific meridian points, as is the case in acupuncture or reflexology, this would benefit the health of "related" organs elsewhere in the body and restore the balance of energy. Similarly, the penis and vagina were considered to possess meridian points which, if massaged correctly, would have a re-energizing effect on the glands relating to sexual function (see right).

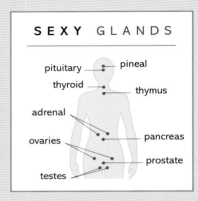

SEXY GLANDS

pituitary — pineal
thyroid — thymus
adrenal
ovaries — pancreas
— prostate
testes

SEX FOR HEALTH

Tao sexual positions aim to massage the penis and vagina evenly – this is something that typical sexual intercourse does not always achieve, because of the uneven shape of the vagina and penis. The Tao genital massage, known as the Sets of Nine exercise, is made up of ninety strokes. Its purpose is to massage the genital meridian points so that all the related organs in the body will benefit.

• SEX TIP •

Try resting during intercourse without losing your erection. This is good training for lasting longer.

The Sets of Nine

In this exercise, the man penetrates his partner in a series of strokes as follows:

1 He thrusts just the tip of his penis into the vagina before withdrawing. He does this shallow stroke nine times, before thrusting the entire penis into the vagina once.

2 He then carries out eight shallow strokes (with the tip of the penis only) and two deep strokes (with the entire penis).

3 Next, he makes seven shallow strokes and three deep ones.

4 Then, he performs six shallow strokes and four deep ones.

5 He follows this with five shallow strokes and five deep ones.

6 He then performs four shallow strokes and six deep ones.

7 This is followed by three shallow strokes and seven deep ones.

8 Then, two shallow strokes and eight deep ones.

9 Finally, he makes one shallow stroke and nine deep ones.

INJACULATION

According to Tao theory, ejaculation can be reversed and semen re-absorbed into the man's body. Injaculation is carried out by pressing the Jen-Mo point – this is an acupressure point on the perineum, which is the area halfway between the anus and the scrotum – at the moment before ejaculation. The man will continue to feel aroused. In fact, sensation will be accentuated because the orgasm will happen very slowly – it may even continue for up to five minutes. The man will also retain his erection, or regain it quickly, and so he is able to continue intercourse for longer. According to Tao principles, his energy will be preserved because his semen has not been expelled. Do not try injaculation if you have a prostate infection.

▲
How to injaculate
Just as you are about to ejaculate, press your perineum so that semen is not allowed to travel through the urethra. If you apply pressure too close to the anus, it won't work. If you press too close to the scrotum, the semen will be forced into the bladder.

ENHANCING ORGASM

Tao sexology describes the female orgasm as a series of rising steps, followed by a declining step. Sensuality is built on and increased with each rising step, and these steps are known as the nine levels of orgasm. According to Tao belief, many men do not realize that there are so many stages of female orgasm. During sex, they tend to stop stimulating their partner at around Level Four, and so the woman's climax is often curtailed. It is only through continuing stimulation that Level Nine can be reached – and then the whole of the woman's body is energized.

NINE LEVELS OF ORGASM

EACH OF THE NINE LEVELS of orgasm energize particular parts of the woman's body. As each organ is affected, watch for the signs that show you how your partner's sensation is increasing, so that you know how to take her on through the nine levels of orgasm:

1 Lungs – The woman sighs deeply, breathes heavily, and begins to salivate.

2 Heart – While she's kissing her man, she extends her tongue out to him.

3 Spleen, pancreas, and stomach – As her muscles become activated, she grasps him tightly.

4 Kidneys and bladder – She starts to experience vaginal spasms and her secretions start flowing.

5 Bones – Her joints begin to loosen and she may even start to bite her partner.

6 Liver and nerves – She writhes and tries to wrap her arms and legs about her man.

7 Blood – Her blood is "boiling" and she tries to touch her partner all over.

8 Muscles – Her muscles completely relax. She may bite even more, and grasp her man's nipples.

9 Entire body – She collapses in a "little death", and is emotionally and sensually "opened up".

ANAL SEX

Many heterosexuals as well as homosexuals find anal sex completely natural and spontaneously sensual – the anal area is rich in nerve endings. However, there are many people who dislike the idea, considering it unhygienic, or who find it painful. It is vital to ensure that you are both scrupulously clean, and never go on to vaginal sex without careful washing first. A good lubricant is also essential.

EASY DOES IT

ANAL SEX needs to be done slowly and carefully or it can hurt. First, caress your partner's genitals, then let your fingers brush across the anus a few times as if by accident. Next, deliberately stroke around the outside of the anus, then move to other areas before returning to the anus for a more intense massage with the finger.

FINGER MASSAGE

Moisten your fingers and your partner's anus with a suitable lubricant, such as one of the new colourful lubes (see p.144). Short, neat fingernails are essential. Massage around the outside of the anus first. As your partner becomes more relaxed, insert the tip of your finger 2–3cm (¾–1¼in) into the anus and continue to move your finger around in circles, but on the inside. Gradually make your movements firmer and use your fingertip to stretch the entrance to the anus.

◀ **Gentle exploration**
When exploring the anal area it is vital to probe gently and build up to things gradually. Check to make sure that your partner is happy for you to proceed to the next stage.

SEX FACTS

HOT SPOTS
Think of the anus as a clock, with the 12 o'clock position closest to the vagina or testicles. The most erogenous points are usually at 10 or 2 o'clock.

◀ **Tongue bathing**
The buttocks are an erogenous zone. Using your tongue to lick and probe provides a sensuous build-up to anal sex.

TAKING IT FURTHER

Some people prefer things to go beyond fingering around the anal passage. Many men enjoy their partner stimulating the prostate gland, which lies at the back of the anus' upper wall (see p.93); some women are profoundly turned on by a combination of fingering the anus and clitoral stimulation. Anal sex toys are very effective (see p.144).

If you want anal intercourse, it is vital that you are relaxed. The key to anal sex without pain is to begin by stretching the anus slowly as described on the facing page, and to use plenty of lubricant. Take penetration very gently and by degrees only. For added protection, use an extra-strong condom designed specifically for anal sex.

• SEX TIP •

To make anal intercourse more comfortable, the man should pause as he penetrates so the woman can consciously relax her back passage.

Anal intercourse

Many people, both men and women, find anal intercourse extremely exciting. Make sure the anal passage is well lubricated and sufficiently stretched before penetration, and enter slowly and gently. ▼

FACING OBJECTIONS

AS WITH ANY KIND OF SEX, never force anyone to have anal sex if they don't want to. If your partner objects to anal massage or anal penetration, you may just have to accept that it really doesn't appeal to them and explore something else instead. Sometimes a partner will feel uncomfortable with the idea but will agree to give it a try. If this is the case, take it extremely slowly and guarantee that you will stop as soon as your lover asks you to. It often helps to go back a stage so that you can discuss their anxiety and offer reassurance. To build up trust, your partner must be confident that you will stop straight away.

LEGAL WARNING: Anal sex is not legal between consenting adults in some countries and states.

CHAPTER 5

Sex
Without
Limits

risk

TOYS

play

TANTALIZE

fantasy

BEYOND THE BEDROOM

THE BEDROOM IS NOT THE ONLY room in the house that is good for lovemaking. Virtually any room can be an erotic venue as long as you are assured of privacy. The mantra to remember here is: Go for it. Life is too short to make love only in bed.

After the bedroom, the bathroom is probably the favourite room for lovemaking. Foreplay in the bath is fun and, even if your bath isn't big enough to have sex in, you can make love sitting on the edge of the tub or on the bathroom floor. Bathing before sex makes you feel clean and confident; bathing after sex enhances relaxation and intimacy. If you are feeling tired and sluggish and you want to energize yourself before sex, spend 15 minutes soaking in a hot bath and then stand up and take a quick cold shower. Your pores will close rapidly and leave you feeling

SHOWER GAMES

THE SHOWER IS A NATURAL sex toy: it combines heat, pressure, moisture, and friction all in one device. There are plenty of sensual experiences you and your partner can experiment with and enjoy:

1 Play around in the shower and use the water jets on an alternate pleasure/punishment basis. Pleasure is warm water directed at the genitals; punishment is a blast of cold water on the back.

2 See if you can masturbate your woman to orgasm using only the jets of water from the showerhead.

3 Use the flow of water from the shower hose to massage different parts of the body, such as the perineum, the genitals, the toes, the lips, the soles of the feet, and the backs of the knees.

4 Cover each other in liquid soap and give each other a sensual massage.

5 Surprise your partner with some exciting oral sex in the shower.

6 If you want to move on to shower sex, the best position is one in which the woman bends over and the man penetrates her from behind (see p.109) – this reduces the risk of slipping.

SEX FACTS

SHOWER THRILLS
According to the *Hite Report* (see p.21), having a shower massage is some women's favourite way of reaching orgasm. Combined with a bath, you can lie back and relax while using the shower jets to massage your erogenous zones.

SPONTANEOUS LOVEMAKING in the kitchen can spice up your love life and take your breath away. The discomfort of the hard kitchen worktops gives a raw edge to your lovemaking.

invigorated and alert. On the other hand, if you are totally stressed out, a warm bath can relax you enough to bring on lazy feelings of sensuality.

Shampooing can be highly sensuous. Prepare the bathroom in advance with candles, a hot bath, and some fluffy towels. Now lead your partner into the steam and both get undressed. Ask him or her to step into the bath, lie back, and relax. Explain that you are going to start by washing his or her hair. Make every action as relaxing and sensual as possible. Carry out a luxurious head massage, applying deep, circular pressure with your fingertips at the temples, the hairline, and all over the scalp (see p.63). Take a comb and sensually comb his or her hair, arousing the millions of tiny nerve-endings that lie beneath the skin.

When you're bathing with your partner, try out the pelvic shampoo: wash each other's genital areas. Swirl your finger tips lightly in and out of each other's most intimate crevices. When your man is aroused, start to "wash" his penis by stroking the length of it, and decide whether (and how) you will bring him to orgasm.

The kitchen
Kitchen tables are hard but for sheer change, they make an interesting venue for love. The kitchen is probably most suited for instant passion when sexual desire takes you by surprise and you can't wait a moment longer to have each other. But a word of warning – make sure you remove all sharp knives from the vicinity first!

The living room
Any large armchair or deep-sprung sofa is an inviting spot for lovemaking, but the most erotic spot in the living room tends to be a thick rug on the floor. Preferably, this is stretched out in front of a roaring log fire!

Couples might seize the opportunity to carry out a sensual massage here, surrounded by soft music and candlelight. Single women have been known to make a night of it by locking themselves firmly in, drawing the curtains, putting some atmospheric music on, and going for a slippery self-massage in front of the fire. Single men might invest in a sexy video and go for a personal, individual, and indulgent sex party.

SPENDING AN EVENING in front of a fire with your partner can be a sensual experience. The warmth of the fire will keep you relaxed and mellow, and the location will add a sense of adventure to lovemaking.

SEX OUTSIDE THE HOME

ONE OF THE GREAT KILLERS of good sex is boredom. However much you adore your partner, if you have made love in the same way, in the same bed, in the same room for years things just aren't as erotic as they used to be. Change only one item in that fixed pattern, such as where you make love, and sex takes on a new lease of life. The secret is to keep an open mind and be unafraid to make some slightly different moves.

Love in the great outdoors

It's a beautiful summer's day and the two of you go for a stroll across the meadows. The sun beats down and warms your flesh and you are aware of a lazy prickling of sexual desire. Provided you are certain that no one else can possibly see you, what could be more natural than lying down in the long grass and making love? You can hear insects humming and birds singing as you lie enclosed in this soft, green world. It's a very romantic and different experience. Just one warning: there are laws about committing public nuisance, so it is vital to make love where you definitely cannot be observed or you might find yourself in trouble with the authorities.

SEXFACTS

THE RISK FACTOR

The risk – whether real or imaginary – of being discovered having sex can actually heighten the experience by raising adrenaline and giving an added natural chemical zap to the proceedings. However, some people get so anxious that the reaction will be a negative rather than an arousing one.

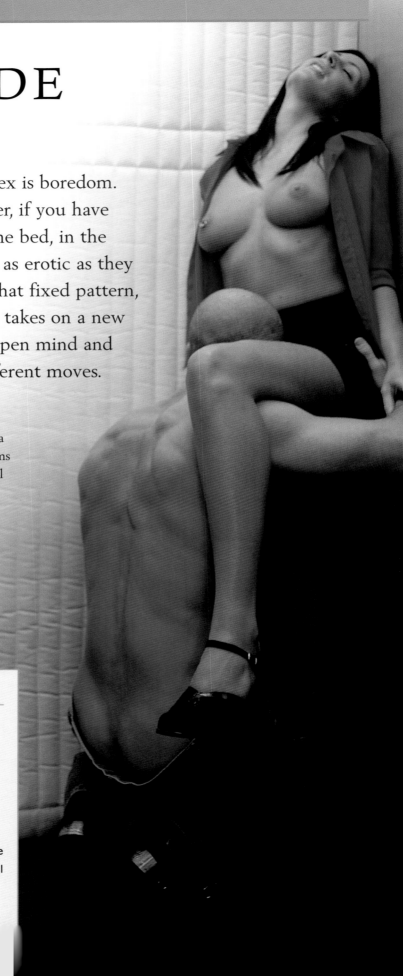

Going to a hotel

Moving to a discreet hotel for an afternoon or evening can allow all kinds of unspoken fantasies to spring into reality. One woman I know walked across the park wearing nothing but her fur coat. When she presented herself at her lover's hotel room, she was already faint with apprehension, and when he understood what she wasn't wearing he was overwhelmed. Another couple specifically booked a room with a four-poster bed and spent a happy night playing Elizabethan "torture" games. The bed posts were wonderful for silken ropes, while sexy blindfolds went with the bigger picture. If your idea of luxurious sex would be to wallow in food and drink, the advantage of a good hotel is that room service will deliver goodies to your door without you having to take a step outside.

Sex in the office

Of course we shouldn't do it. The risk of a colleague finding out, even if you have closed and locked the door of the office, is high. And if this does happen, you're in trouble. Yet many people brave the possible complications for incredible experiences. One couple I know locked the office door in the lunch hour, hung out a "do not disturb" sign, and rolled around on a deep-pile rug. Another couple, who worked in an estate agency, refrained from tearing each other's clothes off in the office and instead borrowed a colleague's apartment around the corner for steamy sex.

Phone sex

Anyone can dial into a sex chat line and be talked through self-stimulation. There's nothing very special about this. Nor is there anything very personal. But when you are

talking erotica down the line with someone you know and like and who really turns you on that is quite different.

Before you embark on phone sex, make sure the circumstances are absolutely right. Give yourself open-ended time when you are unlikely to get interrupted and make the setting as pleasant as possible – warmth, candlelight, and perfume in the air are all delicious ingredients. Sit or lie somewhere comfortable and private, and make sure that anything you might want to use during sex is within arm's reach – you don't want to have to interrupt the proceedings.

GOOD PHONE SEX

IF YOU ARE MISSING your partner let them know it. If there are things you wish they were doing to you, voice this. Be truthful. Tell it like you are really feeling it and don't fake anything. Here are a few tips for great phone sex:

1 If there are things you know they would like done to them, let them know how you would carry out these actions if you happened to be on the spot.

2 Describe your self-stimulation as eloquently as possible. Talk your partner through what you are doing and what you imagine he or she is up to. If you use a vibrator, do so letting your man know that in your imagination he is holding this sex toy. If you are a man applying lubricant to ease the progress of self-stimulation, let your partner know that in your head this feels as if she were applying this from the very act of intercourse…your hand is her vagina, your oils are her very own sweet-smelling juices.

EXPLORING FANTASY

MANY PEOPLE LOVE playing games in the bedroom, and sharing a fantasy is the best sort of spontaneous sex game. There are lots of ways to act out the blue movies of your imagination: you can wear costumes or masks, you can use props, you can decorate your bedroom in erotic style, or you can rely on imagination, role-play, and story-telling.

Get together with your partner and discuss the fantasies that you enjoy, the ones you're ambivalent about, and the ones that you dislike. This helps establish the ground rules for game-playing. Be completely honest, but also be non-judgmental. You can explain to your partner that you don't want to participate in a particular fantasy, but don't criticize his or her sexuality. Always bear in mind that revealing fantasies takes courage. Many people fear that they may disgust or shock their partner if they tell them their secret thoughts. The best way to overcome this inhibition is to agree to swap fantasies with your partner. Start in a mild way and heat up your fantasies progressively. It's important that you both swap scenarios of equal magnitude – if your fantasy is hot, your partner must exchange one of similar sexiness.

FANTASY GAMES

SOME PEOPLE FIND IT EASIER to liberate their imaginations and vocalize their fantasies by playing games – somehow it helps free themselves from their usual inhibitions. Agree any ground rules with your partner first, and then start letting your imaginations go wild!

- On separate slips of paper, write down different fantasy roles or characters, such as a doctor or a nurse (for other ideas, see p.136). You can also use names of famous people. Mix them up and get your partner to pull one out of a hat. Now you must both interact as if he or she is that character.
- Choose a favourite sex scene from a film. Act it out with your partner in the same surroundings – try and use the same props, too.
- Pick a fantasy theme and create it in your own home. For example, turn your bedroom into a palace bedroom, an Arabian tent, or a den of sex toys. If you want to transform a room quickly, the bathroom is ideal: turn the light off and just add candles, perfumed oil, bouquets of flowers, and clouds of steam.

Bear in mind that if your fantasies focus on someone who is not your lover – even someone inaccessible, such as a film star – you should tread with caution. Although you may know that you have no intention of sleeping with your new colleague at work, you can easily make your partner feel insecure and this can be destructive.

Exploring taboos

The idea of a fantasy taboo is a contradiction in terms. The whole point of a fantasy is that it is something your brain produces, virtually in spite of yourself. And yet people speak of "forbidden thoughts". We may dream of passion with someone of the same sex, or with a famous movie star. We may even dream of sex with someone "forbidden" such as a relative or a best friend's partner. Our dreams do not necessarily mean we want to make the fantasy a reality.

The notion that you can police your imagination is an old-fashioned one – you can't. But many people might take reassurance from the fact that their "unacceptable" thoughts are simply methods of exploring possibilities. They are not signs of deviance, and they would only be that if we actually went out and did the things we might have mentally pictured. And most of us don't. We experience fantasies of all sorts as a way of safely exploring something that we wouldn't actually dream of doing.

IF YOU'RE STRIPTEASING for your partner, make sure that the clothes you are taking off are sexy, such as seductive underwear – this will all add to the sensual effect.

If you have a fantasy that you are nervous about, here is a game to help you: Choose one "strand" or aspect of your fantasy and explain it to your partner. The strand you choose should capture the most erotic aspect of your fantasy. For example, if you fantasize about being forced to have sex by a stranger, tell your partner that you want him to make love to you when you are least expecting it and that he must continue his seduction even if you protest.

Acting out a fantasy

The beauty of sexual intimacy, especially in its early stages, is that you feel you can re-visit activities that you last considered during childhood, such as playing out imaginary roles. Many adults want to act out imaginary scenarios with their partner. Acting out fantasies is one of the teasing activities that makes a tantalized partner desperate to get as close to you as humanly possible. Since much of the essence of erotic imagination lies in the unexpected or in novelty, it is often a good idea to choose a new venue as a backdrop for your fantasy. Choose somewhere unfamiliar – a hotel, for example, or a friend's apartment.

The beauty of sexual games is that you can stop at any stage you want. If you feel uneasy, all you have to do is call a halt. If you fear that your partner may not take your requests to stop seriously, establish a code word before you begin. And if you fear that your partner might not honour this code word, despite having prearranged it, you should respectfully decline to play.

Putting on a show

Visual stimulation is very important to a man's arousal – a normal sex drive can get an extra boost and a depressed one be awakened by the sight of a female stripping. No one expects an "amateur" stripper to be as good as a professional but it's worth practising in front of the mirror to help improve your undressing technique. Before you begin your striptease, ensure that the lighting is soft and moody and the room is warm. Use "bump and grind" music to enhance your performance. If you are wearing stockings and heels, consider leaving them on for as long as possible, and even during any sexual intercourse that may follow.

Mirrors placed at strategic points around your room of love can be used for special scenarios of exhibitionism and voyeurism. These always add a certain frisson to sexual proceedings, and they have the advantage of not seeming to be premeditated. Your sexual "acting" in front of them can therefore evolve completely naturally.

TOP FOUR FANTASY ROLES

THERE ARE A NUMBER OF fantasy scenarios that you and your partner can play out together – take it in turns to be the submissive or dominant characters:

1 The virgin and brigand are a good first fantasy for couples. It's easy to make it an extension of her being the meek female and him being the rampaging male.

2 Teacher and pupil is another fantasy that couples often find easily acceptable. In this scenario, one partner attempts to teach, while the other deliberately makes mistakes and is then sexually "punished".

3 Nurse and patient – many people get incredibly turned on seeing their partner in uniform. You can expect it to do more for him than for her.

4 Slave and mistress – not all domination games have the woman as victim. He can take a turn in being the slave and accept his due chastisement.

MIRROR SCENARIOS

USING MIRRORS CAN ADD excitement to your lovemaking in all sorts of ways – seeing yourself and your partner in imaginative sexual positions can be highly arousing. Find out for yourself:

- You might pretend that the mirror is a window into the room next door. In that room, there are two lovers who are performing specially for you.
- You might angle your lovemaking so that you can actually see the penis moving in and out of the vagina. The reflection in the mirror becomes a kind of porn movie. You might position yourself right in front of the mirror so that watching yourself becomes part of a game of submission and domination.
- One of you might order the other to do something specifically sexual that they may never have viewed before. This might be the act of fellatio or cunnilingus, or having sex on a chair in front of the mirror.
- Your lover might tell you that it is your job to turn him or her on. You could do this by stimulating yourself while your partner is watching you in the reflection.
- Your lover might assist you by masturbating as he or she becomes increasingly aroused by your reflected activities.

Reading out loud

While many people enjoy acting out their fantasies, others prefer to keep fantasy in the realm of the imagination. Although men tend to respond to sexy photographs and high-action literature, many women actually freeze when they come across hard-core porn. But if you give them something suggestive to read – not overtly sexual yet with a frisson of sexual thrill – you suddenly generate powerful sexual excitement. This is why one of the best things men can do in bed with women is read out loud to them. Although men may not necessarily see what all the fuss is about, they will certainly enjoy the result of their partner being sexually aroused.

So, if you want to give a memorable sexual experience, shut yourself up one cosy winter's afternoon with your partner. Take a seat in front of a roaring log fire, with drapes drawn against the cold and the dark. Having equipped yourself with a sexy book, let the reading session begin! Linger lovingly over the erotic paragraphs and really conjure up an atmosphere. Sexy authors may be found on the Internet by typing "erotica" into the search engine.

WATCHING YOURSELF AND YOUR PARTNER in a mirror can be a voyeuristic experience – it can seem as if you are watching a film, and this can add to the eroticism of the occasion.

SUBMISSION AND DOMINATION

MANY MEN AND WOMEN love playing sex games of domination and submission – they enjoy role-playing and letting their sexual fantasies come to life. Couples who enjoy sex games are often happy to take turns being the dominant or submissive party.

What might sub/dom games consist of? The list of role-plays, such as client and dominatrix, is as long as the imagination. But, whatever the scenario, there are always certain aims in these games. If you are in charge, your aim will be to create anticipation in your partner. In turn, you will gain reassurance that your own behaviour is acceptable and, if you lead the game well, you will feel a sense of strength. The games should be highly arousing to both parties and should promote trust. Punishments for disobedience play a part, and might include light spanking, genital exposure, and vaginal or anal penetration.

Bondage

This is the sensual art of tying up your partner to render him or her helpless. Once he or she is secured, it is the dominator or dominatrix who then tickles and teases the victim into erotic submission. So what is the attraction of bondage? Some people need to feel securely contained: they find it very hard to "let go" enough to enjoy sexuality, but if they are rendered helpless then there's nothing they can do to prevent erotic stimulation. The constraint somehow makes it okay to experience pleasure. Alternatively, some men and women have explored many other aspects of

SEX FACTS

TANTALIZING YOUR PARTNER

The aim of many sub/dom games is to stir your partner's X-rated imagination, and to frustrate him or her by tantalizing and teasing as much as giving satisfaction. What's the reasoning behind frustrating your partner? Because not being able to have what you desire arouses many people, and this increases the degree of sexual turn-on.

BONDAGE GAME

"YOU ARE MY SEXUAL SLAVE" – Blindfold your partner and tie his or her wrists to a piece of furniture, such as a bed post. Tell your partner that he or she will now be the sexual slave of you and another person and must be ready to obey every instruction. There is no other person present in the room, but its your job to convince your partner that there is. Disguise your voice, change the way you walk and move, and vary your usual sexual techniques. Try using sex toys (see pp.142–45), such as vibrators and dildos – anything that is safe to use. Meanwhile, your partner cannot see who is performing the sexual acts on him or her – the imagination is free to run wild!

sexuality and no longer get the same thrill as they did at the beginning of their sex lives. Games of domination and submission may be seen as a new direction to explore and can help re-arouse slumbering sexual imaginations.

Many people are afraid of the idea of bondage, fearing that by putting themselves so utterly at someone's mercy they might be seriously harmed. If you were to practise bondage with a complete stranger, a degree of risk would certainly be involved. However, if you are in a close relationship there should be nothing to fear. It is necessary to have complete trust in a partner to be able to "let go". And before you can develop such trust, you usually have to establish a good relationship first. So it's for this reason that most bondage fans will tell you that their relationships are more open and more trusting than most others. In this way, bondage can epitomize an extreme degree of trust.

Laying down the boundaries

Talk to your partner about what is and isn't acceptable before you get to tying each other up. Agree that one of you is in charge and the other is passive, because bondage doesn't work if you are both striving to be the dominant one. The person who is in charge should also agree to stay "in character" and persevere despite "protests" from the other partner.

S E X F A C T S

W A R N I N G

In many countries, sexual activities that involve physically hurting others are illegal, even if they are between consenting adults.

SPANKING GAMES

BEFORE YOU PLAY SPANKING GAMES, agree guidelines between yourselves. Safe spanking instruments include carpet beaters, soft flails, paddles, and spatulas — if used properly, these objects do not hurt. However, crops, rulers, and canes do hurt and should be used carefully. Here are some games you could try:

"SAY THANK YOU"

- Every time you paddle your lover he or she must say "thank you".
- If your partner forgets to thank you, probably owing to the eroticism of the spanking, he or she must be "penalized" by another stroke.
- If your partner doesn't sound enthusiastic enough, you can increase the punishment.
- If your partner sounds too enthusiastic, punish him or her for over-doing it.
- Make your partner count the strokes but then insist that he or she has got it wrong — even (especially) when this isn't the case.

"WHERE WOULD YOU LIKE IT?"

- You offer your partner light spanking or caning — whichever would be most acceptable to him or her.
- You ask, "Where would you like it? Here or there?" When your partner says, "Here," then spank or cane somewhere else.
- When your partner protests, do it somewhere else again. The idea is to tease and tantalize, although sometimes you will spank in the desired place.

Agree on a code word. This is so that when your partner shouts "stop it", you know that you can carry on. After all, it is this kind of phrase that adds to the drama of the game. But when he or she shouts the code word, you know your partner is serious and that you must stop — always respect your partner's wishes. And if you have even the mildest suspicion that your partner may not play by the rules, do not even start this activity.

Bondage games

If your partner is keen to join you in a bondage game, you might start off with mild sexual role-play. If, on the other hand, he or she is clearly unwilling to be tied up, do not insist they go against their inner wishes or force them. Your sexual role-play doesn't need to include bondage at all. It could be as simple as the seducer having his or her wicked way with the virgin. But with follow-up lovemaking, you might continue with a slave and sultan scenario where the sultan strongly believes in the helpless passivity of his harem concubines! In other words, build up to the stronger scenarios slowly. That way, you can find out whether you both enjoy the experience, but you can still back out if necessary. Also, make sure you take it in turns to play different roles.

When it comes to bondage itself, as long as you and your partner both agree to take part in a particular sex act, you both respect each other's wishes, and there is no other person involved, you are hurting no one. You could tie your partner to the bed with silken cords and tantalize him or her to climax. Alternatively, you could give your partner rules and punish him or her for breaking them – this might involve a light caning. To make the game more fun, choose rules that will be difficult to stick to.

There are a variety of bondage props you can choose from, such as silken scarves, ties, and haberdashery-style ropes. There are commercial bondage kits consisting of specially designed couches where you can be tied up with your body at the ultimate angle for stimulation and penetration; special "swings" to strap yourself into; and even sets of "love stirrups" to wear during intercourse.

Spanking and caning

Caning and spanking may sound like painful experiences to some but, to many people, a light slap of the hand or a playful tap with a cane brings the blood pleasantly to the surface. The tingling and warming of the skin are all precursors of erotic arousal, and this degree of spanking or caning stings, but does not hurt. If you are spanking, remove rings from your fingers first. If you are tempted to cane lightly, try the instrument out on your own hand first. And when you know just how much of a sting it provides, think carefully. Work out what your partner wants to take in the way of punishment. Do not impose your own ideas. And if your administrations begin to cause pain, call a halt. Pretend pain is one thing, real torture is totally unacceptable.

BEDROOM TOYS

MOST OF THE BEST sex games use props and other items to extend and enhance the action. If straight sex is your favourite, then a vibrator still manages to add to the excitement. If something darker gets your pulse racing, look to blindfolds, restraints, and a variety of other sex toys to extend your experience of sensuality.

SMALL AND DISCREET, this dolphin-shaped vibrator slips over a finger and needs only one tiny battery. It is water-proof, so is ideal for sex in the shower.

Vibrators

There's a small revolution going on in the sex-toys industry. Although the old-fashioned, hard, penis-shaped vibrators are still available, manufacturers have been concentrating on improving the design and texture of vibrators. Many are made from exciting new materials – some are soft and malleable, feeling like real skin, and there are those made from a translucent, jelly-feel substance. Many are gorgeous and jewel-like in colour. Another fantastic feature of modern vibrators is that they tend to be a lot quieter than they used to be. Vibrator designers are beginning to think seriously (and creatively) about the acts that men and women actually want their vibrators for. The result of this is a variety of very distinct shapes that are intended to carry out specific tasks. One of the most popular designs, a dual-action model, vibrates the clitoris while simultaneously probing the vagina or anus. Another new innovation is the pulsating vibrator, pulsation for some women being integral to their style of orgasm, especially for G-spot stimulation. It comes with a variable speed and throb

THIS STRAP-ON harness consists of a dildo and a clitoral vibrator. It can either be worn by a man, or a woman can use it with a female lover or to penetrate her partner's anus.

SLEEK and modern, this vibrator is designed to offer fairly firm stimulation during penetration.

THIS COLOURFUL, translucent, penis-shaped vibrator has a sexy, jelly-like feel and is relatively quiet.

DUAL-ACTION vibrators feature a shaft for penetration plus a "finger" to stimulate the clitoris.

A SKITTLE-SHAPED vibrator offers varied sensations, from light probing to feelings of pressure and fullness.

THIS SMOOTH, hi-tech model is designed for those who like deep, full pressure during penetration.

MANY VIBRATORS have changeable heads to vary the intensity of pressure and stimulation.

dial. For women who have difficulty climaxing during intercourse, there's a strap-on model that's held in place over the clitoris to provide extra stimulation while the man penetrates the vagina. The tiny finger vibrator is one of the most ingenious of the new sex toys (see facing page). It's good for surprises during intercourse, since it's virtually undetectable. Some kits include textured rubber pads for varying finger sensation.

Dildos

Penis-substitutes, or dildos, have been used as sex toys since time immemorial. They are non-vibrating, and are designed for vaginal or anal penetration (or sometimes both at the same time) by women or men. Today, dildos are usually made of latex or silicone. They may be held in the hand, or some can be slipped into a harness that is worn around the hips. The benefit of this is that the wearer keeps his or her hands free for other stimulating activity. Some

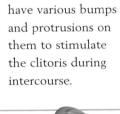

THE FLARED BASE of this dildo makes it ideal for slipping into a harness to create a strap-on (see facing page). The dildo could also be used by hand.

models fit into a vibrating cock ring, which provides clitoral stimulation at the same time. There are also double dildos available, which work in a push-pull fashion, and enable you and your partner to enjoy simultaneous vaginal or anal penetration.

Cock rings

The cock ring fits around the base of the penis. Its tight grip restricts blood from flowing back out of the penis, thus strengthening the erection and giving a feeling of fullness and pressure. It is especially useful for men who suffer from venous leakage problems (see p.206). The more fun versions vibrate, and have various bumps and protrusions on them to stimulate the clitoris during intercourse.

COCK RINGS come in many shapes and sizes, from the basic remedial penis ring to the knobbly, jelly-like clitoral tickler.

THE WELL-STOCKED TOY BOX

ANY ENTHUSIASTIC sex-game player will have at least some of the following erotic accessories in his or her toy box:

- Vibrators, both vaginal and anal, dildos, cock rings, anal wands, and butt plugs (see p.144), for additional stimulation before and during penetration (NB: Don't use vaginal toys for anal sex)
- Lubricating jelly, or some other sex lubricant, for enhanced sensation (see p.144)
- Squares of satin, silk, and velvet, for blindfolding and stroking or massage (see p.152)
- A fur mitt, for stroking and massage
- Feathers, for teasing and tickling (see p.153)
- A paddle or a cane, for spanking (see pp.140–41)
- Silken cords or "safe" handcuffs, for bondage games (see pp.138–41)
- Edible body paints, for smearing on then slowly licking off your lover's body
- Ice (in the freezer), for games of "torture" and submission (see p.80)
- Face masks and disguises, for erotic fantasy games

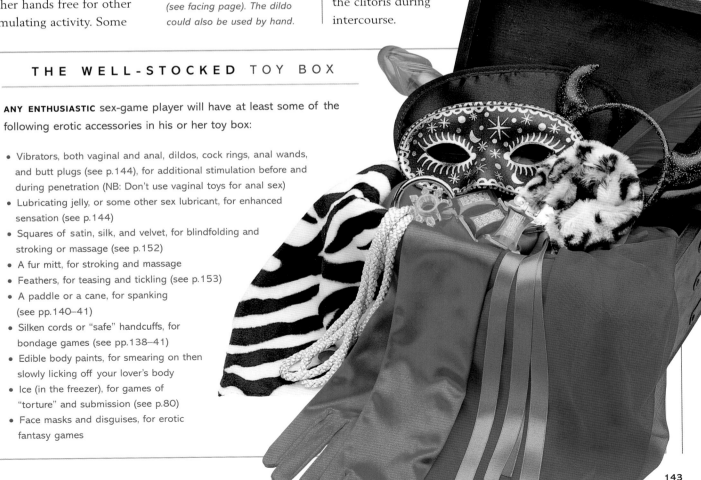

Anal wands

There are now several vibrators specially designed to penetrate the anus comfortably and massage the super-sensitive prostate gland situated at the far end (see p.93). This gland, which exists primarily for the purpose of manufacturing semen, is so sensitive that only brief massage can trigger climax. The anal wand is ideal for those who like a feeling of pressure combined with vibration and movement. Vibrating anal toys help relax the anal muscles if tense, and can be immensely pleasurable.

ALL ANAL TOYS should have a large or flared base to prevent them from slipping inside and getting lost. This sizable wand, with speed adjustments on the handle, is easily long enough to reach the prostate gland.

Butt plugs

Butt plugs are used in the anus or vagina, and are designed to be worn for a feeling of fullness. They are made in silicone or rubber, and are available in a variety of shapes and sizes. There is a long, thin, pointed plug (see right), a shorter, fatter, slightly curved version, and a small, squat, beaded version.

BUTT PLUG

Electrical toys

Many of you will have heard of TENS machines. These are used in physiotherapy to relieve pain, and work by pulsating a tiny electrical charge into the skin. Now there's a sexual version – a wand that, when held near your body, bombards you with a continuous stream of safe, low-voltage, mini-lightning bolts. The sensations are fantastic.

Blindfolds and restraints

A blindfold offers a sense of helplessness, and makes you feel vulnerable. You don't know where you are when you wear it, and you have no idea what obstacles you may be facing. Your mind starts racing as you imagine the hazards that lie outside, and your anxiety levels rise. It's these swirling emotions that the astute partner tunes into and utilizes – generally, the greater the anxiety level, the more intense are the emotions involved.

Most games of restraint involve one partner wearing a blindfold (see pp.138–41 and p.152). For comfort, use a soft material such as a silk scarf, a black velvet eye mask, or a sleep mask. Make sure that you don't tie the blindfold

FUN LUBES

LUBES ENABLE wonderful, warm, slippery sex, and are a great help for some women at certain "dry" times of the month. They are also essential for all anal play, since the anus doesn't provide a natural lubricant. Lubes come in all colours, textures, and scents. For sheer variety, you might consider edible lubes, which are small, gelatine-filled capsules that you bite on during oral sex to flood your partner's genitals with sweet-smelling, edible gel (chocolate flavour is a popular choice). Some of the best-equipped bedrooms display rows of little gelatine pots to choose from.

too tight, which could be painful, or too loosely, unless partial sight is intended as part of a game. Unless you know that your partner is into really serious bondage, it's best to use restraints made of soft fabrics, such as a man's silky tie, or the silky cord from a dressing gown. Alternatively, most of the sex-toy manufacturers sell "safe" handcuffs, specially designed for the purpose of sex-play.

Making your own recordings

Apart from stocking up on what you consider to be really sexy music, it's worth thinking about making your own recordings. The seduction of music is one thing, but the power of your own voice is quite another. You can record all kinds of sexy blandishments to excite your partner on nights when you aren't together, or to give your partner a special frisson as he or she plays a cassette in the car on the way to work. You might record some erotic short stories, a series of S & M commands, an endless list of sexual praise, or conversations or commands in two voices, so that your partner is able to fantasize about the presence of two of you in the room. Everything is subjective, and what one person thinks is erotic may not be for another, so you'll need to experiment with your lover.

The bedroom camera

A camera can capture certain erotic moments. If you want to recollect your naked partner, standing half in the shadow, looking at you with desire, the next best thing to reality is to keep his or her celluloid alter ego in your wallet. You could dress up and send your lover a selection of photographs of you in different costumes – the period clothing of an Edwardian pin-up, a dominatrix with thigh-high shiny boots and whip, or an exotic, sultry houri.

It's worth spending some time considering what you and your partner hope to achieve by your photography. If the imagination counts for a lot with you, you probably won't want an explicit, full-frontal view, where one of you is stimulating yourself directly to the camera. Instead, you could set the camera on automatic, then pose, with your partner, in a compromising position, but behind the clouded glass of a shower door, for example. You won't be able to see everything in the picture, but you'll offer some supremely tempting glimpses.

DIGITAL CAMERAS ARE USEFUL, because it means that your sexy pictures will not need to be processed at a photo lab. The disadvantage is that you might find compromising shots of yourself beamed around the planet by a proud partner via the Internet. Polaroids might prove safer.

SEX BOOSTERS

THERE ARE NUMEROUS WAYS of giving your sex life a boost. Using your imagination is paramount, but the sex-toy industry and drug companies have developed an increasing range of products designed to help reduce inhibition and enhance sexual response.

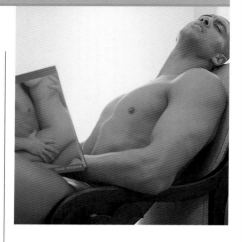

Sexy magazines and books

There is no doubt that men are turned on by sexy pictures of women, and sex tests have shown that men are also frequently turned on by hard porn. Women, on the other hand, tend to be aroused by suggestive, less overtly sexual literature, and generally don't find visual images as exciting. These sex tests seem to have pointed to an innate sex difference between men and women (see pp.24–25). But whatever your preference, the imagination is one of the biggest sex enhancers of all, and erotic books and magazines act as an excellent starting point for the imagination.

Erotic clothing

Dressing up can act as an extremely exciting forerunner to an erotic encounter. In addition to sexy underwear, shoes, and stockings (see pp.148–50), there is now a wide range of outfits available in sensual fabrics, such as PVC and shiny rubber (see pp.153 and 157). These hug every crevice of the wearer's body and feel amazingly sexy; they will also drive your partner mad with desire.

Sex toys

The sex-toy industry is increasingly developing new products for both sexes (see pp.142–45), but particularly for women. This is because a revolution has gone on in the bedroom enabling women to become more overtly sexual – like men, they want to overcome inhibitions and enjoy sex, and

TREAT YOURSELF to a private evening in, surrounded by sensuality in the form of warmth, music, and an erotic book.

YOUR PARTNER CAN APPLY Viacreme to your penis or clitoris during foreplay. You will soon start to feel a sexy, tingling sensation.

welcome any product that allows them to do so in the easiest possible way. Sex-tool products range from new and exciting vibrators, specially designed to suit women's eroticism and sensibilities, as well as anal wands and other products aimed at men.

Some sex toys work by pulsating an electrical charge into the skin and sending out a continuous stream of tiny sparks, producing an incredible array of sensations.

Reducing inhibitions

A couple of glasses of wine can improve your love life because the alcohol relaxes you while lowering your inhibitions, and this lets your naturally sexy, raunchy side emerge. But if you drink more than two glasses, it can begin to have the opposite effect: it can depress sex drive, and make you feel sleepy and uncoordinated. In men, it can lead to "brewer's droop", where it becomes difficult to maintain an erection.

Sex doctors now know that the drug phentolamine works on the "inhibitor" brain centre by loosening up a person's inhibitions and allowing sexual desire to come to the surface,

where previously it may have been repressed. This drug is available by prescription only.

Viagra and Viacreme

A small revolution occurred with the recent development of Viagra (see p.207), which provides impotent men with a good erection. The beauty of Viagra is that it can only function when the brain thinks sexy thoughts, so it does not reduce stimulation to a purely mechanical act. The drug works by boosting the nitric oxide level in the region of the genitals, allowing erections to be sustained. Some women find their sexual response is improved by taking Viagra, but since the drug was designed for men, it is not advisable for women to take it.

Viacreme is a cream that you rub on to your penis or clitoris. It draws the blood to your genitals, and helps trigger the start of your erection (or the female equivalent). See the Internet for more details.

Testosterone

The hormone testosterone is a strong chemical component of male physiological make up (see p.48).

However, a few men have a testosterone deficiency, which is sometimes associated with the andropause (see p.209) – these men could perk up their sex lives if they took testosterone supplements (see p.203). Similarly, women who find it difficult to experience orgasm (see p.210) should get a blood test to check their testosterone levels. If these are low, testosterone therapy may help to improve their sexual response.

Testosterone is available in gel form. Since there are health implications to taking it, it is wise to see a doctor and get it on prescription. However, many doctors are still unfamiliar with testosterone replacement therapy. The gel is also available on the Internet.

DRESSING FOR SEX

WHEN DRESSING FOR SEX, the rules are simple: wear tight clothes that emphasize the curves and contours of the body and draw the eye to the genitals, chest, or buttocks. Clothes should either be difficult to take off – the idea being that you tease your partner into submission while remaining inaccessible – or extremely easy to slip out of.

Shocking your partner by wearing something unexpected always has erotic power. To spice up your sex life, try subverting your normal dress codes. For example, if you normally dress down in your everyday life, try dressing up for sex. If you tend to wear conservative clothes, dress provocatively for a change. Devote a special part of your wardrobe to sex games. If you're a woman who usually wears pale cosmetics, try experimenting with crimson lipstick: huge dark lips are universally seen as sensual. Eyeshadow on a man can also be attractive to some women.

Choosing underwear

Because underwear is the last item of clothing that you shed before sex, it has an important symbolic value. When that underwear is silky and sexy, it can have a wonderfully sensual effect, making you feel great and your partner long to get his or her hands on you. Men have fewer types of underwear to choose from but, rather than get complacent about your choice, buy something that you know your partner finds attractive – black silk boxers are often popular. If you don't know what he or she likes, try drawing up a humorous list with your partner, covering the types of underwear that you find sexy and those that you dislike.

Take each other's vital measurements, and then go shopping together. Let sexual tension start in the underwear department and build on the way home. Some sex shops specialize in erotic underwear, from crotchless panties and G-strings to leather and rubber ware. You can even buy edible underwear. When undressing each other, try a game of removing each other's underwear with your teeth – the only thing that you're allowed to use your hands for is her bra clip.

UNDERWEAR CAN HELP you play a sexual role – white underwear conjures up ideas of virginity, and this can be a real turn-on for men.

USE UNDERWEAR AS A SEXUAL SHORTHAND *to tell your partner what kind of sex to expect — black, lacy underwear expresses confidence and sexual assurance, and shows your man that you want to take control.*

SEXY UNDRESSING

IF YOU'RE NOT USED TO STRIPPING, the following exercise can help. Stand in front of a full-length mirror, pretend that you're alone, and very slowly take off all of your clothes. Take time to really look at your body in the mirror and touch yourself in whatever way you want to. This takes away the performance aspect of stripping and gives your partner the sense of being a voyeur. If it makes you feel better, let your partner hide in the next room and watch you from behind the door.

WHEN MEN strip for a partner, they should make the most of their best assets — for example, wear a tight shirt, which has to be squeezed over your manly shoulders.

THROW A PARTY

ORGANIZE A FANCY DRESS PARTY — the condition of entry is that guests must dress as their favourite sexual fetish or fantasy:

- Tight leather – anything made of leather has sadomasochistic overtones, especially when belts and chains are added.
- Fake fur – this suggests decadence, especially if you are completely naked beneath a fake fur coat.
- Tribal and ethnic clothes – exotic clothing from foreign cultures can be flattering and suggestive. Wear saris, sarongs, grass skirts, bikinis made of flowers, feathers, or veils. Dress up as a belly- or limbo dancer.
- Uniforms – symbols of authority are always sexy. Dress up as a policeman, fireman, doctor, nurse, or teacher. Alternatively, servant and schoolgirl uniforms suggest servility and innocence.
- Cross-dressing – try to create at least a moment's uncertainty when you make your entrance as to your true gender.

MANY MEN AND WOMEN find uniforms very attractive — the clothes convey a strong, powerful image, which can be irresistible.

Shoes

For years the foot, and its clothing – the shoe – have been seen as an erotic symbol of the female body. Indeed, there were generations of men who equated a dainty foot with powerful sex appeal. But that was back in the days when nice women didn't show their legs. Today, we are not focused on the foot in quite the same way. However, if you plant a tall, slim woman, wearing sheer black stockings, a short skirt, and tremendously high stiletto heels in front of

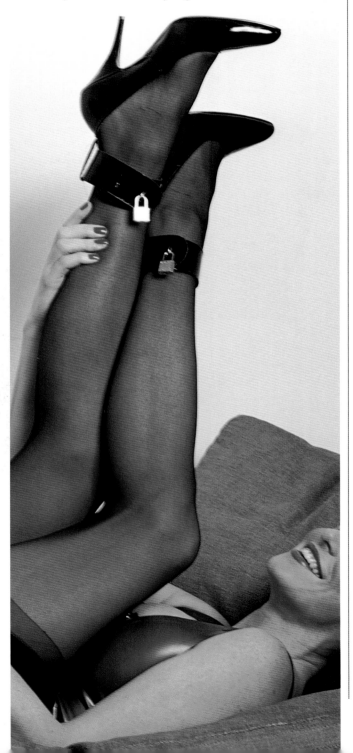

THE EROTIC FOOT

FEET HAVE LONG BEEN ASSOCIATED with sex – in both men and women, toes tend to curl involuntarily during orgasm. In fact, the feet are so rich in nerve endings that some people are able to climax from foot caresses alone. In literature, the foot has been used to symbolize the female genitals – for example, the story of Cinderella can be read as a story about sexual fit. And in Japanese erotic art, curled toes have been one of the stylized symbols of erotic response for hundreds of years. There is a form of lovemaking called pedic lovemaking. This includes the man having his penis massaged by the woman's feet. It also includes sucking the toes of a female partner, using the big toe to stimulate the clitoris or vagina. Many women enjoy having their feet held and caressed during sexual intercourse. Experiment with these techniques with your partner to see if they have the desired effect.

a male you will see a fascinating phenomenon – presented with such a vision of a long-legged woman, men virtually froth at the mouth. Today's psychologists believe that this is a result of males becoming fixated as children on particular sights or objects that they accidentally associate with sexuality (see pp.24–25). Out of this, a thriving industry of high-heeled shoes has grown – these used to be called tart's shoes because prostitutes were so aware of their pulling power. Seamed stockings and high black leather boots also dramatically outline and draw attention to a sexy leg.

Body adornments

Body piercing and tattoos used to be regarded as a very primitive and even mutilating form of art. Indeed, there are many people who still see them like this and dislike the look of them. But in the past five years a new middle-class phenomenon has grown up, mainly among the younger generation. Many young men and women sprout a plethora of earrings, nose rings, and body jewellery with pride.

Piercing and tattoos are often a means of a young person distinguishing him or herself from parents or other members of the older generation. They can be a statement of independence and confidence. There is also a sense of taking part in a rite of passage – couples, or even bunches of friends, go to the tattooist or piercer together.

It's no accident that both being pierced and being tattooed involve a certain amount of pain. Yet both experiences are regularly described as erotic. Certain people associate the pain of skin piercing with the pleasure of sexual arousal. And hidden piercings, such as those through the nipples and the genitals, are associated with the sex act.

Considering tattoos

Hidden tattoos, on the inner arms, thighs, and buttocks can be sexy discoveries for lovers to make. Even the genitals can be tattooed. However, a permanent tattoo is a major commitment – once the skin has been injected with indelible dye, you gain a body adornment that lasts for a lifetime. Always consider carefully where a tattoo will be positioned, and what it will show – because whatever you choose will be with you through your life, and you don't want to grow tired of it. It is probably best to experiment first with henna tattoos that last for a few days and can be removed with oil. You can even have temporary tattoos custom-made, which may be a preferable option.

TATTOOS GIVE THE IMPRESSION of strength and confidence, which can be very attractive to others. They can relate specifically to a lover, such as a name, and can be an indelible statement of enduring love. Or they may be a symbol or pattern that makes a statement about the wearer, working to create an air of mystery.

SENSUAL MATERIALS

WHEN VENTURING into the world of exotic sex, among the first delights to incorporate into your love life are sensual props. If you've never experienced the teasing of velvet or the slither of silk across your skin, you can now anticipate a range of exquisite sensations.

Set time aside for the two of you to indulge in a really sensuous evening. Equip yourselves with squares of sensual fabrics such as silk, velvet, and fur. Using a long strand of velvet, blindfold your partner and lead him or her into an excessively heated room. Make sure that the room is already scented with perfume or a burning, sweet-smelling joss stick. As your partner stands there blindfolded, say that he or she must submit to anything you choose to do. This is the cue to slowly peel off your lover's clothes and lay him or her on a spacious sofa or a bed covered by a large piece of velvet. Tell your partner it is imperative that he or she lies there with legs apart.

Now is the cue to stroke every inch of his or her skin with each of your sensual fabrics. You can whisk them across the main part of the body, use them to tickle and tease, and finally use the materials to actually massage the body with, avoiding the genitals at this stage. Throughout this experience, your partner will be wondering what is going to happen between the legs. Keep your lover waiting for as long as possible: the anticipation will serve to heighten the pleasure. Not until you have thoroughly pleasured the rest of the body do you then repeat the process with the genitals.

SOFT, LIGHT FABRICS *such as silks and satins can be run quickly along your partner's body to tease and tempt. A blindfold adds to feelings of anticipation and excitement.*

TOP MATERIALS

CERTAIN MATERIALS have extremely sensual or suggestive textures:

- Velvet
- Satin
- Silk
- Feathers
- Fur
- Leather
- Rubber
- PVC
- Clingfilm
- Canvas (harness, straps)

Getting into rubber and leather

You don't have to be a fetishist to admire your lover's appearance when he or she dresses up in shiny black rubber. It's also extremely sexy for the wearer: rubber clings to every pore of your skin, grasps and squeezes your flesh, and slips and slides as you heat up and perspire within its tight confines. The heat that your body generates raises the temperature in more ways than one: rubber lovers report feeling so feverish that they fall upon each other with passion.

Leather, particularly wet-look leather, can also be extremely sensual. It is a recognized fashion material, and fetish fashion shows for leather lovers are a regular part of the clothing industry season. You could hold your own private fashion shows for fun. When your partner "buys" something, force him or her to pay in kind.

THERE IS A VAST RANGE of stunning, close-fitting PVC, rubber, and leather clothing available. Get dressed up, and insist that your partner does likewise before you agree to sex.

TEASING WITH FEATHERS

ONE OF THE MOST EXOTIC touch temptations is the feather massage, which you could use as a preliminary to a sensual or genital massage (see pp.58–64). Feathers look gorgeous, skim lightly across the skin, and tickle the innocent recipient into wriggling submission. You could use a feather boa, or a single peacock feather for more directed sensation:

1 Tickle every inch of your partner's skin with the feather boa or peacock feather, using light, rapid movements.

2 Sprinkle your partner with talc and use the boa or plume to sweep the powder across their body in long strokes.

3 Sweep the boa or plume from the knees upwards along your partner's inside thigh, "accidentally" touching the genitals when you reach them.

FETISHES

FETISHISTS ARE PEOPLE who are sexually stimulated by a particular object, and whose fetishes do not conform to heterosexual or homosexual sex. While many people possess minor fetishes that have no great impact on their sex lives, major sexual variations inevitably influence relationships.

> ### WARNING
>
> If you do not want to take part in a certain sexual activity, do not hesitate to say no. No one should be forced to have sex that is repugnant to them.

According to the theories, the fetishist (usually male) is often extremely introverted and anxious about forming relationships. Afraid of rejection, he unconsciously attaches himself to something inanimate or partial that could not reject him. As a child, he may have accidentally associated an object with the stirrings of sexual arousal and may subconsciously "remember" this association the next time he sees the object or feels sexy. The two memories become irrevocably linked, and the fetish is born.

It doesn't necessarily have to be sexual arousal that causes sexual associations – in situations where adrenaline (the "fight and flight" hormone) is aroused, people are put into a state of extra awareness. In 1980, psychologists Chris Gosselin and Glenn Wilson made a study of "rubberites", particularly rubber mackintosh enthusiasts. Most of their subjects felt that their interest had developed in their childhood, during World War II. Gosselin and Wilson surmised that the anxiety-provoking circumstances of war, plus a lot of rubber articles in use at the time, provided fertile ground for this particular interest.

Learning theorists argue that individuals can virtually programme themselves to become fetishists. An example of this would be the young man who masturbated to pictures of women wearing red lace underwear and who eventually found that the underwear itself (without the woman inside) was just as effective.

Women and fetishes

Very few women are fetishists. This is probably because many girls, unlike boys, often don't discover their sexual response until their late teenage years or even their twenties, by which time they have learned to associate sex with a relationship rather than an attraction to specific parts of the body or even objects. Women fetishists often (but not always) associate their special sexual interests with some kind of emotional wounding.

TYING UP A PARTNER is something many couples do occasionally for fun (see pp.138–41). However, if a person has been emotionally wounded, restraint can become an integral part of their sexual make-up.

> ### SEXFACTS
>
> **VISUAL-MENTAL LINK**
> Dr. Glenn Wilson of the Institute of Psychiatry (UK) believes that the area in the male brain which is responsible for male sexuality is situated extremely close to the area that is responsible for seeing. This may account for the theory that men are more turned on by visual stimuli than women, and that experiences can "leak" from one section of the brain to the other.

FETISH AND PHILIA GLOSSARY

Virtually anything can become a fetish, although fetishes change with the times and fashions. In the 19th century, for example, when ladies wore gloves, hand fetishes were common. Today, this fetish has all but disappeared. Over the past 50 years or so, new fetishes for modern, man-made fabrics, such as PVC, have emerged. Below is a list of the most common fetishes:

★ **AMPUTEE FETISH**
Some people (usually men) are sexually stimulated by people who are missing certain limbs. The theory behind this attraction is that if the male fetishist feels sexually inadequate, the realization that he has a physical advantage over the disabled individual allows him to feel powerful and sexually aroused.

★ **AUTOEROTIC ASPHYXIA**
A highly dangerous activity in which a male or female restricts their breathing in order to prolong or accentuate orgasm, often by hanging or putting a plastic bag over the head. This lowers oxygen and blood pressure, and increases carbon dioxide intake. Don't do it!

★ **BONDAGE**
An activity where a dominant partner binds a submissive one so that they cannot escape (see pp.138–41). A major effect of bondage is the release of normal inhibitions on the grounds that there is nothing the submissive partner can do to prevent the activity. (See also String or clingfilm bondage, p.157)

★ **CINDERELLA FETISH (PODOPHILIA)**
One of the most common fetishes among both men and women, this is a passion for shoes. Imelda Marcos of the Philippines possessed rooms full of shoes – we don't know if she derived sexual pleasure from them, but there must have been some special emotion here in order to collect so many pairs so avidly. (See also High-heel fetish, p.156)

★ **DEFILEMENT FETISH**
Some fetishists get very turned-on by looking at people covered in mud, slime, and other messy substances.

SOME MEN have a hair fixation. They can spend hours twining their fingers through hair and like to be wrapped in it or have it whipped against their body.

★ **EXHIBITIONISM**
Some men and women get a major frisson from knowing they might be observed doing something sexual. Sex in the open air, for example, is particularly attractive to many individuals.

★ **FROTTAGE**
The activity of rubbing genitals against someone's body in order to arouse sexual excitement is attractive to many people. It can be done during sexual intercourse but also, more sinisterly, in public places to strangers, such as on a crowded train.

★ **GOLDEN SHOWERS (UROLAGNIA)**
Many people find urinating on their partner or being urinated on enhances sexual pleasure, relishing the warmth and the mess involved. Couples spray "golden rain" onto the face, body, or genitals of a partner, often during sex or while bathing or showering.

★ **HAIR FETISH (TRICHOPHILIA)**
An obsession with hair sometimes leads to hair fetishists creeping up behind strangers in the street or on public transport and snipping off their locks.

MUD WRESTLING contests are very popular with defilement fetishists, who get sexual excitement from seeing naked people covered in slime. There are special clubs for mud enthusiasts.

★ HIGH-HEEL FETISH
(ALTOCALCIPHILIA)
This is an advanced form of the
Cinderella fetish (see p.155), where
the male enthusiast gets carried away by
the sight of women's high-heeled shoes.
This fascination probably develops
when the fetishist is a young boy,
when unconsciously he sees high heels
looming over him, accidentally associates
the sight with sexual sensation, and can
never forget it.

★ INFANTILISM
A sex game, usually played by fairly
powerful men, which involves being
looked after like a baby. Infantilism
fetishists enjoy being dressed in baby
clothes, especially nappies, given bottles
of milk to drink, and having their
nappies changed. The final touch to the
game would be stimulation by "nanny"
to orgasm, although not all men want to
go that far. The common explanation for
this fetish is that powerful men with a
lot of responsibility sometimes need to

feel totally helpless and without
responsibility of any sort. There are
weekend breaks on offer, where business
men can go to be "nannied".

★ KOKIGAMI
A Japanese enthusiasm, where the male
wraps his penis in a paper costume (the
name means origami of the penis). This
idea originated in Japan in the 8th
century, when aristocrats wrapped their
genitals in silky trimmings and then
offered them as gifts to their lovers,
enjoying the sensual experience of
them being unwrapped.

★ MUD-WRESTLING FETISH
See Defilement fetish, p.155.

★ NECROPHILIA
Literally speaking, this means making
love to a corpse, and no doubt there are
some disturbed individuals who do just
that. But it can also mean making love
to a victim who plays dead, lying totally
inert, regardless of what is done to him
or her. The attraction for the fetishist is
total control.

★ PONY-RACING FETISH
The competitive activity of "pony-racing"
is an extension of sado-masochistic
gaming. The "drivers" tend to be male
and the "ponies", often pulling real (but
lightweight) pony carts, are usually
women, partially nude but bound with
harness straps. Often there is an element
of pain to their pulling, and the driver is
likely to encourage speed by using his
whip. Pony-racing clubs hold regular
racing events for their members.

★ PUBLIC-SPEAKING FETISH
(HOMILOPHILIA)
Some people get turned-on by standing
up in front of an audience and making a
sexually fuelled speech; others become
excited by listening to such a speech and
may end up bouncing compulsively on
the edge of his or her seat.

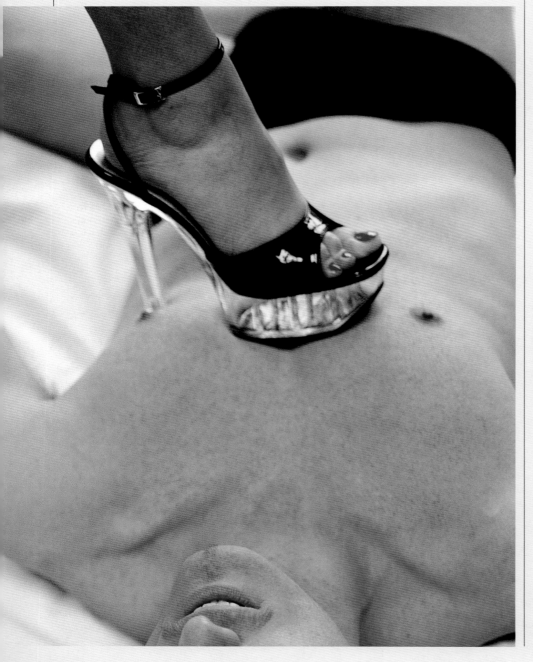

*MANY MEN ENJOY looking at women in high-
heeled shoes, and many women enjoy
wearing them. Taken a stage further, some
men also enjoy the masochistic connotations
of a powerful woman walking all over them.*

RUBBER is one of the most common fetish fabrics. The texture and odour are a great turn-on for rubber enthusiasts. In addition, it makes the wearer very hot and sweaty, thereby adding to the appeal.

★ TELEPHONICOPHILIA

Telephone fetishists get a thrill from calling strangers and shocking them with the use of sexual conversation. Alternatively, they may be enthusiasts of telephone sex in which men and women masturbate while consciously arousing each other on the telephone.

★ VAMPIRISM

This can refer to any sex play where blood is involved. Originally, the expression specifically referred to drinking blood, with Dracula as a prime example of the true vampirist.

Warning: Since vampirism involves exchanging blood, it is considered to constitute unsafe sex, and you run the risk of contracting AIDS.

★ VOYEURISM

Some people, commonly known as "Peeping Toms", get sexually aroused by watching other people engage in sexual activity. Such enthusiasts will often masturbate while watching the activity or will stimulate themselves later while they "relive" the event.

★ ZOOPHILIA

Some people are sexually stimulated either by the thought of sex with animals or by the activity itself. Primitive societies have traditionally engaged in sex with animals when human beings are not available. Since becoming more urban, zoophilia has diminished in Western societies.

CLINGFILM is a relatively new fetish fabric to be used in bondage games. The entire body may be wrapped in it, or only certain parts.

★ RUBBER FETISH

Rubber fetishists are aroused by wellington boots, rubber mackintoshes, and rubber aprons. Many wear underwear made out of latex, and costumes, such as nuns' habits, vests, skirts, and hoods, are also part of the specialist clothing on offer. Rubber sheets are also available.

★ STRING OR CLINGFILM BONDAGE

String bondage is a specialized form of S & M, where the submissive partner is tied up or wrapped with string around certain areas of the body. Clingfilm is a modern material used for the same effect, and can be subtly provocative. Games involve winding the wrap between a woman's legs so that her labia are trapped open under a layer of clingfilm but so that the entrance to her vagina remains unobstructed. Alternatively, a male wraps it around his scrotum to form a kind of testes ring, or around the shaft of his penis with only the head left free. An important word of caution: clingfilm must never be wrapped around the face.

ALTERNATIVE SEXUAL LIFESTYLES

WE LIVE IN CHANGING TIMES. The divorce statistics are high, and it is apparent that marriage does not answer everyone's needs. For those who don't strive for the marital "ideal", numerous alternatives are on offer. Many of the promiscuous lifestyles described have been discontinued, largely owing to AIDS, but shreds of the sexual revolution still linger on.

Couples today frequently opt for cohabitation instead of rushing into marriage. For some, cohabitation is a more carefree way of enjoying a regular sex life without opting for all the responsibilities as well. Real commitment often only happens when the couple starts a family. There's nothing very new about "living together", but what is new is that some very contemporary lifestyles are emerging out of cohabitation.

Singles cohabitation

It sounds a conundrum to say in the same breath that you can be single and cohabit, but that is effectively what many people now choose. There are more single households in the Western world than ever before, and more women are opting not to have children. Enjoying your own company and learning to be self-reliant appear to be today's goals.

In practical terms, this may mean you have a partner with whom you perhaps spend one night during the week and very likely the whole weekend. Or if one of you works overseas, which is becoming increasingly common, your relationship may be carried on by phone, e-mail, and web-cam. And this includes sex! Virtual sex consists of masturbation while talking on the phone, "chatting" while online, or playing "show and tell" on web-cam.

THREESOMES are popular with both men and women, in various configurations. All three can participate at the same time, or one person may take a more voyeuristic role.

SWINGING PARTIES, where couples meet, flirt, and end up having sex with someone else's partner, are still much in evidence today.

Singles cohabitation is a concept of relationship that suits modern lifestyles. In practice, it's a modern-day version of a forces marriage, the situation where the woman manages the home on her own but changes all routines as soon as her partner has home leave.

Communal marriage

Some couples, or accepted singles, agree to enter a group marriage and to stay faithful to it. This may involve actually living together (such communities still exist in both the US and the UK), or it may mean living apart but getting together at regular intervals to enjoy communal sex.

Partner-swapping sex parties

Swinging is very much associated with the 1960s, along with "wife-swapping" parties. But as the many contact magazines bear testimony, it's still alive and well. Swingers are (usually) two or more couples that get together, mainly in each other's homes, and experience sex jointly or exchange partners and have sex separately. Group sex parties grew out of

swinging, and developed in the 1970s. These would offer the opportunity for men and women to meet and have sex together, either in a private bedroom set aside for the purpose, or in a common room where everyone else was having sex too. Sex here was still experienced mainly as an activity for two, with the occasional single "helping out".

Orgies are an extension of the sex party concept with the difference that participants were expected to have sex together *en masse* and indiscriminately. In the 1970s, many sex orgies were enjoyed by gays. The advent of AIDS in the 1980s generally put a stop to this extrovert lifestyle.

Fetish parties

This is a more contemporary concept, in which both friends and strangers get together regularly to play specialized sexual games at fetish parties. These include games of submission and domination (see pp.138–41), as well as aspects of exhibitionism and voyeurism (see pp.155–57). Although sexual intercourse tends to be carried out

only between specific couples, there are still plenty of fetish-related activities that involve other people and end in masturbation, mutual masturbation, and oral sex. Many of these games are carried out with the help of sex toys (see pp.142–45).

Sexual clubbing

Many capital cities today possess specialized clubs where people can go to meet new friends and possible lovers with shared sexual preferences. Many of these encourage sexual action, if not overtly then somewhere concealed on the premises. Clubs for transvestites, gays, lesbians, and fetishists all feature in the entertainment columns of magazines.

TRANSVESTITES AND TRANSSEXUALS

TRANSVESTITES ARE MEN OR WOMEN who take sexual pleasure in dressing up in clothes that are normally associated with the opposite sex. Transsexualism, these days sometimes called "gender dysphoria" (meaning unease with one's gender), is more extreme and may lead to the individual seeking to change his or her sex.

SEXFACTS

TRANSSEXUAL STATISTICS
In 1974 it was estimated in the UK that one in 33,000 biological males was transsexual compared with one in 108,000 females.

The transvestite experience

Contrary to what many people think, the majority of male transvestites are heterosexual, and often within a marriage that they value highly. However, some transvestites are homosexual, while others are not of any particular sexual persuasion.

Transvestites differ from transsexuals in that they do not usually feel "wrongly sexed". Instead, they are effectively clothes fetishists. There are also some female-to-male transvestites, who enjoy wearing overtly masculine clothing. However, today these females tend to go unnoticed since many of the women's fashions are androgynous in style.

TRANSVESTITES LOVE the glamour of make-up and women's clothing, and tend to wear very feminine fashions.

The transsexual experience

A transsexual is someone who believes strongly that he or she is trapped in the body of someone of the opposite sex, and feels quite different from other members of his or her gender, often at an extremely early age. Most specialists observe that the feelings can be present in children as young as six. At this stage, they start to feel depressed because their body does not match up with their own perception of themselves.

Some young transsexuals grow out of their feelings as they get older. However, many do not, and numerous individuals seek corrective measures. Re-assignment surgery, in conjunction with hormone therapy and cosmetic surgery, is now an option in a few major cities throughout the world.

Variety of transsexual types

The word "transsexual" is an umbrella term, since within it there may be as many different types of transsexual as there are heterosexuals. There are male-to-female transsexuals who alter very little of their lifestyle and remain married. There are others who adopt a flamboyant lifestyle and are seen as a very specific gender of their own. And there are "feminist" male-to-female transsexuals, who argue that they see no reason to dress in a particularly feminine manner or wear cosmetics, just as many "real" women don't. Female-to-male transsexuals usually try to look as male as possible, and often grow a beard and spend time weight-training to build muscle.

Male-to-female sex-change

For male transsexuals, the sex-change process consists of taking hormones to feminize the appearance, and experiencing genital surgery, in which the male genitals are amputated and an artificial vagina is created out of folds of the scrotum. In addition, the patient has electrolysis, to remove unwanted body hair, and cosmetic surgery, to emphasize feminine characteristics such as the breasts.

Personal reports from male-to-female transsexuals reveal that although the male sex organs are removed, there continues to be erotic feeling that is now concentrated in or around the pubic mound, just above the new vagina.

The most successful transsexuals are those who learn female deportment – how to hold themselves, and how to walk like women. Instruction in the use of cosmetics and personal grooming advice given to transsexuals include the idea of trying to model themselves on some female icon whom they admire.

Female-to-male treatments

Treatment for this group includes androgens (male hormones) that masculinize the appearance. This encourages beard growth, a deeper voice, greater muscular strength, and sometimes a baldness pattern. Surgery includes breast amputation and construction of a scrotum from the labia, as well as the insertion of synthetic testicles. Penile construction

APRIL ASHLEY

TOP VOGUE MODEL and society hostess April Ashley was born in 1935 and christened George Jamieson. In 1960, male April had the sex-change operation. Although physically traumatic, the surgery greatly enhanced her life.

is unfortunately not very successful, and many female-to-male transsexuals prefer to retain the clitoris, albeit in the enlarged form that has been encouraged as a result of the androgen treatment. The clitoris usually grows to a length of around 9cm (3½in).

RAYMOND THOMPSON

RAYMOND THOMPSON was born a female but felt from the age of five that he should have been a man. After many complex sex-change operations, he finally has an artificial penis made from his own tissue. He now lives with his girlfriend, and feels that the surgery has given him dignity and the ability to identify with his physical form.

CHAPTER 6
Gay Sex

GAY ISSUES

MOST GAY MEN discover around their teens that they're deeply attracted to other males, although some experience feelings from an earlier age. This can be true of lesbians, but it's also very common for a woman to discover her sexual preference in her late twenties, often after she's already married.

How many of us are gay?

Famous sex reports, such as the *Kinsey Report* in the late 1940s, would have us believe that up to 30 per cent of the male population were homosexual. Either times have changed, or this was an unscientific and unbalanced piece of research. The 1994 National Survey of Sexual Attitudes and Lifestyles, carried out in the UK (see box, facing page), found that the figure was rather lower, and this is probably closer to the truth.

When gay people are studied, their sexual preference is usually measured by the number of sexual acts they have performed. Many people find this form of measurement controversial, believing that it is the force of emotion that counts, not actual behaviour.

Gay lifestyle

There are many gay men and women who actively like to be regarded as different from their heterosexual contemporaries. The most high-profile gays wear distinct clothing and often lead an extrovert life, which includes clubbing at gay clubs and mixing mainly with other gays.

However, there are also a vast number of gays who do not subscribe to this lifestyle. Although gay men have traditionally been seen as promiscuous, the 1994 survey showed precisely the opposite. Over 50 per cent of gay men had only had one partner, and out of the small number of men (gay and straight) who reported up to 99 sexual partners in their lifetime, there were 3 per cent more heterosexual men in this category than gay men. Women's same-sex relationships have been traditionally less controversial than those of gay men, perhaps because statistics show that they have far fewer sexual relationships

GAY STATISTICS

THE 1994 NATIONAL SURVEY of Sexual Attitudes and Lifestyles, conducted in the UK, revealed that people's experience of homosexuality was as follows:

- Some kind of homosexual experience: 6.1% of men; 3.4% of women
- Genital contact with a same sex partner: 3.6% of men; 1.7% of women
- Same-sex sexual partner within the last two years: 1.4% of men; 0.6% of women

NB: While 6.1% of British men admit to some kind of gay experience in their lifetime, this contrasts with 4.9% of US males, 4.1% of French males, and 3.5% of Norwegian males.

same-sex relationship. Today, many lesbians opt to have children by artificial insemination. Although there has been criticism of giving children same-sex parenting, British psychological surveys in the 1980s showed that children of lesbian couples appeared to be as well adjusted and as happy as the children of heterosexual couples.

When homosexual male parents have been contrasted with heterosexual male parents, the research shows that gay men appear to be better fathers. They tend to be more sensitive to their children's feelings, and make a point of helping their children work through problems instead of just letting them "get on with it".

What is bisexuality?

A bisexual is a man or a woman who is able to relate sexually to either gender. Famous sex researchers Masters and Johnston considered that bisexuality represents a point of sexual sophistication that human beings are working towards. The 1994 survey showed that there is a group of men who describe themselves as "heterosexual", but who have had same-sex experiences in the past. It also showed that men and women who have had a lot of experience with the opposite sex were also likely to have had a lot of same-sex experiences. This lends itself to a bisexuality theory speculating that men and women with a high sex drive have so much libido that it drives them towards many and varied outlets.

as a group; indeed, according to the 1994 report, two-thirds of lesbian women have only ever had the same sexual partner and no lesbians in the survey reported more than 20 sexual partners.

Gay parenting

Many lesbian households include children, as do some male homosexual ones. Some lesbians already have children when they discover their true sexual identity and the children move with them out of the marriage into the new

DEALING WITH THE OUTSIDE WORLD

OVER THE LAST 50 YEARS, particularly with the repeal of anti-homosexual laws in most Western countries and states, and since homosexuality as a psychiatric problem was removed from the medical text books, society has come a long way in accepting gay men and lesbians. However, prejudice is still rife.

Many openly gay men and women believe that you should reveal your sexuality so that society (including those individuals who are close to you) is forced to come to terms with homosexuality. It's only by doing so, goes the argument, that you can ever obtain overall acceptance. This may or may not be true, but the sad fact is that there are many problems on the road to real gay liberation.

Should you tell your parents?

The vital question of whether or not to tell your parents that you're gay is hotly debated by gay counsellors. Most people believe, in principle, that your mother and father should know and accept who you are, regardless of your sexual inclination. However, sadly, some parents are unable to accept that their child is gay – they may become extremely violent, or throw their son or daughter out of the family home; some even dismiss their gay child as "dead". If you know that you couldn't bear to live disowned in this way, it would be advisable to refrain from revealing your sexual nature unless you're certain that your parents will react positively. Of course, the down side is that a vital part of your life has to be concealed, which may have a negative affect on your relationship with them. If you do decide to tell your parents, try to break the news as tactfully as possible.

GAY CLUBS offer an environment in which gay men and women can meet and show sexual interest in public without being ridiculed or attacked. Most of these clubs are in big cities, where gays tends to be more accepted.

OVER THE PAST 30 years or so, gays have raised their public profile by marching in the streets and lobbying politicians for the right to be treated like any other individuals.

How to tell your parents

When it comes to breaking the news of your sexuality to your parents, it's not a good idea to suddenly blurt out your sexual inclinations in the middle of dinner. A softer tactic tends to be much more effective, where you approach the parent you consider to be most sympathetic. Some methods of disclosure are better than others: the person who explains "I've fallen in love, and I'd like you to know about it, but I feel I must tell you that my friend happens to be a man" is likely to achieve far more in terms of acceptance than the individual who announces bluntly "I'm gay". The latter may be more difficult to accept, whereas the first approach has the reassuring context of a relationship.

Many parents take the news extremely well and offer positive support straight away. However, others can take longer to adjust to the idea. To many it will come as a great

HISTORY FACTS

ANCIENT GREEKS

Homosexuality was much more widely accepted in ancient Greece. The Sacred Band of Thebes, the backbone of the Theban army and the best military force in ancient Greece, was made up entirely of homosexual men. The Sacred Band remained unconquered for 40 years, and when finally it was vanquished the dying soldiers were found lying clasped in each other's arms on the battlefield.

shock, and they might need time to "grieve". They may have seen themselves one day with grandchildren, and might think that your homosexuality now precludes this. They may also be concerned that you, and possibly the whole family, are likely to meet with prejudice and discrimination. The main thing is to be patient and prepared to go over the same ground several times so that they can get used to the idea. You've had a long time to get used to the idea of your gay identity, now they will need some time too.

If you predict that your parents will be upset by your news, it's advisable to take the precaution of seeking out a telephone counselling organization in advance (see p.264).

Meeting other gays

It can still be extremely difficult to make same-sex relationships in country areas, and gay men and women usually find that moving to a big city makes this easier. Good starting points may be gay bars and clubs, classified ads in gay magazines, and of course chat rooms and the

Internet. There are matchmaker sites on the Internet that specialize in putting single people of all types together (see p.263).

If you plan to meet up with someone contacted on the Internet, choose a neutral meeting place, don't take him or her home on the first date, and if possible ensure that a friend or relative is in your home should you do so. This may not sound conducive to intimate friendship, but unfortunately meeting through the Internet can sometimes be dangerous. If anyone is going to be worth knowing, they will understand your attitude and will wait until you feel more ready to trust them.

Pink economy

The gay market is rapidly becoming recognized as a growth area for marketing. Today, there are gay films and gay film festivals, gay insurances, gay financial companies, gay publications, gay characters in popular soap operas, and gay entertainers. All of these go some way towards raising the profile of gays in the outside world, and will hopefully lead to further acceptance of gays generally.

WHY ARE SOME PEOPLE GAY?

WHY ARE SOME PEOPLE HOMOSEXUAL and others heterosexual? The answer is that no one actually knows. One theory is that we inherit our sexual characteristics, and that the cause of any sexuality is genetic. Another is the view that the environment in which we grow up is responsible, since it greatly influences how we think and develop. Some scientists consider that hormones or brain structure are contributing factors.

Environmental factors

For many years, the main explanation for homosexuality was based on Freud's theory, which stated that male homosexuality was caused by a boy growing up with a weak, remote, or absent father and a dominant or over-close mother. This was known as the "nurture" theory, and it is still, to some extent, in evidence today. However, this has never been proved, and many people contest this viewpoint on the grounds that not all homosexuals have poor or unbalanced relationships with their parents, nor do all those with poor father–son or mother–daughter relationships necessarily become gay. In the early part of the 21st century, the nurture theory is losing out to the various "nature" arguments in circulation.

Evolutionary theory

This more positive view of homosexuality is based on ideas put forward in Bruce Bagemihl's book *Biological Exuberance: Animal Homosexuality and Natural Diversity*, as well as the work of psychologists Geoffrey Miller and Susan Blackmore. According to the theory, a natural percentage of homosexuality exists within the population on the grounds that homosexuals may have evolutionary value in helping the rest of the tribe survive. This is because the gay members of a group become important "uncle" figures, thus aiding the survival of children of the group, even though they don't have children themselves. The strength of this view is that it regards homosexuality as extremely valuable.

SEX FACTS

GENETIC RESEARCH

A team of National Cancer Institute researchers in a study of over 100 homosexual men found that many of their uncles and male cousins were also homosexual, suggesting a hereditary factor. In its comparison of the DNA of 40 pairs of same-sex oriented brothers, it was learned that almost all shared genetic markers in the Xq28 region of the X chromosome. Research on the DNA of 36 pairs of lesbian sisters did not reveal a corresponding pattern.

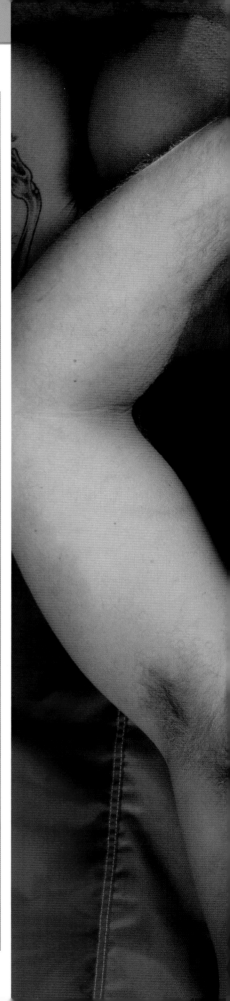

Hormone differences

In the 1970s and 1980s, hormone differences were a fashionable explanation of homosexuality. US psychiatrist John Money stated that the foetal brain is either masculinized or feminized according to which hormones it bathes in within the womb. This could mean that a hormone difference during pregnancy plays a role in sex orientation. However, it has now been proved that over 99 per cent of homosexuals have no measurable hormonal abnormality.

Brain structure

Could homosexuality be the result of differences in the brain? There are conflicting reports about this, and nothing so far has been proved. However, a 1991 study reported that the hypothalamic nucleus INAH3 was smaller in women and homosexual men than in heterosexual men. The study did not show, however, how the area involved had any bearing on sexual behaviour. Nor could it reveal which came first, the sexual orientation or the brain structure.

Is homosexuality genetic?

One popular theory is that homosexuality is genetic. Several studies of brothers, including twins, have been carried out, some of which appeared to prove there is a genetic factor in the case of male, but not female, homosexuality (see box, facing page). However, fault has subsequently been found with some of the studies.

Some people believe that genetics are responsible, but in a more complex and less direct way. For example, a tendency to certain personality traits may be inherited and could predispose someone to developing a homosexual orientation within a certain environment.

CHAPTER 7

Sex for Life

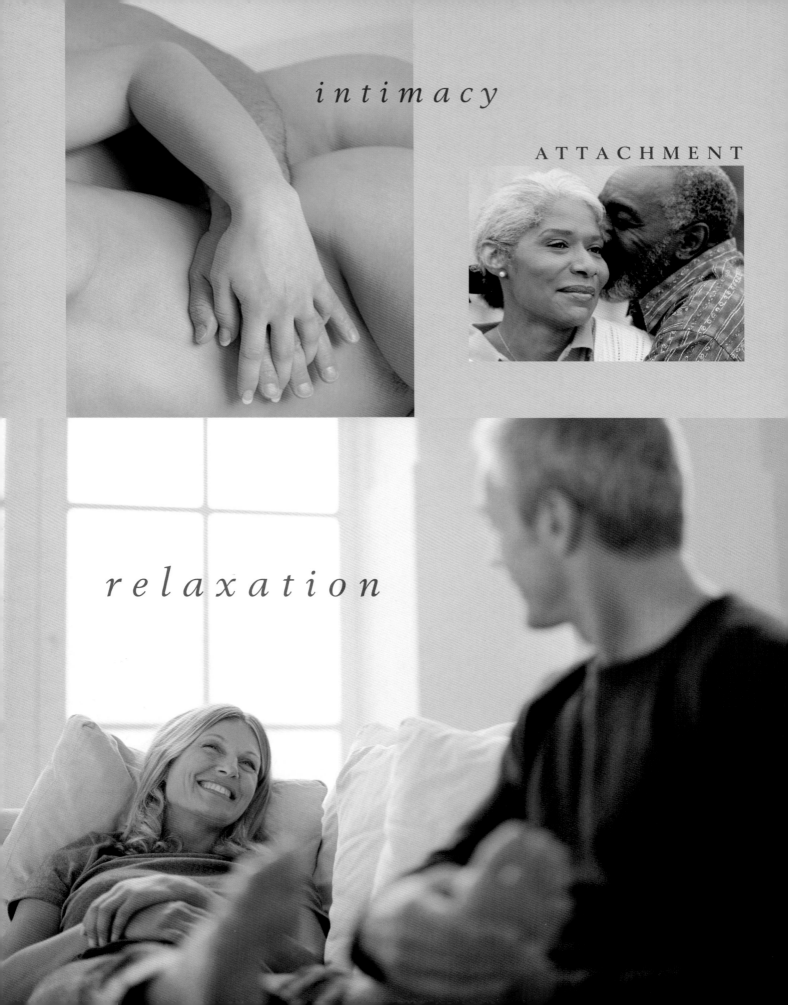

intimacy

ATTACHMENT

relaxation

sharing

T R U S T

SEX EXERCISES

Sexual exercises, or "sexercises", are simple and great fun to do on your own or with a partner. They help you build up strength in the muscles that you use most during sex, and encourage awareness of the sexual energy flow in your pelvis and genitals, which in turn leads to more enjoyable and erotic sex. Some of them also help to delay ejaculation and prevent incontinence.

<table>
<tr><td>

RELAXATION ROUTINE

SEX ISN'T ENJOYABLE WHEN you're feeling stressed or anxious, so you need to learn how to relax effectively. Take long, deep breaths, drawing each breath down into your abdomen. As you exhale, imagine that tension is floating out of your body.

</td></tr>
</table>

PELVIC LIFTS

Exercising the muscles of your pelvis makes you toned and flexible in this area. It also enhances the flow of blood to the sexual organs and releases sexual energy.

▲
Lifting the pelvis
Lie on your back with your knees bent and the soles of your feet flat on the floor. Place your arms by your sides with your palms facing down. Lift your pelvis as high as you can so that only your feet, head, neck, and shoulders are on the floor, and breathe deeply. Warning: Do not attempt this exercise if you have back problems.

PELVIC CIRCLING

This exercise is a fantastic way of reducing stiffness in the hips and freeing up energy in the pelvis.

Circling exercise ▶
Stand with your feet hip-width apart and start to move your hips slowly in small circles. Now gradually make the circles bigger and bigger as if you were twirling a hula-hoop around your waist. Aim to make the circles as fluid and rhythmic as possible. A sexy variation of this exercise is to stand close to your partner, wrap your arms around him or her, close your eyes, and rotate your hips in unison.

PELVIC-FLOOR EXERCISES FOR WOMEN

Pelvic-floor exercises, also known as Kegel exercises, were originally designed for women suffering from incontinence, since they strengthen the pelvic-floor and sphincter muscles which support and control the bladder. Another bonus is that they enhance sexual sensation by toning the vagina so that it hugs the penis tightly during intercourse.

The pelvic-floor muscles surround the urethra, vagina, and anus. To locate them, imagine that you are trying to stop yourself urinating and tense the appropriate area. Practise the exercises by drawing up the muscles as tightly as you can, holding them in a contracted state, and then releasing them. Now repeat this as often as you can. Vary the speed of the contractions by doing ten fast contractions followed by ten slow ones. Aim to do a combination of up to 300 fast and slow contractions over a day.

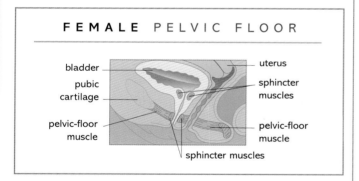

FEMALE PELVIC FLOOR

bladder

pubic cartilage

pelvic-floor muscle

uterus

sphincter muscles

pelvic-floor muscle

sphincter muscles

PELVIC-FLOOR EXERCISES FOR MEN

Men can also reap the sexual benefits of a tightly toned pelvic floor. Strong muscles in this area can assist you to achieve and maintain a firm erection; some men also find that drawing up the pelvic-floor muscles can stop the urge to ejaculate, helping them to last longer during intercourse.

To locate the correct muscles, imagine that you are trying to stop the flow of urine through the penis (or the passage of wind through the anus). Once you've found the muscles, tense them as hard as you can and work up to holding this contraction for ten seconds. Then let go. Now repeat this up to 12 times, concentrating on holding the contraction at its height. Do this several times a day.

OVERCOMING STIFFNESS

A common obstacle to good sex, particularly in later life, is stiffness and joint inflexibility which mean that you can't move in the way you want to during lovemaking. Two great ways to overcome this problem and stay toned, flexible, and mobile are yoga and Pilates. Both are gentle forms of exercise that emphasize the importance of posture, alignment, and breathing, and let you go at your own pace. The best way to learn yoga and Pilates is from a qualified teacher who will guide you through the movements, but you could try this exercise at home:

The Pilates squeeze
This Pilates exercise works the muscles of the lower abdomen, pelvic floor, buttocks, and inner thighs.

▲
1 Lie face down on a comfortable surface and place a small pillow or cushion between your upper thighs. Rest your head on the backs of your hand. Put your toes together but keep your heels apart.

2 Inhale and draw up your stomach muscles. Tighten your buttock muscles, squeeze the cushion between your inner thighs, and put your heels together. Count to five and release. Do ten times in total. ▼

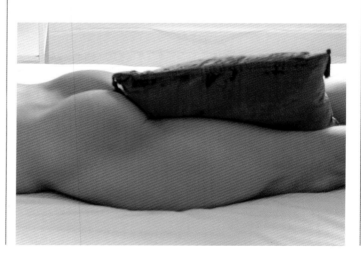

DIET AND FOOD SUPPLEMENTS

PEOPLE HAVE TURNED to an enormous variety of substances throughout history in their attempts to intensify the sexual experience, from powdered rhino horn to oysters. Today, the general consensus is that very few of these aphrodisiacs actually work. Instead, attention has turned to substances that promote the sexual health and well-being of the whole body.

Although there is some evidence that drugs derived from yohimbine (a compound in the bark of the yohimbe tree) can improve sex, there are very few other substances that act as reliable aphrodisiacs. A much better option is to try to improve your sex life using techniques pioneered by sex therapy, or to consult your doctor about pharmacologically approved drugs such as Viagra (see p.207) or hormone supplements such as testosterone (see p.147 and p.203).

A diet that is rich in antioxidant vitamins and minerals is thought to prevent degenerative diseases, such as heart disease and cancer, and retain healthy sexual function. It is also thought to preserve youthful looks and vitality, both of which are important for sexual confidence. Antioxidant vitamins and minerals include vitamins A, C, and E, co-enzyme Q10, betacarotene, selenium, and zinc. A good way to ensure that you get enough antioxidants is to eat plenty of fresh fruit and green, leafy vegetables or to take a general antioxidant supplement. Zinc and vitamin E are both particularly good for sexual health and fertility. In addition, zinc is good for the prostate gland (see p.181). A deficiency of vitamin E is thought to result in a low sex drive.

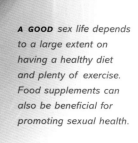

A GOOD sex life depends to a large extent on having a healthy diet and plenty of exercise. Food supplements can also be beneficial for promoting sexual health.

HERBAL SUPPLEMENTS

THERE ARE MANY HERBAL SUPPLEMENTS on the market. Some of them can benefit your sex life indirectly by alleviating problems such as stress and fatigue, or by promoting vitality and energy. If you have any doubts about whether it is appropriate to take herbal remedies, consult a qualified medical herbalist, naturopath, or doctor. Among the herbs that are worth investigating are the following:

♥ AGNUS CASTUS
Works on the pituitary gland and has a balancing effect on the hormones, particularly during the second half of the menstrual cycle and the menopause, when hot flushes can occur. Also useful in reducing excessive prolactin levels.
WARNING: Do not take if you are already taking HRT or other hormonal treatment.

♥ GINKGO BILOBA
Improves blood circulation, reduces pre-menstrual breast pain, and improves learning ability, memory, and concentration. Is an effective agent for inhibiting PAFs (platelet-activating factors), which can lead to thrombosis and bronchial constriction.

♥ GINSENG
One of the most highly prized of all medicinal herbs, ginseng regulates the metabolic rate, stimulates blood sugar levels, maintains vitality, and protects against mental and emotional stress.

GINSENG is useful if you have been under severe stress. Take for three months.

♥ L-ARGININE
Can increase both sperm count and quality of sperm.
WARNING: Herpes sufferers should not use the supplement L-arginine because it stimulates the virus.

♥ LINSEED
An alternative to cod-liver oil, this increases immune function, regularizes the menstrual cycle, lowers blood pressure, and reduces the risk of heart disease.

♥ RHODIOLA ROSEA
Regulates stress hormones, boosts physical energy (it is particularly useful for improving recovery after illness), and may improve sexual function.

RHODIOLA ROSEA is used by Russian athletes and cosmonauts to increase physical energy.

♥ SAW PALMETTO
Treats prostate problems caused by too much testosterone. Strengthens the neck of the bladder, reduces frequent urination, and acts as a tonic for general debility.
WARNING: Not to be taken by pregnant or breast-feeding women.

SAW PALMETTO BERRIES are mentioned as a remedy for several problems in Native American medicinal texts of the 1800s.

RECOMMENDATIONS FOR LATER LIFE

In addition to the other supplements and dietary recommendations mentioned on these pages, the following are useful to improve or maintain a good sex life in the middle or later years:

♥ GLUCOSAMINE
An amino sugar, glucosamine builds up cartilage that may otherwise have worn down in older men and women. It also helps counteract stiffness, which can cause sexual problems.

♥ PHYTOESTROGENS
Naturally occurring oestrogens found in plants can supplement natural hormones. Phytoestrogens maintain hormone production in post-menopausal women and help to prevent prostate enlargement in men (see p.181).
WARNING: Phytoestrogen supplements must not be taken together with HRT.

CELERY is a natural provider of phytoestrogens, as are fennel and pulses.

♥ SALVIA OFFICINALIS (SAGE)
Sage acts as an antispasmodic, antiseptic, astringent, and tonic. May be used in an infusion. Helps to control menopausal symptoms in women (see p.211).

♥ VITAMIN E
Vitamin E capsules taken orally relieve menstrual cramps, endometriosis pain, and pre-menstrual tension. Oil applied locally encourages healing. A capsule inserted into the vagina offers resistance to chlamydia and relieves menopausal vaginal dryness.

PERSONAL CARE

You can look after your sexual health in several ways. Personal hygiene is crucial, and you should also always practise safer sex (see pp.182–83). For your general health, it is vital to check yourself for any abnormalities such as lumps or swellings on the breasts or testicles. There are also professional medical checks such as smear tests and prostate examinations that are extremely important (see pp.180–81).

Perhaps the most basic aspect of caring for your sexual health is to pay attention to your personal hygiene. Wash the genitals and perineum daily with water and perfume-free soap to prevent the build up of smegma under the foreskin and to wash away stale vaginal secretions.

Tampons should be changed every four to six hours and removed before sexual intercourse. Don't forget to remove a tampon at the end of a period – tampons that remain in the vagina for too long can cause an infection known as bacterial vaginosis (see p.220).

OVERDOING HYGIENE

We are often wrongly encouraged to think that all bodily smells and secretions are dirty and unnatural. Cosmetic companies in particular target us with a bewildering array of products, from genital deodorants to fragranced sanitary towels. In fact, the smell of fresh genital secretion plays an important part in sexual arousal – if you are too vigilant about washing, you may be depriving yourself of an important natural aphrodisiac!

Too much washing with highly perfumed bath products or soaps can also irritate the delicate tissues of genitals, and may lead to a common infection of the vagina known as candidiasis, or thrush (see p.220). Although candidiasis isn't technically speaking a sexually transmitted infection, it's easily passed on to a sexual partner, manifesting itself as an infection of the glans of the penis.

◀ **Keep it simple**
When bathing, use simple, unperfumed products. These are gentler on the skin, and unlike scented soaps do not mask the natural scents of vaginal juices that so excite your partner.

GOLDEN RULE

THE MOST BASIC hygiene rule during sex is not to let anything that touches the anus go on to touch the female genitals – this way, you prevent the transmission of anal bacteria to the vagina or the urethra. In practical terms, this means washing the penis *after* it has touched the anus and *before* vaginal intercourse, and disinfecting sex toys such as vibrators or dildos that have been in contact with the anus. It is vital to be scrupulous about genital hygiene during lovemaking sessions that involve anal sex.

BREAST SELF-EXAMINATION

All women should check their breasts regularly for signs of any abnormalities. Although most breast changes are completely benign, a few may signify breast cancer. As with all cancers, early diagnosis will maximize your chances of effective treatment and recovery. Because the breasts are often naturally lumpy in the days leading up to a period, the best time to examine them is just after you have stopped bleeding (postmenopausal women can examine their breasts at any time). Some women find it easiest to check their breasts in the bath or shower, with soapy hands.

How to examine your breasts

▲
1 Lie down, and hold your first three fingers flat against your breast. Press down gently and, starting at the nipple, trace a circle around your breast. Now make the circles larger until you have covered your entire breast. Also check the area above and underneath your collar bone and in your armpits. Repeat on the other breast.

2 Stand up, and repeat step 1. Then, standing in front of a well-lit mirror, look at the contours of each breast, first with your arms by your sides, then with your arms behind your head, then leaning forwards slightly with your hands on your hips. Look for any irregularities, and squeeze each nipple to check for discharge.

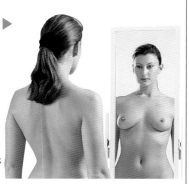

WHAT TO LOOK FOR

IF YOU NOTICE any of the irregularities listed below, seek prompt medical advice:

- A small painless lump or mass on or around the breast
- Unusual or bloody discharge from the nipple
- A nipple that becomes inverted
- Puckered, dimpled, or scaly skin on the breast

TESTICULAR SELF-EXAMINATION

From puberty onwards, all men should carry out regular testicular self-examinations in order to detect problems such as testicular cancer at an early stage. If treatment is prompt, testicular cancer has one of the best cure rates. Report anything that looks or feels unusual to your doctor as soon as possible. Note that the soft, slightly bumpy area at the back of the testicles is the epididymis, so don't get this confused with an abnormality. In addition to testicular self-examinations, older men will need to have regular prostate checks carried out by a doctor (see p.181).

How to examine your testicles

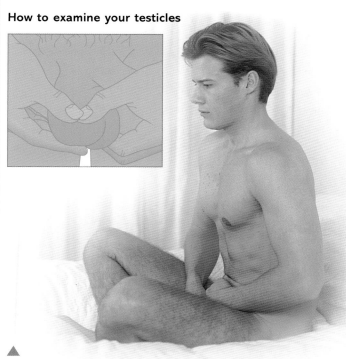

▲
Checking for abnormalities

After a warm bath or shower, when the scrotum is relaxed, palpate each testicle in turn between your thumb and fingers. The surface should feel smooth and the skin of the scrotum should move freely. Check for signs of any change or irregularities.

WHAT TO LOOK FOR

EXAMINE YOUR TESTICLES for any of these changes. If you spot any abnormalities, consult your doctor:

- Alterations in testicle size or texture
- Hard but painless, pea-sized lump in the testicle
- Swellings in the testicle
- Changes in the skin of the scrotum, such as ulceration

MEDICAL CHECK-UPS

Early detection of any illness always means that there is a better chance of curing it more quickly. Since no one is more familiar with your body than you, it is well worth carrying out regular self-checks (see p.179), and always seek medical advice straight away if you spot any irregularities. Also, make sure you undertake the screening tests provided at doctor's surgeries and hospitals. If you are worried about your sexual health, visit a sexual health clinic and have a thorough check-up.

VISITING A CLINIC

There are various reasons for visiting a sexual health clinic. Some people are aware that they have contracted a sex-related disease because they have an obvious symptom such as an unhealthy discharge, or an unusual sore or lump on their genitals (see pages 220–23). Others may have no noticeable symptoms but may have been told by a sexual partner that they have been exposed to a sex-related disease. Those who indulge in casual sex sometimes seek routine sexual check-ups to reassure themselves that they are healthy. They may just decide to have a check-up before they embark on a new sexual relationship so that they can confidently tell their partner that they have a clean bill of health.

Most major hospitals have sexual health clinics – usually called genito-urinary clinics – that offer free and impartial advice. Doctors who work in sexual health clinics are specially trained to diagnose and treat sex-related diseases and are professional and discreet. You don't even need to disclose your identity if you don't want to.

AT THE CLINIC

IF IT IS YOUR FIRST VISIT to a genito-urinary clinic, it is helpful to know what to expect:

1 A doctor will make a physical examination of your genitals to check for any obvious sores, ulcers, rashes, or other signs of infection.

2 He or she is also likely to take a urine and a blood sample and a swab from your genital area (the cervix, vagina, urethra, and anus in women, and the urethra and anus in men). Your blood, urine, and genital swabs are then tested for the presence of disease-causing micro-organisms. Although some test results may be available immediately, others may take several days or even weeks to come back. Ask the doctor how long you will need to wait for the results, and what sexual precautions you should take in the meantime.

3 If you do have a sexually transmitted infection, you will probably be offered treatment immediately at the clinic. This may consist of antibiotics or anti-viral drugs. In some cases, you will need to return to the clinic for further treatment or for a follow-up check to make sure that your treatment has been successful. You may also be given advice about how to prevent transmission to (or re-infection by) sexual partners and how to avoid sexually transmitted infections in future. Some clinics also offer counselling.

MAMMOGRAPHY

A mammogram is a sophisticated way of examining the breast tissue for lumps using X-ray, and is an excellent tool in the early diagnosis of breast cancer. Mammograms can reveal precancerous cells as well as tumours – if detected early, these often respond well to treatment. Women over the age of 40 should have regular mammograms.

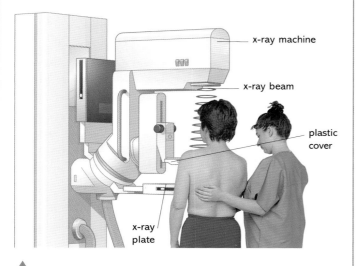

Having a mammogram

The woman places her breast between the plastic cover and the X-ray plate, where it is firmly compressed. X-rays pass down through the breast and onto the plate, where an X-ray image is produced.

PROSTATE EXAMINATION

Many men are unaware of the prostate gland until late in life, when it can start to enlarge and put pressure on the urethra. This means that even when you have a full bladder and feel the need to urinate, the flow of urine is weak and impeded, leaving you with the feeling that you haven't emptied your bladder properly. The medical name for this is benign prostatic hyperplasia (BPH).

Cancer is another problem that commonly affects the prostate in men over the age of 50. Prostate cancer is often symptomless until it is quite advanced, although sometimes it causes symptoms similar to BPH. Both BPH and prostate cancer can often be detected at a very early stage by a simple rectal examination carried out by a doctor.

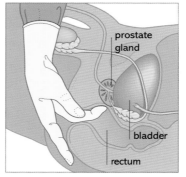

◄ Checking the prostate

The prostate is a walnut-sized gland that lies just below the bladder and circles the urethra. If a rectal examination reveals that the prostate gland is enlarged, there are a number of treatment options available to prevent further problems.

SMEAR TEST

The cervical smear test, also known as the "Pap smear", detects cervical cells that could become cancerous in the future. If cells show signs of being pre-cancerous, you will be referred for further diagnostic tests and treatment to prevent cancer occurring. Ask for a smear test within six months of having sexual intercourse for the first time, and then about every three years thereafter.

Having a smear test ►

A lubricated speculum is inserted into the vagina and a sample of cells are scraped from the cervix's surface using a spatula. The cells are smeared on a slide and later looked at under a microscope.

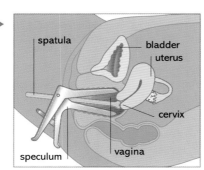

During the procedure

This painless, quick procedure involves the woman lying on her back, resting her legs on the support provided. The doctor or nurse holds the patient's vagina open with a speculum and gently scrapes cells from the surface of the cervix (see left).

SAFER SEX

SAFER SEX IS A WAY of making love that will help you reduce the chance of getting a sexually transmitted infection. It will also protect you from an unwanted pregnancy. By wearing a condom or, better still, by having sex that is non-penetrative, you can still have fun and relax in the knowledge that you're not putting your health at risk.

Everyone who has uncertainties about the sexual health of the person they are sleeping with should have safer sex. This means using a male or female condom every time you have penetrative sex (see p.185), or substituting penetrative sex with a lower-risk activity, such as mutual masturbation or sensual massage (see box, right).

People who are in high-risk groups for HIV and other sex-related diseases, such as gonorrhea, genital warts, or herpes (see pp.220–23), need to be particularly scrupulous about safer sex. High-risk groups include people who have penetrative sex with multiple partners; prostitutes and their clients; and those who have anal sex (see pp.124–25). Anal sex is considered high risk because it can cause tears and abrasions to the lining of the rectum, which provide a route

WHAT IS SAFE?

THE GOLDEN RULE to remember when practising safer sex is to avoid any activities that involve the exchange of bodily fluids with your partner. Condoms provide a barrier and greatly reduce the chances of contamination. Below is a list of sexual activities in order of risk:

HIGH RISK

- Vaginal or anal intercourse without a condom
- Oral sex without a condom or latex barrier
- Inserting shared sex toys into the vagina or anus
- Any sexual activity that results in bleeding

LOWER RISK

- Mouth-to-mouth kissing – although HIV is present in saliva, it is much less concentrated than in blood, semen, or vaginal juices
- Mutual masturbation, providing neither of you have cuts, sores, or abrasions on your hands and fingers or genitals, and as long as no vaginal fluids or semen come into contact with broken skin anywhere on your body
- Vaginal sex using a condom
- Oral sex using protection

LITTLE OR NO RISK

- Dry kissing
- Cuddling
- Massaging unbroken skin
- Using clean sex toys that you don't share
- Semen or vaginal fluids coming into contact with intact skin
- Self-masturbation

in for bacteria and viruses. If you have anal sex, you should use plenty of water-based lubricant together with an extra-strong condom that is specially designed for anal intercourse. Take things very slowly and gently, and never go directly on to vaginal intercourse without washing the genitals very carefully first.

Talk about it

An important principle of safer sex is to initiate frank and honest conversations about sexual health every time you consider making love with someone new. Many people find this difficult, mainly because they're afraid of appearing

KISSING AND LICKING your partner's body are low-risk activities. However, if you're planning to move on to oral sex you'll need to use a latex mouthshield or condom, unless you both have a clean bill of health.

A SENSUAL MASSAGE is both sexy and relaxing. It's ideal in the early days of a relationship, when you're uncertain of your partner's sexual history, since it carries no danger of any sexual infection.

presumptuous. Also, they may be concerned that they might destroy the romance of a new relationship. Added to this is the reticence that many people feel about discussing sex in intimate detail.

The best way to tackle this problem is to wait until a time when you have shared some sexual intimacy but you haven't actually made love. Then describe your own health status first and invite your potential lover to do the same. You could suggest a joint visit to a sexual health clinic to get checked out for any sexually transmitted infections (see p.180). Explain to your partner that you feel this would be a sign of your mutual commitment to a sexual relationship. If you're both free of disease and choose to have unprotected sex, you need to know for sure that your partner will be monogamous.

The joy of touch

It's a myth that great sex has to include penetration. Some of the most erotic lovemaking consists of sharing fantasies (see pp.134–37), giving each other a long, tantalizing massage (see pp.58–65), or bringing each other to orgasm by hand (see pp.76–77). If you're new to the idea of non-

penetrative sex, resolve to spend an evening in bed with your partner exploring every part of each other's body with your hands. This is not only a fabulous way to find out new and exciting things about your partner, it's also a way to break out of old sexual ruts and patterns and breathe new life into your lovemaking.

CONDOM FUN

MANY PEOPLE dislike using condoms. However, there are many ways of making the experience more enjoyable:

1 Use them suggestively. Slip one under the sheets on your partner's side before he or she gets into bed.

2 Go shopping for novelty coloured, shaped, and flavoured condoms that you can have fun experimenting with (always look for the safety kitemark).

3 Girls – put one on your partner using your mouth. Hold the condom tip between your lips and then smooth it along the length of his shaft.

4 Use lots of water-based lubricant to make the condom glide smoothly onto your penis.

5 Don't stop to put the condom on, or you may lose the sexual momentum. Touch her breasts while she puts it on, or ask her to stroke your buttocks while you put it on yourself.

CONTRACEPTION

The word "contraception" literally means "against conception", preventing the union of male sperm and female ovum. There are numerous types of contraceptives, which work in a variety of different ways. Barrier methods physically prevent the sperm travelling as far as the ovum, while the Pill prevents ovulation from taking place. An intrauterine device (IUD) inserted into the uterus reduces the chance of a fertilized egg being implanted.

NATURAL METHODS

Some couples favour a natural approach to birth control, which relies on accurately detecting ovulation and either avoiding intercourse or using a barrier contraceptive around this time. Ovulation detection has become much easier in recent years with the invention of home ovulation tests and electronic fertility monitors, which measure hormones found in urine. Alternative but less reliable methods involve monitoring cervical mucus (see p.51), which increases around ovulation, and body temperature.

Monitoring body temperature ▶
Take your temperature at the same time every day, before getting up. Just after ovulation, your temperature will rise and remain high for about three days. Refrain from sex during ovulation as well as for several days before and afterwards to be safe.

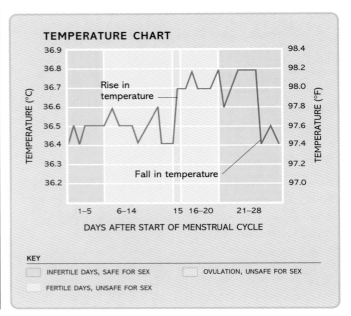

TEMPERATURE CHART

Rise in temperature

Fall in temperature

DAYS AFTER START OF MENSTRUAL CYCLE

KEY

INFERTILE DAYS, SAFE FOR SEX OVULATION, UNSAFE FOR SEX

FERTILE DAYS, UNSAFE FOR SEX

CONTRACEPTIVE EFFECTIVENESS

WHEN CHOOSING A CONTRACEPTIVE you need to be fully aware of the efficiency and limitations of each method. Listed below is the percentage of women who become pregnant over a period of a year using different methods correctly and consistently.

BARRIER METHODS

- Male condom — 3%
- Female condom — 5%
- Diaphragm with spermicide — 6%

HORMONAL METHODS

- Combined pill — 0.1%
- Progestogen-only pill — 0.1%
- Hormonal implants and injections — 0.1%

INTRAUTERINE CONTRACEPTIVES

- Intrauterine device — 1%
- Intrauterine system — 1%

STERILIZATION

- Tubal ligation — 0.5%
- Vasectomy — 0.5%

NATURAL METHODS

- No contraception — 70–85%
- Abstinence on fertile days — 25%

BARRIER METHODS

Contraceptives that work on the barrier principle prevent the sperm from reaching the ovum. The advantages are that there are no side-effects and they reduce the chance of transmitting disease. The drawback is that foreplay may be interrupted while the contraceptive is put on or inserted.

MALE CONDOM

The male condom is the most popular barrier method of contraception and is a vital accessory for safer sex (see pp.182–83). By trapping semen inside a rubber sheath (usually coated in spermicide), sperm are prevented from entering the woman's body. After ejaculation, the penis and condom must be withdrawn from the vagina before the penis becomes flaccid.

COLOURED CONDOMS

Putting on a condom ▶

When the penis is erect, place the opening of the condom over the head of the penis and pull it down along the shaft. It is vital to ensure that no bubble of air remains in the tip and that the condom is fully unrolled so that it covers the length of the penis.

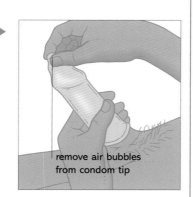

remove air bubbles from condom tip

SPERMICIDES

SPERMICIDES ARE CHEMICALS that immobilize or destroy sperm. They are not widely used as contraceptives in their own right, but they increase the efficacy of other contraceptives such as condoms, caps, and diaphragms. Spermicides come in various forms including creams, gels, foams, and pessaries (vaginal suppositories). They should be applied as close to the woman's cervix as possible, or on the concave part of a cap or diaphragm. The popular spermicide nonoxynol-9 has been shown to destroy HIV and disable some types of bacteria that cause sex-related diseases.

FEMALE CONDOM

The female condom is designed to line the inside of the vagina. It consists of a thin polyurethane tube with one open end and one closed end. The ring at the closed end of the tube sits in the upper part of the vagina while the ring at the open end lies outside. During intercourse, the man inserts his penis into the tube. Female condoms are almost as effective as male ones, but they are often more expensive.

FEMALE CONDOM

Inserting a female condom ▶

Taking care not to puncture the condom with sharp fingernails, insert the sheath into the vagina. Push it back towards the cervix, leaving the outer ring of the condom at the vaginal entrance.

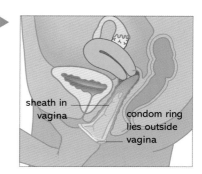

sheath in vagina

condom ring lies outside vagina

DIAPHRAGM AND CAP

The diaphragm and cap are two barrier methods of contraception that work by blocking the entrance to the cervix so that sperm cannot penetrate the uterus. The diaphragm is a circular rubber dome with a springy rim; the cap, also made of rubber, is smaller and thimble shaped. Initially, these devices should be fitted by a nurse or doctor, who will choose the right size for you. Caps and diaphragms should always be used with a spermicide and inserted prior to intercourse. To be effective they must always be positioned correctly and must remain in the vagina for six hours after the man has ejaculated.

CERVICAL CAP

DIAPHRAGM

Position of a diaphragm ▶

In the squatting position, insert the spermicide-coated diaphragm into the vagina in an upward and backward motion. It should fit snugly across the far end of the vagina and must cover the cervix.

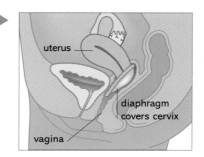

uterus

diaphragm covers cervix

vagina

HORMONAL METHODS

Hormonal contraceptives work by altering the natural processes of a woman's menstrual cycle so that conception cannot take place. They involve the woman taking laboratory-made substitutes of one or more female sex hormones in the form of a pill, an injection, or an implant. Hormonal methods offer a high degree of long-term protection but they can cause side-effects.

COMBINED PILL

The combined Pill consists of oestrogen and progestogen (the artificial version of the female hormone progesterone, see p.49), and it works by suppressing ovulation. It is taken in a 28-day cycle: you take one pill every day for 21 days, then you stop for seven days (alternatively, some brands of the Pill offer seven dummy or placebo pills). During your Pill-free week you have a withdrawal bleed that is similar to a period but tends to be lighter. Many women like taking the Pill because it regulates bleeding, doesn't disrupt sex, and offers a high degree of contraceptive protection (used correctly, it is at least 99 per cent effective).

However, disadvantages can include side-effects such as headaches, weight gain, and increased body hair. The combined Pill may be unsuitable for women who smoke, are over the age of 35, or who have a history of heart disease, high blood pressure, or diabetes.

COMBINED PILL

PROGESTOGEN-ONLY PILL

The progestogen-only Pill (POP) contains progestogen (progesterone-substitute), but unlike the combined Pill it contains no oestrogen. It works by thickening the cervical mucus so that sperm cannot penetrate, and by making the uterus less hospitable to a fertilized ovum. In some women, the POP also suppresses ovulation. You take one pill daily – it's very important that you take it at more or less the same time each day to be protected (if taken correctly, it is at least 99 per cent effective). Unlike the combined Pill, the POP may be taken by women who smoke and/or are over 35. It is also fine to take if you are breast-feeding.

POP

HORMONAL IMPLANTS AND INJECTIONS

Implants and injections are less common than hormones in pill form, but they do offer very effective, long-term protection for those who find the daily routine of taking the Pill difficult (the failure rate is less than 1 per cent). Implants deliver a steady, low dose of progestogen for up to five years. Injections also use progestogen but, unlike implants, they only last for eight to 12 weeks. Both methods have potential side-effects such as weight gain, breast tenderness, and mood swings.

Implant site

Hormonal implants are usually inserted just below the skin on the upper arm, always by a medical professional. However, some doctors prefer to position the implants on the side of the buttocks to avoid visible scars and swelling.

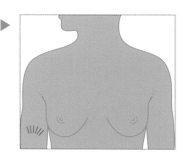

Always prepared

Hormonal methods of contraception have the advantage of enabling spontaneous lovemaking sessions to take place without interruption. ▼

INTRAUTERINE CONTRACEPTIVES

Intrauterine devices and systems offer effective long-term protection and are most popular among older women who have completed their families. They prevent conception by decreasing the chance of a fertilized ovum being implanted in the wall of the uterus by creating a "hostile" environment.

INTRAUTERINE DEVICE

Popularly referred to as the IUD, the intrauterine device is made of plastic, sometimes but not always incorporating copper wire. The device acts as a "foreign body" within the uterus, and sets up a mild uterine inflammation, which prevents the ovum from implanting. The IUD must always be inserted and removed by a professional – after insertion, plastic threads should hang down into the vagina, enabling the woman to check periodically that the IUD is still in place. It will also need to be checked by a doctor every five years. The advantage of the IUD is that the woman does not have to do anything else to protect herself. The disadvantages are that in some women the IUD increases the risk of pelvic inflammatory disease and ectopic pregnancy (pregnancy taking place outside the uterus). The IUD can be used as a method of postcoital contraception in emergencies.

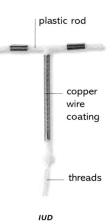

plastic rod

copper wire coating

threads

IUD

Inserting an IUD

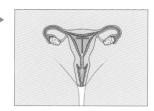

The doctor pushes the IUD into the vagina, then along the cervical canal and into the uterus, where it remains. Ideally, this takes place in the last days of menstruation.

INTRAUTERINE SYSTEM

The intrauterine system (IUS) is a type of IUD that releases a low dose of the artificial hormone progestogen into the uterus. This causes the cervical mucus to thicken and become inhospitable to sperm. The advantages of the IUS over the conventional IUD is that it is less likely to result in pelvic inflammatory disease or ectopic pregnancy. The IUS needs to be checked by a doctor every five years.

STERILIZATION

Couples who do not wish to have more children may prefer a permanent method of birth control. The woman may choose to have an operation known as tubal ligation, or tubal sterilization, or the man may opt for a vasectomy. Both are fairly simple surgical procedures.

TUBAL LIGATION

This operation will permanently prevent pregnancy. There are no side-effects, and the couple need to take no other precautions. After the operation, the ovaries continue to produce the female sex hormones and sexual desire is not diminished. They also continue to release eggs, although these are reabsorbed. Periods usually remain unchanged.

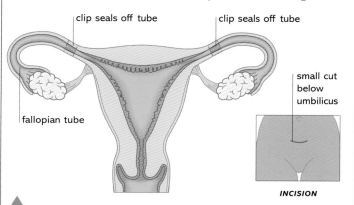

clip seals off tube   clip seals off tube

small cut below umbilicus

fallopian tube

INCISION

Female sterilization operation

This operation is usually done using a laparoscope, which is inserted through a tiny cut in the abdomen. Each fallopian tube is clipped or tied and sealed off, preventing any sperm from reaching the ovum.

VASECTOMY

This relatively painless operation makes the man sterile without interfering with sexual arousal, enjoyment, or ejaculation. The only change is that seminal fluid will be ejaculated without the sperm. Many men claim that their sex life actually improves after vasectomy.

Having a vasectomy

Two tiny cuts are made in the scrotum, and each vas deferens is cut and sealed so that sperm cannot pass through. The couple will need to use contraception until test results confirm that sperm are no longer present.

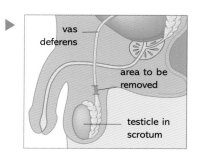

vas deferens

area to be removed

testicle in scrotum

SEX IN ADOLESCENCE

TEENAGERS IN THE WESTERN WORLD tend to start their sex lives early now – often as early as 14 or 15. While this shows that young people today are more comfortable with the idea of sex than their forebears, the peer pressure to become sexually active can be intense, often before the individuals are emotionally ready, and frequently leads to disappointment in a variety of ways.

A major problem of adolescents tends to be the female's lack of sexual sensation, usually because the young woman and her partner have as yet little knowledge about how to stimulate her. This lack of knowledge seems to be a direct result of a change in how young people today experience sex. Prior to the availability of reliable contraception, individuals spent months, even years sometimes, getting to know each other sexually but without intercourse. This activity was known as "heavy petting", and most of the sexual stimulation was done by hand. Petting was a bonus, because it meant there was time to develop trust and to build up knowledge of a partner's body responses. It also meant that many avenues for stimulation were discovered which led to rich experience. Many of today's teenagers go for intercourse very early on, missing out on this all-important "in between" stage. Self-masturbation and foreplay (see chapter 3) with a partner in the form of kissing, mutual exploration using

SEXFACTS

FIRST-TIME SEX

A sizeable majority of young people are now sexually active before they reach 16. A 1994 UK survey of sexual lifestyles showed that 18.7% of women and 27.6% of men aged 16–19 had experienced intercourse before the age of 16, compared with fewer than 1% of women and only 5.8% of men in the 55–59 age group.

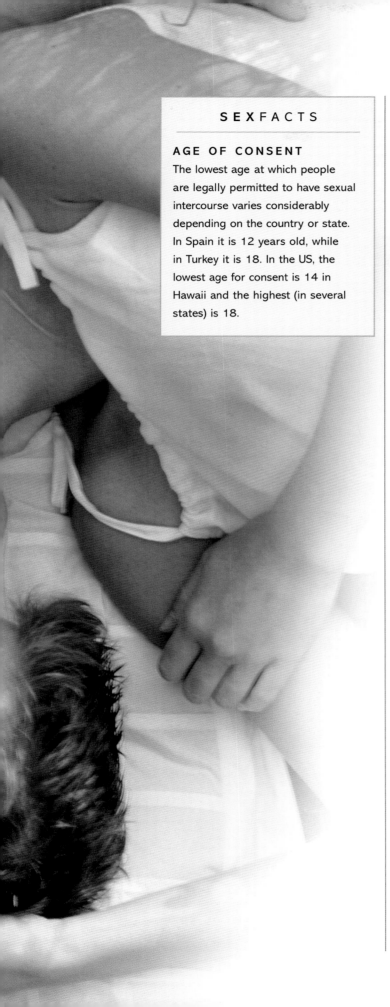

SEX FACTS

AGE OF CONSENT

The lowest age at which people are legally permitted to have sexual intercourse varies considerably depending on the country or state. In Spain it is 12 years old, while in Turkey it is 18. In the US, the lowest age for consent is 14 in Hawaii and the highest (in several states) is 18.

hands and tongue, and massage are all excellent preliminaries before embarking on full sexual intercourse, and give young people a much greater understanding of their own as well as their partner's response.

A further component to sexual problems in the early years is that young men naturally tend to climax quickly, often owing to over-excitement and anxiety. Time and experience tend to remedy this, but there are also some exercises that can help a man of any age to delay premature ejaculation (see pp.208–209).

Sex and the media

Teenage magazines are very explicit now about sexual matters. While there is a positive side to this, it results in younger teenagers having some curious peaks and troughs in their sexual knowledge. They may well be aware of a diverse range of sex toys available but, surprisingly, they do not know where the clitoris is. They may litter their conversation with references to sex but still find it difficult to talk frankly in bed. In homes where parents talk about sex with comfort, and where the children are well-informed, teenage pregnancies are less likely to be a problem than in families where the children are left in ignorance. The key to a more mature sex life for teenagers appears to be good and detailed communication with the adults who are close to them.

Practise safe sex

Contraception is all-too frequently ignored during early sexual experience. Pregnancies, terminations, and live births to teenagers have increased in the Western world. The main problem seems to be that many young women fear that they will be regarded as over-experienced in sexual matters if they come to their relationship complete with contraceptive protection. Even though the use of condoms has been greatly promoted since the onset of AIDS in the 1980s, these are not being used enough. Genital warts, genital herpes, and other sex-related diseases (see pp.220–23) are practically epidemic in certain groups of young people, and would not be so common if barrier protection were regularly used (see pp.182–83 and p.185). In addition, young people are more prone to sexual infection, a fact that offers an argument for delaying sexual intercourse until the later teens. One of the most useful sexual skills for young men and women is to build up the confidence to say "no" if it seems too early in the relationship to have sex, or if the sex is going to be unprotected and therefore unsafe.

SEX DRIVE DURING PREGNANCY

MANY WOMEN experience some change in their libido in pregnancy. The most typical pattern is for sex drive to decrease during the first trimester (three months), when you may be feeling tired and nauseous, to return during the second trimester (the "blooming" period), and then to decrease again during the third trimester, when you are likely to be feeling heavy and fatigued.

Right from the moment you conceive, your body starts to adjust to the new life that is growing inside you. Levels of hormones, such as oestrogen, progesterone, and human chorionic gonadotrophin, surge and cause multiple changes throughout your body. Some of these changes are easily confused with premenstrual syndrome (PMS) but, unlike PMS, which abates when your period comes, the signs of pregnancy intensify over days or weeks and no period comes to relieve them. During pregnancy, the hormonal and physiological changes that take place are likely to affect your sex life over the forthcoming months in various ways.

Sex drive by trimester

Many women report feeling very tired during the first trimester. This, together with "morning sickness" (which in many women isn't just restricted to the morning), can make the first trimester quite debilitating. Add painful and swollen breasts to the equation and it's highly likely that sex will slip down your list of priorities. However, not all women suffer from these debilitating symptoms, and a few are lucky enough to enjoy a normal or even a heightened sex drive.

It's likely that by the time you reach the second trimester your body will have adapted to your new hormone levels and you'll be feeling much more normal and able to enjoy sex. In this so-called "bloom of pregnancy" your energy levels will be high, your appearance healthy, and your sex life increased. Your body will retain more fluid than usual, which means that it will be permanently partially aroused and responsive.

In the third semester, you're likely to feel very large, tired, and immobile and sex will probably not be your priority. In addition, common third trimester symptoms, such as heavy vaginal discharge and leaking colostrum from your breasts, may also

BIG IS BEAUTIFUL

YOUR SELF-IMAGE can have a huge knock-on effect on your sex life. If you're proud of your new swelling belly and fuller breasts, and you feel close and connected to your partner, pregnancy can be a wonderfully intimate time.

On the other hand, if you feel fat, unattractive, self-conscious, and you are worried that your partner no longer finds you attractive, this can put a huge dampener on your libido. If the latter describes you, try to explore your feelings about pregnancy and talk over any feelings of ambivalence with your partner or a friend. Remind yourself that you and your partner are together in this — enjoying and exploring your sexuality in pregnancy can be great fun as well as being a romantic and bonding experience.

deter you from frequent intercourse, and you may choose to have other forms of sex instead that do not involve penetration.

Better orgasms

One potential advantage of pregnancy is that blood flow increases to all parts of the body, including the genitals. As a result, your vulva may feel particularly engorged and sensitive – this can lead to more intense orgasms than usual, or even first-time multiple orgasms. Your engorged vagina also hugs the penis more tightly during intercourse, and this can feel great for both you and your partner. Genital engorgement can occasionally be counterproductive though, in that the genitals continue to feel full even after orgasm so that you feel you "haven't quite got there".

IF YOU DON'T FEEL like sex, you can still enjoy being physically intimate with your partner by giving each other a massage or a foot-rub.

SEX DURING PREGNANCY

You can make love in any position during pregnancy as long as it feels comfortable, although the sheer size of your belly, particularly in the third trimester, can make some positions uncomfortable, difficult, or even impossible. Some couples choose this time to stay sexy using non-penetrative sex such as masturbation or sensual massage.

<table>
<tr><td>

WARNING

AVOID SEXUAL INTERCOURSE if you have unexplained bleeding at any stage of your pregnancy or if your waters have broken. If you have had previous problem pregnancies, consult your doctor about whether or not intercourse is advisable.

</td></tr>
</table>

Masturbation during pregnancy

Sometimes you don't feel like having intercourse but you want sexual relief, particularly if your genitals feel full and sensitive. This is where masturbation comes in. It's a great way to relieve sexual tension, and you can do it on your own or with your partner. You may experience stronger and more powerful orgasms during masturbation than you did before pregnancy. Some women find this disconcerting, especially when the contractions of a powerful orgasm ripple up and over the enlarged uterus – but don't worry: orgasmic contractions are very unlikely to stimulate labour.

SACRAL MASSAGE

MASSAGE OF THE SACRUM (the large, wedge-shaped bone at the base of the spine) is ideal for a man to give his pregnant partner, since a build-up of tension in the lower back is common at this time. Sacral massage is also widely recommended by active birth experts as a form of pain relief during labour.

1 Ask your partner to kneel, leaning forward on some cushions so that her whole body is supported. Rub some almond oil (or other base massage oil) into the palms of your hands, coating them thoroughly.

2 Place your palms firmly on either side of your partner's spine, just below her neck. Slowly smooth your hands down the length of her back. Ask her to exhale and to imagine any tension, pain, or discomfort flowing away.

3 Let your palms come to rest on your partner's sacrum. Move your hands in slow, firm circles around her sacrum while she breathes deeply into her abdomen. Repeat the strokes as often as you wish.

POSITIONS FOR SEX

Most women find that sexual positions that involve the man being on top become increasingly unviable as their bump gets larger. Women-on-top or side-by-side positions, such as the spoons position (see p.111), are often easier and more enjoyable in the mid- to late stages of pregnancy.

You may have fun trying to initiate labour by having intercourse at the very end of the third trimester. This is a time-honoured way to kick-start childbirth – it's thought that substances called prostaglandins in semen may help to trigger contractions. But don't worry – if you're not ready to give birth, intercourse won't cause premature labour. If you have a history of premature labour, it is always best to consult your doctor about sex during your pregnancy.

She straddles him

This position takes pressure off her abdomen but may be difficult to keep up. Never be ashamed of owning up to physical fatigue when you're pregnant – just naturally slide into a more relaxed pose.

Side-by-side position

One of the most comfortable positions for later pregnancy, this owes its popularity to the fact that all pressure is taken off her abdomen while he still has access to her clitoris with his fingers.

Legs in the air

In this way, sex is possible even in the very late stages of pregnancy. The man is more likely to enjoy it than the woman, so he needs to make sure of her climax in other ways, perhaps by masturbation.

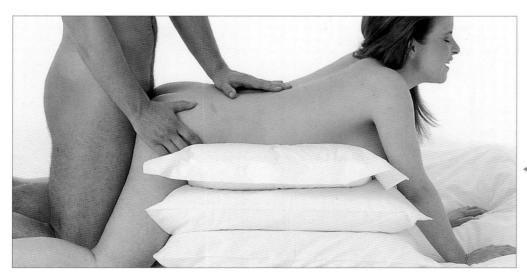

• SEX TIP •

In late pregnancy, pressure in the pelvic area intensifies the need for orgasm. If you find intercourse difficult, try masturbating instead.

◀ With a pillow on all fours

In the first and second trimesters of pregnancy, this rear-entry position is ideal for variation. However, it is not advisable later on since it puts pressure on her middle.

SEX AFTER CHILDBIRTH

IT IS STANDARD MEDICAL ADVICE to wait between three and six weeks after giving birth before resuming sex. Women frequently receive a six-week postnatal check-up, and this is an excellent time to discuss with the doctor whether it is advisable to resume lovemaking at this stage and to consider the various contraceptive options (see pp.184–87).

When couples do get the green light to resume lovemaking, some find that their libido is low (at least for the woman) or that sex has become difficult. For example, both men and women may be fearful of another pregnancy or anxious about inflicting or receiving pain or discomfort. Sheer fatigue and exhaustion are also impediments to an active sex life, not to mention the fact that you might feel inhibited by the presence of the baby in your bedroom. Women may worry that their body is no longer sexually attractive, or that sex won't feel as enjoyable because of slack vaginal muscles.

Solving sexual difficulties

To counter these problems, sex needs to be tackled slowly and gently, with plenty of frank communication. Talk to your partner about what feels good and what doesn't, and find different ways to express yourself sexually. For example, experiment with mutual masturbation (see pp.76–77) if penetrative sex is uncomfortable. It also helps to work around your baby's schedule: if possible, plan to have sex during your baby's nap break. If your baby's presence in your bedroom inhibits you, make love in a different room, but remember that to a baby the sounds of lovemaking are no more significant than a cough or a snore. Women can get back into sexual shape by doing pelvic exercises (pp.174–75).

THE SHARED EXPERIENCE of having a baby adds an entirely new dimension to the relationship with your partner, and you may find that you feel closer than ever before.

*A **NEW BABY** inevitably takes up most of your physical and emotional energy, and will almost certainly take first place, for a few months at least. However, it is very important to make the time to spend together as a couple.*

Retaining intimacy

A good relationship will be able to accommodate the changes and pressures that a new baby brings, but it does take time and effort. Try to make sure that you and your partner find ways of staying intimate. For example, take a bath together after the baby has gone to bed, hire a babysitter and go out for dinner once in a while, or let your parents have the honour of caring for their grandchild so that you get a weekend off together. Above all, keep talking, have a sense of humour, and share your anxieties with each other. The good news is that couples often feel so emotionally drawn together by the extraordinary experience of birth that even if sex itself doesn't work too well immediately, they feel incredibly close and intimate.

Breast-feeding and sex

Breast-feeding can both enhance and impair your sex life. If you and your partner find your enlarged breasts sexy and enjoyable to touch, your lovemaking can benefit greatly. On the other hand, you may find that breast-feeding hormones lower your libido so that you simply don't have the desire for sexual activity. You and your partner may feel that your breasts are no longer erotic territory and that they belong temporarily to your baby. Leaking milk may be off-putting for some couples during sex.

Even if breast-feeding dampens your libido, your sex drive will return in full after you have weaned your baby – if it doesn't, then it is advisable to consult your doctor.

AFTER THE BIRTH

THE POST-NATAL PERIOD can be a real challenge to both new parents. Never make the common mistake of expecting too much of yourselves too early on.

TIPS FOR WOMEN

- Be patient; don't expect your body and sexual responses to immediately revert back to their pre-pregnancy state.
- If you are low on natural lubrication, use a water-based lubricant to make sex more comfortable and enjoyable.
- Keep doing pelvic-floor exercises to strengthen your muscles and to improve sexual sensation (see p.175).
- Make time for sex by letting other less important things slip – new mothers don't have time for everything. Make an "appointment" for sex at a time when you're feeling energetic. Don't leave it until the end of the day when you're exhausted.

TIPS FOR MEN

- Be patient; let your partner guide you as to what feels comfortable and what doesn't.
- Tell your partner that you still find her sexy. Pay her compliments and be romantic.
- Don't nag her for sex. Talk to her about your sexual needs and what kind of sex life you want. Seek shared solutions and compromises.
- If your partner finds intercourse uncomfortable, suggest non-penetrative sex such as sensual massage (pp.58–65) or mutual masturbation (see pp.76–77).

SEX IN THE MIDDLE YEARS

TURNING 40 OR 50 is a major milestone for many people. Although you don't yet consider yourself old, you don't feel young either. On the positive side, you have a wealth of experience behind you; however, physical changes can erode your self-confidence. It's important to stay positive and to express yourself sexually in the way that suits you best.

If media depictions of sex are to be believed, few people over the age of 30 enjoy an active sex life. Sex is often portrayed as the preserve of the young and beautiful. Slowly but surely, this can have the effect of making older people feel marginalized sexually. So it's important to know that privately, if not publicly, many middle-aged people say that they enjoy a great sex life, and that age brings with it many sexual advantages. Among these bonuses are confidence gleaned from years of experience, greater privacy and time if children have left home, being relaxed enough with your partner to ask for what you really want in bed and, if you are a post-menopausal woman, being able to forget about contraception.

Adapting to physical changes

The main changes that affect middle-aged men and women are the andropause (see box, below, and p.209) and the menopause (see box, facing page, and p.211). There is still controversy about whether the andropause exists, but a number of leading experts say that a decline in testosterone in some men does give rise to a range of debilitating

SEX CAN BE FANTASTIC in mid-life – you can benefit from your years of experience, and are more able to communicate your sexual needs. If you don't feel like having intercourse as often, you can stay sexy by kissing and cuddling.

SEX FACTS

ANDROPAUSE

The andropause is the male equivalent of the menopause, although not all men are affected. It occurs when a man's testosterone levels have reached a critical point of decline and he becomes aware of aging. It may be a time of emotional upheaval, with some men struggling to regain a youthful lifestyle and sexual virility.

AS YOU GET OLDER, make sure that you spend time with your partner simply enjoying yourselves. Don't be afraid of showing affection in public, as well as in private, and challenge or ignore negative sterotypes of how middle-aged people are meant to behave.

symptoms in the middle years, such as low libido, fatigue, and less powerful erections (see pp.203–207). The majority of women experience some menopausal symptoms – the most common being hot flushes and sweats, but also vaginal dryness (see p.211). Hormone replacement therapy (HRT, see p.211) can counterbalance menopausal changes. It's important for you to know that both menopausal and andropausal symptoms can dampen your sex drive. In fact, two of the commonest sexual traps of middle age are, firstly, to get into the rut of boring lovemaking and, secondly, to stop having sex altogether.

Adapting to emotional changes

Everyone responds differently to turning 40 or 50, but there are some feelings that frequently predominate. Women, for instance, may feel apprehensive about the decline and end of fertility that comes with the menopause, especially if they have not had children and wanted to. Both men and women may be concerned that they are looking old and are less desirable. Some people experience a full-blown mid-life crisis, when they feel compelled to reassess everything in their life, from their relationship to their career.

1 0 TIPS FOR DEALING WITH MIDDLE AGE

HOWEVER YOU NAVIGATE the emotional and physical changes that come with the middle years, there are various tools that can help you:

1 Practise positive thinking. Remind yourself of all the good things about growing older. Work out the things that you enjoy in life and spend more time doing them.

2 Keep your mind active. Make sure that you're always learning something new. It doesn't matter what it is as long as it's a challenge.

3 Develop your spiritual side. If you don't subscribe to a particular religion, try exploring an ancient discipline such as yoga or meditation.

4 Keep communicating with people close to you. Tell your partner if you're feeling depressed, anxious, or insecure and accept his or her support and reassurance.

5 Don't ever think "I'm too old to do that". Do things that feel naughty or decadent, such as spending a day in bed with a bottle of champagne or renting a sexy film.

6 Resolve to stay sexy. Be naked together, share erotic thoughts, and pay each other compliments. If you get out of touch now, it's harder to get back in touch later on.

7 Stay fit by exercising as much as you can. Exercise helps to prevent depression and makes you feel good about yourself.

8 Complement your exercise routine with a healthy diet: eat plenty of olive oil, garlic, unrefined carbohydrate, and fruit and vegetables.

9 Don't keep using fatigue as an excuse for inactivity. Whether you choose to have sex or go for a swim, make sure you do *something*. You'll feel better for it.

10 It isn't vain to care about your appearance. Invest in new clothes, a professional make-over, a new hairstyle, or a day in a health spa every so often.

SEX IN LATER LIFE

ONE OF THE BIGGEST CHALLENGES that older people face when it comes to sex is not so much the problem posed by an aging body, but the assumption that older people are no longer expected to want, need, or enjoy sexual activity. Learning to think positively about sex is the first step to great lovemaking.

Your body may be getting older but that doesn't mean you can't cherish it to the end of your life. It's important to value your body and sexuality, not just for your own sense of self-esteem, but also to provide a positive role model for children, grandchildren, and younger people in general.

Think positively

It may sound like a cliché, but positive thinking really can have an effect on your mood and behaviour. Positive affirmations are short statements, such as "this day finds me happy and content", that you repeat to yourself throughout the day. They work because your unconscious mind faithfully catalogues all of your emotional responses – good, bad, happy, or sad. Therefore, if you keep telling yourself that you feel confident, happy, and peaceful, these messages will be instilled in your unconscious and reflected in your day-to-day moods and feelings. Practise positive thinking while you are lying in bed, getting dressed, in the shower, travelling to work, or listening to a piece of music. You can even practise in front of the mirror. Make up your own affirmations to suit your mood, such as "I am strong, supple, and sexy", "I am a sexual being", and "I am as energetic now as I have ever been". Also, read and act on the list of

tips for dealing with middle age (see p.197) – these points are just as relevant to people in later life.

Take care of yourself

It's worth bearing in mind that although physical aging is natural, there are some things that can speed up the aging process and are best avoided in the interests of your long-term health. The five biggest age-accelerators are frequent exposure to the sun and to cigarette smoke, drinking an excessive amount of alcohol, and stress and pollution. All of these things create toxic chemicals known as "free radicals" in the body, and may increase your risk of degenerative diseases such as cancer.

Looking after your body should never be a chore. Avoid restrictive diets and exhausting exercise programmes. Instead, eat healthy and delicious food and lavish treats upon your body. Treats can be sexual, in the form of intercourse or masturbation; sensual, in the form of massage and stroking; or physical, in the form of

MYTHS OF AGING

WHEN IT COMES TO sex and aging, many of our beliefs are often clouded by negative stereotypes. The media, for example, often present older people as asexual. Below are just some of these attitudes, all of which can be dismissed by positive thinking:

- People lose the desire for sex after the age of 60
- Impotence is inevitable with age
- Older people are unfanciable
- It's inappropriate for older people to talk about sex
- There's something wrong if an old person has a relationship with someone much younger
- You need to have a fit, agile body to enjoy yourself sexually
- Sex isn't complete without orgasm

gentle exercise. Never feel that you're too old to indulge yourself by having a professional massage, or going to a sauna, steam room, or health spa. Try taking some food supplements to give you an extra boost (see pp.176–77), particularly those that are specifically helpful in later life.

Possible changes in later life

Many older people report that they simply don't have the same desire for sex at the age of 60 or 70 that they did when they were 20 or 30. On the other hand, when they do have sex it can be as enjoyable and satisfying as it ever was. The key, say older people, is quality rather than quantity.

As women get older, they may experience delayed sexual response (see p.204), including vaginal dryness (see p.211). Older men may become more likely to experience difficulties getting and keeping an erection (see pp.206–207), although this is not inevitable. If you do experience problems it is important to consult your doctor to ensure that there isn't another underlying reason, such as illness (see pp.212–15) or medication (see pp.216–17), both of which can affect sexual response. Try out forms of non-penetrative sex such as mutual masturbation (see pp.76–77) and sensual massage (see pp.58–65).

Stiff joints can also be an obstacle to sexual intercourse when people become older. Experiment with yoga or Pilates, preferably by joining an exercise class. Both are gentle forms of exercise and are also extremely relaxing. The Pilates squeeze is a simple exercise you can try at home to alleviate stiffness (see p.175).

*A **GREAT ADVANTAGE** of getting older is that you can spend time with your partner without the stresses of work and raising a family.*

CHAPTER 8

When Sex Goes Wrong

COMMON SEX PROBLEMS

ALTHOUGH ALL RELATIONSHIPS are affected by emotions, sex problems can also be purely technical. However well a couple may communicate and however long they may try, if some part of their sexual system is not functioning then sex will not necessarily improve. Fortunately, most issues can now be helped by sex therapy and drug therapy.

Although self-help works for many people, others feel the need to consult the professionals. Regular counselling sessions with a sex therapist can often work extremely well for many sexual problems (see box, below), and frequently it is not necessary to see a doctor.

However, if you have any anxieties about your sexual health, or if your therapist has recommended that you get a physical check-up, don't hesitate to seek medical advice. Bear in mind that if you want to claim for sex therapy on a health insurance policy, you will probably need a doctor's referral to qualify for it.

Lack of sexual desire

Some men and women find that they rarely, if ever, experience a desire for sex. They may have relatively undeveloped sexual characteristics, for example, they may lack body hair and their genitals may be immature.

There may be several reasons for a primary lack of sexual interest and ability but one of the main ones is inadequate natural testosterone circulating within the body. Hormone supplementation can often help here (see facing page) – a sex therapist or doctor could pinpoint the most appropriate treatment.

VISITING A SEX THERAPIST

IN ORDER TO FEEL COMFORTABLE with the idea of seeking clinical advice, it helps to know what actually happens at sex therapy. Treatment could involve a one-off session with a counsellor, or a course of sessions at weekly or fortnightly intervals over a period of months. This will depend upon you and the type of problem you're experiencing. During the first session, you will usually have to give the counsellor a brief history of yourself so that he or she can see your problem in context and decide what the best approach will be for you. The counsellor may refer you to a doctor for a medical examination. Or you may be asked to do some "exercises" at home. You will then be expected to discuss your results at the next session.

SEX FACTS

HORMONE THERAPY

Some hormones taken as supplements can enhance sexual function. For example, testosterone can help to revive a flagging sex drive in both men and women. Dehydroepiandrosterone (DHEA) is a chemical that gives rise to testosterone in men and progesterone and oestrogen in women, and supplements of this have been found to increase energy levels and a sense of well-being. A doctor or a sex therapist would be able to recommend the right treatment for you.

Low libido in later life

Mid-life, for some people, is the time when their libido fades. They simply stop having sexual thoughts and they stop desiring sex with a partner. If celibacy is a lifestyle choice, then this is fine, but you should be aware that sexual desire doesn't have to fade irretrievably. The causes of lack of sex drive can be complex and are likely to be unique to you.

Loss of sexual desire

When men and women have originally enjoyed normal sex lives but have then lost interest, secondary causes need to be looked for. These could include:
- Prolonged stress (see p.205)
- Depression (see pp. 204–205)
- The period following childbirth (see pp.194–95)

LOSS OF SEXUAL DESIRE can cause anger, confusion, and frustration, but it's important to realize that there are ways to boost a flagging libido.

- Low testosterone levels (see p.147)
- Alcohol or drug abuse (see pp.218–19)
- Prescribed drugs for medical conditions (see pp.216–17)
- Relationship complications
- Diabetes (see p.213)
- Aging (see pp.196–99 and 204)

Correct diagnosis is essential: ask your doctor for a check-up to exclude any physical causes of low libido. Solutions range from changing your lifestyle to popping a few pills. They may involve alleviating stress or depression, correcting hormone fluctuations, coming off alcohol or drugs, finding alternative medications, or consulting a relationship therapist.

SENSATE FOCUS THERAPY

ONE OF THE BEST NON-DRUG treatments for loss of desire is a technique known as sensate focus, which has been pioneered by sex therapists. Sensate focus is carried out in the privacy of your own home. It involves a series of exercises designed to help a couple rediscover each other's sensual and sexual responses without the pressure to have penetrative sex. Exercises might include giving each other sensual massages so that both partners understand each other's arousal patterns.

IF YOU HAVE PROBLEMS WITH your sexual response, try not to get tense about it because stress will accentuate the problem further.

each other lots of feedback. If you don't have a partner, you can embark on a delicious process of self-exploration through self-massage and masturbation (see pp.68–71).

Delayed sexual response

You may notice that, with age, the immediate signs of arousal such as vaginal lubrication in women (see p.211) and erection in men, take longer to appear. You may feel mentally aroused, but it seems that your genitals need a bit more time to catch up with your thoughts. Sometimes this problem has an emotional cause, for example, feeling angry with your partner, but often the cause is hormonal. Your best response to delayed arousal is, very simply, not to worry about it. Instead, carry on regardless; spend longer on foreplay; or try things that you find extra-titillating in order to boost your arousal levels. If these measures don't work, or you are worried that you have a more intractable problem, seek the advice of a doctor or sex therapist.

Coping with depression

One of the hallmarks of depression is the inability to enjoy normally pleasurable activities such as eating, socializing, and making love. When we are depressed we feel apathetic and indifferent to events around us – and sex is one of the first things that we lose interest in.

Increasing your libido in later life

As long as you don't have any physical problems, such as women experiencing pain or discomfort during sex (see pp.210–11), or men experiencing problems with erections (see pp.206–207), then all that you really need to do is to find a sexual pattern that suits you and your partner.

One of the secrets of great sex when you are older is to slow things right down. Now is the time for sex to stop being goal-orientated and instead become a long, slow, sensual voyage of discovery. It doesn't matter if you don't have an orgasm, the important thing is to wallow in erotic enjoyment. If you have a partner, this could mean learning to massage each other, spending a long time stimulating each other's genitals with your hands or mouth, and giving

---

RECOGNIZING DEPRESSION

PSYCHOLOGISTS SAY that when we are depressed we tend to make certain "errors" in our thinking. It's worth being aware of these behavioural traits, both in yourself and in others. They include:

1 Magnification and minimization: dramatizing the negative things in life and downplaying the positive things.

2 Personalization: thinking that negative events are always your fault.

3 Arbitrary inference: believing that something is negative without any supporting evidence.

4 Overgeneralization: making sweeping negative generalizations such as "this is hopeless" or "I'll never be able to change".

A two-pronged approach to depression that includes psychotherapy and drug therapy in the form of anti-depressants yields very good results. Alternatively, some people who are prone to depression have their own personal coping strategies, for example, taking lots of aerobic exercise such as running or cycling, talking to friends, keeping busy, eating healthily, getting plenty of sleep, and cutting out depressant drugs such as alcohol. These kinds of self-help measures may be particularly good for mild or transient depression.

If you are prescribed anti-depressants by your doctor, it is important to know that some types have the side-effect of decreasing your sex drive. This is true of one of the most popular anti-depressants: Prozac (fluoxetine hydrochloride). This drug can impair women's ability to reach orgasm and men's ability to ejaculate. If you are on anti-depressants, ask your doctor what sort, if any, sexual side-effects to expect. And rest assured that, as soon as you stop the medication, your sexual responses will return to normal. See the drugs table (pp.216–17) for more details of the impact of prescription drugs on sexuality.

Dealing with stress and fatigue

No matter how old you are, stress and fatigue will always have a detrimental effect on sex, but when you find that you spend most of your time feeling anxious or tired, or both, then it's time to take action.

Low levels of the male and female sex hormones testosterone and oestrogen can contribute directly to feelings of tiredness, so consider asking your doctor about hormone replacement therapy (this applies to men as well as women; see p.203). It's also worth acting directly on the causes of stress. Work out where your priorities lie: if your quality of life is diminishing because you have a stressful job, ask yourself whether it's possible to downscale and live on a smaller salary. Alternatively, if you can't reduce or eliminate stress, try relaxing therapies such as massage, aromatherapy, yoga, tai chi, creative visualization, meditation, or yogic breathing exercises.

MEN'S PROBLEMS

THERE ARE SEVERAL sexual problems that may affect men at different stages of life. Unfortunately, many males are reluctant to discuss their sex lives with a doctor. Remember that most sexual problems can be treated successfully with the help of a professional.

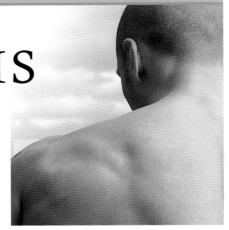

Erection difficulties

Of all the sexual problems that men experience, erectile dysfunction is the most common. Erectile dysfunction describes several problems, ranging from being able to retain an erection for only a short time to the inability to get an erection at all. It's quite normal for men to experience this at some point in their lives.

One of the commonest causes of erectile dysfunction is a condition known as "venous leakage". Although blood flows into the penis in the usual way during an erection, it then leaks out again so that your penis droops and becomes flaccid. This is because the "locking system" that normally keeps blood inside the penis stops working effectively. The problem of venous leakage can be counteracted by the man wearing a medically designed ring that fits around the base of the penis (see details on facing page).

Erectile problems can be psychological in origin. For example, if you're worried about your sexual performance, or are harbouring feelings of inadequacy, guilt, or resentment, these may manifest themselves as an inability to get or keep an erection. This form may be quite easy to diagnose because you will be able to have an erection sometimes, but just not with a partner. Sex therapy is usually the best treatment for this problem.

Illness and aging

Various illnesses can affect erectile function (see pp.212–15) as well as certain medications (see pp.216–17). Impotence is more likely to strike in later life, although fortunately this is not inevitable. As you get older, your levels of the male sex hormone testosterone decline and one side-effect may be less powerful erections. This isn't necessarily a problem; you simply need to find what gives you the best erection, usually plenty of direct friction in the genital area. You may also like to consider taking a hormone treatment (see facing page).

SEXFACTS

SMOKERS AND DRINKERS

Two groups of men who are particularly vulnerable to impotence are long-term smokers and drinkers. Both heavy smoking and alcohol consumption can cause major damage to the body's cardiovascular and nervous systems. Alcohol abuse in particular causes men's testosterone levels to drop and interferes with nerve impulses to the genitals. It also kills sex drive and makes sperm abnormalities more likely.

TREATMENTS FOR ERECTILE DYSFUNCTION

WHEN A MAN has erection difficulties, it's very important to have a general medical check-up in case of illness. The good news for men with erectile dysfunction is that there are numerous remedies available. Successful treatment must always be tailored to the cause of the problem.

• SEX THERAPY
A qualified counsellor helps the couple overcome any psychological difficulty that may be causing the problem. Behavioural exercises often focus on massage, and all performance anxiety is removed by forbidding intercourse. The woman is taught how to stimulate and hold back as appropriate.

BENEFITS/FUNCTION: The forbidding of sexual intercourse means that the man no longer feels performance anxiety. He relaxes, and his ability to have an erection returns.

• PENIS RING
Ideal for those suffering from venous leakage, the penis ring is like a specially designed rubber band (don't substitute one for the other or you could damage the blood vessels!). Once you have an erection, you put the ring around the base of your penis. The ring, which can be worn for up to 30 minutes at a time, can also be used with a penis pump if you have difficulty getting an erection (see below).

BENEFITS/FUNCTION: Constricts blood vessels at the base of the penis and stops blood draining away from the erection.

• PENIS PUMP
The penis or vacuum pump consists of a plastic cylinder attached to a hand pump. Because the penis pump is purely mechanical, you don't have to take drugs in the form of pills or injections. To use the penis pump, place the plastic cylinder around your flaccid penis and then pump air out. Once the penis is erect, if you need to, you can put on a penis ring to keep your erection firm (see above).

BENEFITS/FUNCTION: Draws blood into the penis and makes it erect.

• PENILE IMPLANT
The penile implant or rod is a surgical method for the treatment of long-term erectile dysfunction. Some implants leave the penis in a permanent state of semi-erection; others (such as the one shown below) are designed to be inflated by means of a squeeze pump, which is installed inside the scrotum.

BENEFITS/FUNCTION: Enables erection when required and a measure of control.

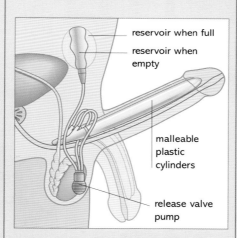

reservoir when full

reservoir when empty

malleable plastic cylinders

release valve pump

A PENILE IMPLANT consists of a pump inserted in the scrotum. This draws fluid from a reservoir placed in the abdomen, causing the two rods fitted inside the penis to inflate and become rigid.

• PENILE SURGERY
If you're suffering from erectile dysfunction caused by venous leakage, it's possible to have microsurgery to improve the problem. However, this kind of surgery is relatively unusual and isn't always successful. The majority of doctors recommend the penis ring as a more practical solution (see left).

BENEFITS/FUNCTION: If successful, surgery repairs the penis' locking mechanism.

• HORMONE TREATMENT
Although treatment with the male sex hormone testosterone (see p.48) isn't a treatment for impotence per se, it may help with erectile problems in mid- and later life. A blood test can reveal your testosterone levels – if they are low you may benefit from treatment.

BENEFITS/FUNCTION: Testosterone increases libido and may give more powerful erections.

• PENILE INJECTIONS
Some drugs (e.g. Caverject) can be used locally on the penis to induce erection. They are administered either in the form of an injection into the shaft of the penis (men are taught how to do this themselves at home) or as a pellet inserted into the urethra.

BENEFITS/FUNCTION: Relaxes the smooth muscle of the penis to enable erection.

• VIAGRA
Although Viagra works very well for many impotence sufferers, it isn't a true aphrodisiac. It doesn't magically produce an erection or make you desperate to have sex – it simply improves the ability to get and sustain an erection. You still have to feel aroused by usual means, such as touching and kissing a partner first. The effects of Viagra last up to four hours. Common side-effects include headache, flushes, and dyspepsia. Never use Viagra if you're taking nitrate drugs, commonly found in angina medications and in amyl nitrate or "poppers".

BENEFITS/FUNCTION: Increases blood flow to the penis giving better and stronger erections.

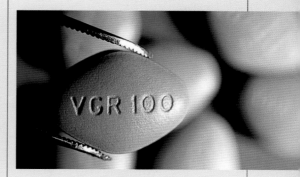

VGR 100

VIAGRA comes in pill form and should be taken around one hour before you make love.

Premature ejaculation

This is the inability of the man to delay orgasm long enough for sexual pleasure within a relationship. It is considered to be mainly a young man's problem, and is associated with anxiety, inexperience, and having sex in conditions where you are anxious to get the sex act over and done with quickly. The trouble with premature ejaculation is that if this is how you start off experiencing sex, sometimes you can unconsciously train yourself to always experience sex in this fashion.

Fortunately, premature ejaculation is one of the easier sex difficulties to improve – there are self-help methods, as well as techniques to try with a partner. However, a tiny percentage of men finds their ejaculation problem is so acute that the training method doesn't work. Sex specialists believe these days that drug therapy (using beta-blockers) is the best line of help for such extreme cases. The drugs work by either controlling acute anxiety (which seems to trigger ejaculation), or by slowing ejaculation down.

Overcoming premature ejaculation with a partner

Sensate focus massage is a form of therapy often used to overcome premature ejaculation. The first step is for a couple to give each other a sensual massage (see pp.58–63). For the first few days, this is done without touching the genitals. When you've both enjoyed this general pleasuring, you may move on to exploration and stimulation of the genitals, such as erotic massage (see pp.64–65). When the man feels an orgasm is imminent, he should signal to his partner, who should give him the squeeze technique to prevent ejaculation (see below). His erection may subside a little at this stage, but she can simply massage him once more until he regains his erection. As he gets used to this, his confidence will grow and he will come to believe he can last longer during sex.

Now is the time to move on to intercourse. The woman sits astride and thrusts gently, while her partner remains on his back, immobile. He should try to refrain from having an orgasm for 15 minutes and, again, he should signal when he

SQUEEZE TECHNIQUE

THE PENILE SQUEEZE is a sex therapy technique that has the effect of preventing ejaculation. Your partner may squeeze your penis for you (you'll need to let her know when to do it), or you may find it easier to do yourself:

1 Firmly grasp the penis on the coronal ridge (the ridge around the head of the penis) between the forefingers and thumb.

2 When you feel that you are close to ejaculating, ask or signal to your partner to squeeze hard.

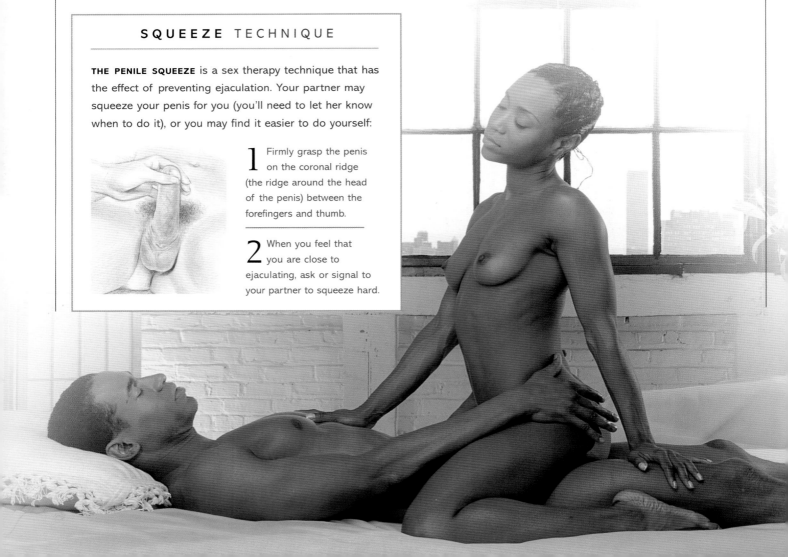

OVERCOMING PREMATURE EJACULATION
ON YOUR OWN

MANY MEN want to overcome premature ejaculation on their own so that they can venture into new relationships without any anxiety. One method of learning how to control ejaculation is to masturbate in a specific and controlled way over a period of several weeks, as shown here:

1. Masturbate with a dry hand – see if you can last for a full 15 minutes
2. Masturbate with a wet hand, again trying to last for 15 minutes or more
3. Learn to perform the squeeze technique on yourself (see facing page) to help your dry and wet hand masturbation

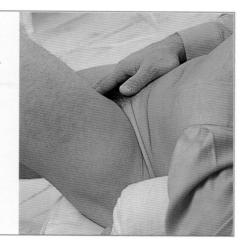

thinks he's reaching the point of no return so that his woman can climb off him and apply the squeeze technique. Once she's done this, she repeats the massage until he gets an erection and then sits astride him again. This time, he thrusts gently for 15 minutes, letting her know if ejaculation is imminent as before, so that she can apply the squeeze. Finally, both partners thrust for 15 minutes, after which the man is allowed to ejaculate.

Retarded ejaculation

This is a condition which involves the male finding it very difficult to have an orgasm. He may grow excited and he may want to climax, but the actual experience of ejaculation proves to be complicated for some reason.

Retarded ejaculation usually responds to professional sex therapy methods. Behavioural therapy is a practical treatment, and involves helping a male to relax sexually in the presence of a female. Methods include the man first using self-stimulation while his partner is in the next room, then within the same room but a distance away, and eventually with her up close to him. Talking therapy simultaneously helps the man discover where his anxiety concerning women hails from. A few cases of retarded ejaculation are solved by testosterone supplements.

The andropause

The andropause is characterized by a decline in testosterone levels in later life, and can lead to emotional and sexual problems (see pp.196–97). If you suffer from decreased sex drive and weaker erections, and in addition are experiencing three or more of the symptoms listed

THE WOMAN-ON-TOP position is recommended for premature ejaculation therapy, since the woman can slip quickly off her partner to apply the squeeze technique.

below, it's worth seeking advice from a doctor or hormone specialist, who should be able to supply testosterone medication in the form of gel or patches.

The main symptoms of the andropause include:
1. Decreased sex drive
2. Erections that are less strong
3. Reduced strength and endurance
4. Loss of height
5. Diminished enjoyment of life
6. Sadness and/or grumpiness
7. Lack of energy
8. Deterioration in sporting ability
9. Tiredness
10. Deterioration in work performance

NB: Many of these symptoms may be caused by other problems, such as depression or thyroid disorder.

WOMEN'S PROBLEMS

BY VIRTUE OF THEIR HORMONAL make-up, women may experience sexual difficulties that are both physical and emotional. It has only recently been understood that the ebb and flow of female hormones affects women's sexual experience and responses (see pp.25 and 49).

Some women find it very difficult to experience orgasm through sexual intercourse, even though they may find it possible through masturbation. In some cases, they may suffer inhibitions and find that they are not able to let go and be open with a partner. Perhaps they have not explored their own sensuality, and so they are unable to show a partner how to stimulate and arouse them effectively. In rarer cases, some women simply have a lack of testosterone, the hormone that sexologists believe is responsible for sex drive.

If a woman shows through tests that she has very low testosterone, she can be prescribed supplements (see pp.147 and 203). Some women can be helped to learn how to climax by being taught how to masturbate (see pp.70–71), either with fingers or with a vibrator. Sex therapy for couples often helps men and women work out the best way to do this together. If extreme inhibition is holding a woman back, the drug phentolamine can remove some of that inhibition.

Some women find that Viagra, the impotence pill for men, helps. However, this is not specifically recommended, because the drug is designed for men, not women. Meanwhile, work is currently being carried out to develop a version of the drug for women. A substance called Viacreme (see p.147) can help stimulate the external genitals but doesn't necessarily guarantee orgasm. There is still a need for research into this sex problem.

Vaginismus

Some women suffer from a condition in which the vagina goes into a muscular spasm when a partner's penis tries to penetrate during sexual intercourse. This makes sex either painful or, in some cases, impossible.

Tranquillizers can be effective, because they help reduce muscular tension. However, there is also a sex therapy technique in which a woman is gently encouraged to get used to inserting safe objects, such as "training cylinders", into her vagina. By getting used to the presence of these objects, the woman slowly starts to lose the tension she previously felt.

SEX FACTS

FEMALE ORGASM

Many women do not automatically learn to masturbate, but discovering how to in later life often results in climaxes. The *Hite Report on Female Sexuality* found that only 29 per cent of women climaxed during sexual intercourse. However, up to 82 per cent climaxed as a result of masturbation.

SELF-HELP METHODS

IF YOUR SEX LIFE is adversely affected by the menopause – and this isn't the case for all women – there are lots of self-help measures you can try:

1 Make sure you are well lubricated before you have sex. Spend a long time on foreplay or use a lubricant (don't forget, saliva is an excellent lubricant).

2 After the menopause, the vagina and urethra are less well cushioned and the urethra may be irritated by the thrusting movements of intercourse. So, if you are susceptible to urinary tract infections, empty your bladder after you have made love.

3 Take plenty of exercise and eat foods that will nourish your skin and hair. Keep your body in good shape. Boost your health with dietary supplements (see pp.176–77).

4 Explore complementary therapies for help with menopausal symptoms. Medical herbalists offer a range of treatments for menopausal women; so do Chinese herbalists, acupuncturists, homeopaths, and naturopaths.

5 Nurture your self-esteem and body image by following the advice about adapting to mid- and later life (see pp.196–99).

Vaginal dryness
A lack of the female hormone oestrogen in postmenopausal women can cause the tissues of the vagina and vulva to shrink and dry so that even when you feel aroused you don't get lubricated in the way that you used to.

If this is the case, invest in a good-quality lubricant and use it liberally during sex. Alternatively, oestrogen cream or HRT in pill, patch, or implant form can help you to produce natural lubrication.

The menopause
Marking the end of a woman's fertility, the menopause usually occurs between 45 and 55 years of age. In the build up to the menopause, your oestrogen levels fluctuate and ovulation becomes erratic. During this phase, known as the perimenopause, you may menstruate some months and then have a period-free break for one or several months. Sometimes you may bleed heavily and sometimes the flow is very light. In other words, expect your menstrual cycle to become unpredictable.

Menopausal side-effects
During this time, you may also start to experience an array of physical and emotional – and even intellectual – symptoms as a side-effect of fluctuating and declining oestrogen levels. The most well known of these symptoms are hot flushes and night sweats, but other perimenopausal signs include anxiety, irritability, depressed moods and mood swings, forgetfulness, poor concentration, aching joints, fatigue and lethargy, and dryness of the skin, hair, eyes, and mouth.

These can all have a negative effect on your libido and your sexual self-esteem. In addition, some women experience itchiness of the vulva and vagina, which can make sex difficult or painful.

Relief and treatment
If you have problems with sex owing to the menopause, try out some self-help methods (see box, left). Alternatively, you can take hormone replacement therapy (HRT). This treatment restores your oestrogen levels to their pre-menopausal levels and, in addition to relieving troublesome symptoms, such as hot flushes, it can also protect you from several serious diseases. Talk to your doctor about finding the right treatment for you.

TAKING HRT

HRT RELIEVES menopausal symptoms and prevents the long-term changes associated with the menopause such as genital atrophy and change in body shape. It is also considered to protect you from some diseases such as osteoporosis and cancer of the uterus. There are several types and doses of HRT. The most commonly prescribed forms of HRT are pills, patches, and implants. Oestrogen creams are also available for local application to the vulva and vagina. As well as oestrogen, most forms of HRT contain progestogen, which causes the uterus to bleed periodically. Doctors can also prescribe the male hormone testosterone as part of your HRT, to help revive a flagging libido.

ILLNESS AND SEXUALITY

ONLY RECENTLY HAS IT been fully appreciated that physical problems can be the cause of diminished sexual response. This deterioration can be a symptom of the disease itself or, as is frequently the case, it may be a psychosomatic response to being ill.

• ANGINA

Bouts of energetic movement may cause painful spasms around the heart; understandably, this restricts enthusiasm for sexual intercourse.

TREATMENT: Nitrate drugs are commonly used to reduce attacks of angina. If you feel a tightening in the chest when having intercourse, stop. Alternatively, you might prefer to undertake less strenuous sexual activity, such as mutual masturbation.

• ARTHRITIS

Arthritic pain often adversely affects the movements of the sufferer, making it difficult, for example, to enjoy straightforward missionary position intercourse. Arthritic hips are especially troublesome for women. Generally, arthritic pain can inhibit overall enjoyment of lovemaking.

TREATMENT: The disability can be eased by use of specially prescribed drugs and by having a hot bath prior to sex. Lovemaking can be encouraged to take forms other than intercourse. If intercourse is particularly desired, then working out which positions are most comfortable and using cushions or pillows as supports is most helpful.

• ASTHMA

Some people suffer from activity-induced asthma. This can make them wary of enjoying sexual intercourse.

TREATMENT: In most cases, preparation by taking appropriate medication beforehand, such as using a bronchodilator, should inhibit an attack and allow relaxed enjoyment of sex.

A HOT BATH enjoyed prior to lovemaking can ease the painful symptoms of arthritis as well as making you feel warm and relaxed.

• BLOOD DISORDERS AFFECTING GENITALS

Impairment to the blood supply, as in the case of arterial disease, may be responsible for obstructing sexual response, such as erection in males, and vaginal lubrication, swelling of the labia and vaginal wall, and clitoral erection in females. Scar tissue as a result of a wound or surgery may also be a cause of obstruction. Third-degree tears during

IF YOUR PARTNER is ill, understand that he or she may not feel like intercourse, and that this lack of interest has nothing to do with you.

childbirth, general vaginal repair surgery, and surgery affecting the rectum (such as prostate operations) may all inhibit perineal blood supply with the side-effect of lessening sexual response.

TREATMENT: Cosmetic repair surgery may help in some cases.

• DIABETES

Diabetes tends to damage peripheral and autonomic nerves and to cause degenerative changes in small blood vessels. It causes problems of impotence in men. Diabetic women do not usually have problems with sexual response, except that vaginal lubrication may be slightly impaired. However, they are prone to vaginal infections, such as thrush, which may make intercourse uncomfortable. They also tend to have

more hazardous pregnancies and larger than average babies. The psychological effect of this may mean that post-birth sexuality becomes problematic. Diabetic women may also experience greater vaginal atrophy during menopause. In addition, hormonal methods of contraception disturb diabetic control.

TREATMENT: The first priority is to control the diabetes. This means eating healthy foods, cutting down drastically on alcohol consumption, and giving up smoking. Avoid blood sugar lows by eating regularly. Viagra (see p.207) may help erections in diabetic men. Barrier methods of birth control are preferable to hormone-based ones for diabetic women (see p.185).

WOMEN WHO HAVE experienced vaginal repair surgery, perhaps after a difficult birth, may need to take things slowly when they begin their sensual life again.

SEXFACTS

MEDICAL CHECK-UPS

Recent estimates of people visiting their doctor with sex problems puts the incidence of physical causes as high as 30 per cent. On this basis, anyone suspecting they may have a sex problem would be wise to ask for a thorough physical check-up before going on to seek counselling in case the problems may be symptomatic of a more serious underlying illness.

• EPILEPSY

The majority of people suffering from epilepsy have normal sex lives and do not suffer from sexual difficulties. It is rare for a fit to be triggered off by intercourse or orgasm. However, epileptic sedation can sometimes cause problems and so can difficulties in adjusting to the epileptic state. Fear of orgasm can be a complication.

Temporal lobe epilepsy, however, has definite association with a low or non-existent interest in sexual activity, lack of sexual curiosity, sexual fantasy, or sensual activity. Much more rarely, hypersexuality (excessive display of sexual activity) is shown, and this sometimes takes the form of an abnormal sexual preference such as transsexualism, excessive masturbation, and aimless attempts at intercourse.

Drug treatment complicates the issue, since it has recently been recognized that anti-convulsant drugs prescribed in the past impair sexual development and others, such as phenobarbitone, affect hormone levels and diminish sex drive.

TREATMENT: Counselling and sex therapy can help many couples with epilepsy. In addition, switching to newer, less sexually invasive anti-epileptic preparations is advisable.

MUTUAL MASTURBATION and oral sex offer happy alternatives to couples nervous of undertaking sexual intercourse for fear that it will adversely affect their health.

• HEART ATTACK/DISEASE

The majority of people with heart disease are capable of enjoying a normal and full sex life. However, a few (who have suffered heart attacks) may change their attitudes regarding sexual intercourse through fear that something too energetic will put them at risk of a further attack. The psychological effects of heart attack may have an impact on general feelings of well-being. Often, the patient recovering from a first attack understands that, for safety's sake, an entire way of life needs to be altered. This can be unnerving and disorienting. Combined with feelings of vulnerability

PEOPLE OFTEN BELIEVE that their illness has diminished their libido. However, with a little encouragement from an understanding partner they frequently rediscover their desire.

and anxiety, these make poor conditions for enjoying energetic activity.

TREATMENT: Research shows that sexual intercourse is less demanding on the heart than other forms of moderate exercise, and that keeping fit is important for a healthy heart. If intercourse becomes seriously anxiety-provoking, learning to value other less energetic forms of sexual activity, such as mutual masturbation, solitary masturbation, and oral sex, may be beneficial.

SEX FACTS

HEART ATTACKS

There is some evidence to suggest that sexual intercourse in stressed situations is more likely to lead to heart attack than regular sexual intercourse with a constant partner. Japanese research shows that, although rare, sudden death during sex is more likely to occur in an extra-marital sexual encounter (when presumably stress levels are higher) than within a stable relationship.

• HYPERTENSION

One of the side-effects of heart disease can be hypertension. The effects of hypertension on sexuality are uncertain. Some drugs used in its treatment appear to interfere with sexual function, and men and women also sometimes fear that sexual activity will increase blood pressure to a dangerous level.

TREATMENT: Resumption of sexual activity is best taken in gradual steps. The patient would be wise to begin with solitary masturbation, then to practise masturbation with a partner, slowly combining it with gentle intercourse taken at a very easy pace with a lot of mutual caresses. If the drugs you're taking interfere with sexual function, consult your doctor and attempt to alter the drug regimen.

• MULTIPLE SCLEROSIS

About one-third of multiple sclerosis sufferers report difficulty in achieving orgasm, a lowered sexual appetite, or reduced sensation in the genitals. The causes vary from impaired nerve function to other physical or psychological illnesses. As the symptoms of the disease flare up, so too can related sexual disorders.

TREATMENT: Treatments for the sexual problem depend on treatments for the disease itself. There have been no sure-fire cures, although evening primrose oil was hailed as a saviour in

SEX FACTS

MULTIPLE SCLEROSIS

Research has shown that although male MS sufferers failed to respond to fantasy or erotica with an erection they did respond to genital touch. This means that even if they don't initially feel like sex, if they're given genital massage they may respond.

the 1980s. In periods of remission, sufferers should not assume that sexual response is still impaired but should carefully experiment with sexual stimulation.

• RENAL FAILURE (CHRONIC)

Uraemia results in a loss of sexual appetite and a general feeling of uncertainty regarding sexual activity. Many people also develop a degree of sexual unresponsiveness.

TREATMENT: Haemodialysis or renal transplant usually gives the patient confidence to resume sex, but response is not always fully restored. Sufferers from renal disease often become depressed as a result of the illness; in these cases, careful counselling can sometimes lift the depression and aid lovemaking.

MEN AND WOMEN *who have suffered from a stroke are often anxious about making love. However, sexual problems are more likely to be caused by anxiety than the stroke itself.*

• SPINAL CHORD INJURY

Spinal injuries appear to affect men sexually more than women. Two major studies showed that men who had injuries were more likely to suffer from loss of erection, although they still experienced sexual sensation. More women reported satisfactory sexual relationships that included arousal and orgasm (although some stated that their orgasms had changed in quality).

TREATMENT: Sensitive sexual experimentation is needed to discover ways round the difficulties.

• STROKE

Strokes are only likely to impair sexual appetite if a particular part of the brain is involved. However, anxiety as a result of the illness is often responsible for a stressed sexual response. Much of that response stems from the erroneous belief that sexual activity may in some way trigger off another stroke.

TREATMENT: Acceptance that sexual activity is not in any way connected to the occurrence of another stroke is often enough to restore a full and healthy sex life.

SOLITARY MASTURBATION *means that you can set the pace, so it is ideal for those wary of vigorous sexual activity with a partner.*

MEDICINAL DRUGS

MANY PEOPLE TAKE PRESCRIPTION medicines for good reasons but find that they experience undesirable sexual side-effects. It is important to be aware that certain medications carry a risk, and that any problems may just be a side-effect of the drug. In many cases it is the illness, rather than the drug used to treat it, that is the cause of sexual problems (see pp.212–15).

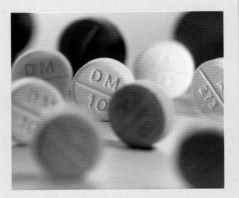

MEDICATION AND SIDE-EFFECTS

THE FOLLOWING TABLE summarizes a number of the major classes of medication. Some of the medicinal drugs mentioned may only cause sexual problems when combined with alcohol or other recreational drugs (see pp.218–19).

CONSULT YOUR DOCTOR if you notice anything different about your sexual drive or response. It may be a result of the drugs you're taking.

• ANTIDEPRESSANTS
Depression itself causes loss of desire (see pp.204–205), so recovery through treatment can help to alleviate this.

Tricyclics including amitriptyline and clomipramine
SIDE-EFFECTS: May decrease sex drive in women and men. They may cause erection and ejaculation problems for men and orgasm problems for women.

Selective serotonin re-uptake inhibitors (SSRIs) including fluoxetine (*Prozac*) and sertraline
SIDE-EFFECTS: Orgasmic delay or inability to reach orgasm in both sexes.

PROZAC may cause problems for a percentage of users. Side-effects include ejaculation problems in men and orgasm problems in women.

Monoamine oxidase inhibitors (MAOIs) including phenelzine
SIDE-EFFECTS: Cause sexual problems for a small percentage of users. Erection and ejaculation problems for men and orgasm problems for women.

• ULCER/ACID SUPPRESSING DRUGS
H2-receptor antagonists including cimetidine
SIDE-EFFECTS: May cause erection problems for some men.

Proton pump inhibitors including omeprazole
SIDE-EFFECTS: May cause erection problems for some men.

• BLOOD-LIPID CONTROL DRUGS
Statins including atorvastatin
SIDE-EFFECTS: May cause erection problems for some men.

Fibrates including bezafibrate
SIDE-EFFECTS: May cause erection problems for some men.

• BLOOD-PRESSURE CONTROL DRUGS
Thiazides including bendroflumethiazide
SIDE-EFFECTS: Women taking these drugs for blood pressure may experience vaginal dryness and men may suffer erection problems.

Potassium-sparing drugs including spironolactone
SIDE-EFFECTS: High dosages can cause a reduction in sexual desire. Women may experience vaginal dryness and men may suffer erection problems.

Beta-blockers including propranolol
SIDE-EFFECTS: May cause erection problems in men and lack of arousal in women.

Alpha-blockers including prazosin
SIDE-EFFECTS: May cause priapism (prolonged, painful, unwanted erection).

Centrally acting drugs including methyldopa
SIDE-EFFECTS: High dosages can cause a decrease in desire for both sexes, and erection and ejaculation problems for men.

• TRANQUILLIZERS
Benzodiazepines including diazepam and lorazepam
SIDE-EFFECTS: May reduce sexual desire in both sexes.

• DRUGS FOR SCHIZOPHRENIA
Phenothiazines including chlorpromazine
SIDE-EFFECTS: Ejaculation problems in some men; high doses may cause erection problems.

Atypical antipsychotic drugs including risperidone
SIDE-EFFECTS: Some men may experience ejaculation problems.

• EPILEPSY DRUGS
Anticonvulsants including carbamazepine
SIDE-EFFECTS: May cause erection problems and decreased fertility.

• ANTIHISTAMINES
Histamine H1-receptor antagonists (in travel sickness, hay fever, cough remedies) including diphenhydramine hydrochloride
SIDE-EFFECTS: Sexual desire may be reduced. Women may experience vaginal dryness.

• HORMONAL PREPARATIONS
Oral contraceptives such as oestrogens and/or progestogens, e.g. combined Pill or POP (progestogen-only Pill)
SIDE-EFFECTS: Women have extremely variable reactions – sexual desire may increase or decrease. May also cause vaginal dryness. Oestrogens can improve vaginal lubrication in post-menopausal women.

Androgens, such as testosterone preparations, can help to restore sex drive and orgasmic ability to both men and women.
SIDE-EFFECTS: High doses can cause problems – development of masculine features in women, impaired sperm production in men.

Antiandrogens
SIDE-EFFECTS: May reduce sexual desire in both men and women. May cause erection and ejaculation problems and impaired sperm production in men.

• BREAST CANCER DRUGS
Antioestrogens including tamoxifen
SIDE-EFFECTS: May cause vaginal dryness.

• PROSTATE CANCER DRUGS
Antiandrogens including flutamide
SIDE-EFFECTS: May cause decreased sexual desire, erection problems, and a reduction in sperm production.

Oestrogens including diethylstilbestrol
SIDE-EFFECTS: May cause decreased sexual desire and erection problems.

Note: Inclusion of a drug in this table only indicates that adverse effects on sexual function have been recorded, and does not include information on the frequency or severity of the problems. For most people, the drugs mentioned should cause no sexual problems. Omission of a drug from the table does not imply that it is free of side-effects.

BE AWARE of the potential side-effects of your medication. Understanding will help to minimize the emotional impact.

RECREATIONAL DRUGS

STIMULANTS, SUCH AS ALCOHOL, nicotine, cannabis, cocaine, and ecstasy are frequently associated with sex. Both the positive and negative affects of recreational drugs on sexual sensation and performance are regularly debated, but what's the real story?

Drinking alcohol is enormously popular in Western culture – people love the way it loosens their inhibitions and makes them feel more relaxed.

The affects that alcohol can have on sex drive and performance are varied. The primary factor is how much or how little alcohol you drink. After the first glass or two, you may notice signs of excitement that are similar to those you experience during sexual arousal – your face flushes and your heartbeat quickens. More significantly, you start to feel at ease and you become more animated and lively – even in social situations where you might normally feel reserved and uncomfortable. The reason for this is that alcohol affects the part of your brain that normally inhibits you – it acts as a sort of social lubrication.

After a few more drinks, however, the affects are less attractive. Your thinking, speech, and co-ordination become impaired. You may experience mood swings, even becoming depressed or violent. There are also the physical consequences of drunkenness to consider – it can cause temporary impotence in men. Meanwhile, alcohol abuse over long periods can cause permanent impotence and loss of sex drive in both men and women.

So, does alcohol increase desire? Researchers have discovered that your expectations influence whether alcohol has an aphrodisiac effect on you or not. If you believe that alcohol makes you feel turned on, then it will have this effect, whereas if you believe that booze kills your desire, you're unlikely to feel sexy.

SMOKING FASHIONS

IN THE HOLLYWOOD MOVIES of the 1930s and 1940s, smoking was portrayed as glamorous and sexy. However, in today's US movies it is frequently associated with failure, depression, and the villain. Smoking and sex make disastrous bedfellows – not only does the smell mask natural body scents, smoking can also dull sensation.

SEX FACTS

TOBACCO
Smoking causes circulatory problems, which can impede blood flow to the genitals, cause impotence, damage general health, and even cause sterility.

A–Z OF ILLICIT DRUGS

SOME PEOPLE TURN TO DRUGS in an attempt to enhance erotic sensation and sex drive. The dangers inherent in this include the risk of short- and long-term side-effects, and the possibility of impairing your sexual drive and performance. It's a far better option to see a sex therapist or consult your doctor about pharmacologically approved drugs such as Viagra (see p.207) and testosterone (see p.147).

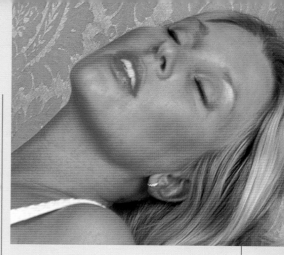

DRUGS may make you feel sexy, but they can damage your sexual health in the long term.

• AMYL NITRATE ("POPPERS")
Effect on libido Not significant.
Sexual sensation Enhances sensation in the genitals when inhaled immediately prior to orgasm.
LONG-TERM EFFECTS: Users with weak hearts who abuse the drug have been known to die from heart attacks. Poppers must not be taken with Viagra since both lower blood pressure.

AMYL NITRATE is sniffed as a vapour from a bottle or capsule. Users claim it produces light-headed, warm feelings and enhances orgasm.

• CANNABIS
Effect on libido Cannabis is a mood amplifier, so if you are already feeling sexy, it can enhance your desire for sex.
Sexual sensation If you are feeling sexually sensitive, cannabis can enhance sensation, whereas if you are feeling sleepy, it will knock you out.
LONG-TERM EFFECTS: It can damage your sex life by reducing testosterone levels in the blood. Cannabis can also be the cause of impotence and sperm damage in men and ovarian damage in women.

• COCAINE
Effect on libido Some people find it increases their sex drive.
Sexual sensation Reduces sensation. Small amounts can cause retarded ejaculation and inflammation of mucous membranes in the vagina. Orgasm may be difficult to achieve.
LONG-TERM EFFECTS: It can cause permanent sexual problems for both men and women.

• ECSTASY
Effect on libido Increases desire for physical closeness but not necessarily for sex.
Sexual sensation Heightens sense of touch and feelings of sensuality.
LONG-TERM EFFECTS: Its long-term effects are the subject of fierce debate. Some consider that it increases the risk of death from heart attack and that it can cause brain damage.

• HEROIN
Effect on libido Generally decreases or destroys sex drive.
Sexual sensation Can make orgasm difficult or impossible.

LONG-TERM EFFECTS: Can cause impotence, ejaculation problems, sterility, and inability to achieve orgasm.

• LSD/MAGIC MUSHROOMS
Effect on libido Unpredictable because the drug can amplify the mood of the user. If the "tripper" is not with someone he or she finds erotic and trustworthy, sex experienced on a bad trip can be so terrifying that all interest in sex will rapidly diminish.
Sexual sensation Variable, depending on the mood of the user. Orgasm on LSD tends to be less absorbing and yet a more prolonged and encompassing experience.
LONG-TERM EFFECTS: Can lead to psychotic symptoms or frightening flashbacks.

• SPEED/AMPHETAMINE
Effect on libido May increase sex drive.
Sexual sensation Can encourage sexual awareness in the short term, but orgasm may be difficult to achieve.
LONG-TERM EFFECTS: May cause depression, which diminishes sexual desire, and paranoia.

CANNABIS RESEARCH

RESEARCH SHOWS that heavy cannabis use leads to memory loss, impairment of attention, and sudden, dark changes of mood – including paranoia, anxiety, and panic. It may even trigger schizophrenia. It is also considered to be more addictive than it once was: recent studies show that up to 15 per cent of cannabis users have become dependents.

SEX-RELATED DISEASES

INTIMATE SEXUAL CONTACT can result in sexually transmitted infections (STIs) and a number of other health problems. During sex, the close proximity of genital mucous membranes allows the exchange of micro-organisms between partners, particularly if you have tiny cuts or tears in the vagina or rectum. Some STIs can even be transmitted without intercourse. Most sex-related diseases are easily diagnosed and treated.

A–Z OF CONDITIONS

MOST OF THE INFECTIONS below are transmitted sexually, although some (e.g. cystitis) may be triggered by sex rather than transmitted. Infections may be the result of viruses, bacteria, yeasts, or parasites and they may be present in semen, blood, and cervical and vaginal fluids.

• BACTERIAL VAGINOSIS (BV)
Most prevalent in sexually active women, bacterial vaginosis is an infection and inflammation of the vagina caused by an upset in the normal balance of micro-organisms in the vagina. The key symptoms include frothy, grey-white vaginal discharge that smells fishy and causes itching or burning around the vagina and vulva. The odour may be particularly strong after sexual intercourse or washing with soap, suggesting that changes in vaginal acidity are responsible.

Bacterial vaginosis can be caused by tampons that remain in the vagina for too long. It is vital that tampons are changed every four to six hours and that they are removed at the end of a period.
TREATMENT: Antibiotics, either in pill form or as a cream applied to the vagina.

• CANDIDIASIS ("Thrush")
Candidiasis is an inflammation of the vagina and vulva caused by an overgrowth of yeasts that are found normally in the vagina. This may be triggered by a course of antibiotics, stress, a high-sugar diet, diabetes, too much washing with highly scented bath products or soaps, or wearing very close-fitting tights or jeans. A thick white vaginal discharge, accompanied by local irritation and a burning sensation during intercourse, are common symptoms. Although candidiasis isn't a sexually transmitted disease as such, women can pass it on to males, who experience it as an inflammation of the glans of the penis. This is known as balanitis.
TREATMENT: Over-the-counter anti-fungal medications in the form of creams or pessaries for women.

HONEST COMMUNICATION is vital when you are about to have sex with a new partner. If you're in any doubt about your sexual health, or your partner's, visit a clinic for a check-up.

• CHLAMYDIA

Infections of the reproductive tract caused by the micro-organism *Chlamydia trachomatis* are generally known as chlamydia infections. The symptoms of chlamydia are usually so mild in women that they often go unnoticed. In fact, many women don't discover that they have chlamydia until it spreads through the reproductive system and causes a complication such as pelvic inflammatory disease (see p.222). Men may also be symptomless or they may experience uncomfortable burning sensations when they urinate (see Non-specific urethritis, p.222).

TREATMENT: Antibiotics.

• CYSTITIS

Most common in women, cystitis occurs when the inner lining of the bladder becomes inflamed causing frequent, painful urination. Sometimes women get cystitis after intercourse because the urethra, which lies close to the vagina, gets bruised by the thrusting movement of the penis. This is more common in rear-entry positions. Women who get post-coital cystitis should empty their bladder within half an hour of sexual intercourse. They should also avoid using soap in the genital area.

TREATMENT: Antibiotics.

CRANBERRY JUICE *is considered by many to alleviate the symptoms and prevent further outbreaks of cystitis.*

SEXFACTS

CYSTITIS

This inflammation of the bladder is often called the "honeymoon illness", since it often first occurs after over-enthusiastic intercourse in the early days of a relationship.

• GENITAL HERPES

Symptoms of genital herpes consist of an itchy, tingling sensation in the genitals followed by blisters that go on to burst, creating painful sores, sometimes accompanied by headaches, fatigue, fever, and muscle pains. Although the virus remains in the body for a person's lifetime, and cannot be destroyed by drugs or the immune system, the good news is that it's dormant for most of the time (only around 50 per cent of sufferers experience recurrent attacks). Later outbreaks tend to be milder than the first few attacks. Herpes on the genitals are caused by a strain of the same virus that causes cold sores around the lips and mouth (if oral sex takes place with a person who has herpes blisters on his or her lips the virus may infect the genitals).

TREATMENT: Symptoms may be alleviated by antiviral drugs.

• GENITAL WARTS (HPV)

Genital warts are the most common STI and they can affect any part of the genitals or the area around the anus. The warts themselves are usually painless, and appear as small or large bumps or outgrowths of skin. You may get just one or two, or large numbers of them. The wart virus stays within the body permanently with the potential to cause further outbreaks. Because specific strains of HPV are associated with an increased risk of cervical cancer, it is vital that female sufferers have annual cervical smear tests.

TREATMENT: Removal of warts using liquid nitrogen, caustic chemicals, or lasers.

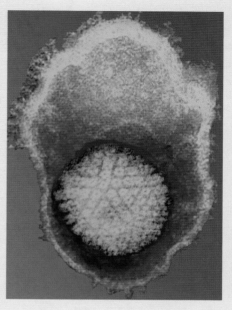

THE HERPES SIMPLEX VIRUS *sets up residence in the nervous system, where it cannot be destroyed by drugs or the immune system.*

• GONORRHOEA ("The clap")

This is a common bacterial infection that causes symptoms such as frequent, painful urination (women may mistake gonorrhoea for cystitis), a pus-like discharge from the penis in men, and a yellow-green discharge from the vagina in women. Alternatively, gonorrhoea may be completely symptomless. Gonorrhoea can infect the throat and rectum as a result of oral or anal sex, causing mild discomfort when swallowing in the case of throat gonorrhoea, and irritation and discharge from the anus in the case of rectal gonorrhoea.

TREATMENT: Antibiotics.

• HEPATITIS B (HBV)

This virus is slightly different from other STIs in that it doesn't produce localized symptoms on the genitals. Nevertheless, it is commonly transmitted by sex with an infected person. It causes inflammation of the liver, tiredness, nausea, lack of appetite, and jaundice (yellowing of the skin). Occasionally hepatitis B may be symptomless.

TREATMENT: No specific treatment except rest, a balanced diet rich in vitamins and minerals, and avoidance of alcohol. There is a preventative vaccine available.

• NON-SPECIFIC URETHRITIS (NSU)

NSU may be caused by chlamydia or it can have a non-sexual origin. Symptoms frequently include a whitish discharge, although some women experience no symptoms at all. NSU is sometimes associated with "red eye", and very occasionally with trichomoniasis (see right). If infection is suspected, both sexes should be treated for NSU even when there are no obvious symptoms, since men and women can be carriers.

TREATMENT: Antibiotics.

• PELVIC INFLAMMATORY DISEASE (PID)

Inflammation of the female reproductive system, particularly the fallopian tubes, ovaries, and uterus, is usually the result of an untreated STI such as gonorrhoea or chlamydia. It can affect women's fertility, often by blocking and scarring the fallopian tubes. The main symptoms are pain in the lower abdomen, fever, backache, and painful, irregular periods.

TREATMENT: Antibiotics or combined drug therapy.

• PUBIC LICE ("Crabs")

Lice that live in pubic hair infest the area by biting the skin, feeding on blood, and laying eggs. Because pubic lice are so tiny they may not be immediately visible, but microscopic examination can yield a conclusive diagnosis. The main symptoms you'll be likely to notice are intense irritation and itching of the pubic region, and possibly small flakes of dried blood in your pubic hair.

TREATMENT: Special insecticidal lotion or shampoo. Your bed linen, towels, and clothes should be washed in very hot water or dry cleaned.

• SYPHILIS

This is transmitted during intercourse, but also by contact with infected sores or skin rashes, blood transfusions, and by sharing infected needles. It develops in three distinct stages. In the first stage, a firm, painless ulcer on the genitals known as a chancre appears – this heals within 6–10 weeks. Local lymph glands in the groin may also become enlarged. In the second stage, bacteria have spread to all parts of the body causing diverse symptoms including skin rashes, headaches, mild fever, hair loss, wart-like growths around the anus and genitals, and swollen lymph glands. In the third stage, which occurs any time between 3–25 years after initial infection, the body's internal tissues start to be destroyed. Eventually, damage to the cardiovascular or nervous system can prove fatal.

TREATMENT: Antibiotics if diagnosed during the first or second stage. If allowed to progress to the third stage, it can be fatal.

CONDOMS should be used whenever you have penetrative sex, unless you know that you and your partner have a clean bill of health.

• TRICHOMONIASIS ("Trich")

Women usually get a greenish yellow, frothy, foul-smelling vaginal discharge and soreness around the vulva, or they may have no symptoms. Men are usually symptomless although they may suffer from a condition known as non-specific urethritis (see left), which causes burning sensations when urinating.

TREATMENT: Antibiotics.

WHAT TO DO IF YOU HAVE AN STI

WHETHER YOU SUSPECT or know you have an STI, it's important to take action quickly. Never ignore suspicious symptoms; many STIs can be successfully treated with antibiotics, and prompt treatment can prevent complications.

1 Go to your doctor or a clinic that specializes in sexual or genito-urinary medicine for professional diagnosis and treatment (see p.180).

2 Talk to the person or people with whom you have had unprotected sex and encourage them also to have a check-up.

3 Avoid all sexual contact until symptoms have abated in order to prevent others from being infected. The doctor will let you know when it is safe to have sex again.

4 Practise scrupulous genital hygiene (see p.178). Avoid transferring infections such as herpes to other parts of your body by washing your hands every time you touch your genitals. Wear loose-fitting, cotton underwear.

5 Make sure that you reduce the likelihood of acquiring an STI in the future by practising safer sex (see pp.182–83).

HIV AND AIDS

HIV (HUMAN IMMUNODEFICIENCY VIRUS) is probably the most feared of all sexually transmitted infections. It can enter the body after exposure to the blood, semen, or vaginal fluids of an infected person, and once inside the body it slowly destroys the immune system so that you can no longer fight off infection (at an advanced stage the disease is known as AIDS).

SEXFACTS

TAKING THE TEST

A simple blood test can reveal if you are suffering from HIV or AIDS. Many organizations offer counselling to people seeking an HIV test.
To prevent the possibility of complications with insurance companies, ensure that your hospital records are anonymous.

How HIV attacks the body

Certain white blood cells (T-cells), a crucial part of the immune system, are destroyed by the HIV virus, resulting in the body's inability to protect itself against disease. Whereas a healthy immune system can destroy hostile bacteria, viruses, parasites, and fungi, a compromised immune system allows them to proliferate to the point where they cause irrevocable damage. At the point where the immune system is no longer capable of resisting disease, the person infected with the HIV virus usually develops full-blown AIDS and suffers from a range of infections.

The stages of infection

There are four stages of HIV infection and the first two are likely to go unnoticed by the majority of people. In fact, lots of people with HIV stay healthy for many years.

1. Seroconversion illness

This is a flu-like illness that may occur six to eight weeks after exposure to HIV.

2. Asymptomatic infection

This is the latent phase during which you may look and feel perfectly healthy. However, the virus is multiplying and your T-cell count is likely to be dropping.

3. Symptomatic infection

This is when the immune system is becoming weak and you are vulnerable to persistent infections that would not normally gain a foothold in the body, such as thrush. Other symptoms may include swollen lymph glands, night sweats, weight loss, diarrhoea, and fatigue.

4. AIDS

When your T-cell count falls below a certain level and you start to suffer from illnesses such as Pneumocystis carinii pneumonia or cytomegalovirus, you are described as having AIDS (acquired immunodeficiency syndrome). Other common AIDS infections include toxoplasmosis, tuberculosis, and gastrointestinal illnesses.

How is HIV transmitted?

HIV can be transmitted by any activity that involves the exchange of bodily fluids, including both heterosexual and homosexual sex. These are the most common routes:

- Unprotected vaginal or anal intercourse – this exposes you to your partner's semen or vaginal fluids. The risk of HIV transmission by intercourse increases if you have torn or ulcerated skin in or around your genitals. This is why genital sores or ulcers caused by herpes or syphilis make HIV transmission more likely.
- Intravenous drug users – those who share needles are exposed to each other's blood.
- Blood transfusions – In the early days of HIV, before blood was screened for the virus, those who had blood transfusions were at risk. Haemophiliacs (who require frequent blood transfusions) were a high-risk group.
- Through the placenta – infected pregnant women can pass HIV to their babies during pregnancy or delivery.
- Via breast-milk – infected mothers can infect their babies through their milk.

Treatment

When HIV was first discovered it was almost invariably fatal. Since the 1980s, however, massive strides have been made in the management of HIV, enabling many sufferers to live normally for years. Combinations of two or more drugs, such as AZT, aim to prevent the virus reproducing. For patients with full-blown AIDS, treatment may also include antibiotic, antiviral, and antifungal drugs to prevent opportunistic infections. These days, people with AIDS have a much better prognosis for the future.

Managing anger

SURPRISINGLY, ANGER CAN SOMETIMES improve a relationship or act as a vehicle to hold it together. It can even improve sex. More commonly though, anger gets in the way of lovemaking and causes major emotional rifts. We may feel angry with the real partner, or we may project anger from a previous relationship on to a new one. The good news is that there are useful methods of overcoming anger to help things heal, as Jane and Simon discovered when they went to see a therapist.

The case

Jane and Simon had been living together for just over six years and had been each other's first lovers. They were both fairly highly sexed, and spent most evenings engaging in fiery arguments, followed by passionate lovemaking. Although they both enjoyed the drama of their relationship, neither enjoyed feeling guilty or disgusted after yet another fierce argument ending in sex. The couple feared they were addicted to rows and that these now formed a part of their sexual foreplay. Another aspect of their problem was that the couple hardly ever saw their friends and had few interests other than sex in common.

Therapist's assessment

Jane and Simon did not necessarily have major emotional problems. Some people accidentally discover that rows trigger passionate sex and then get drawn into repeating the pattern. Jane realized that boredom was a major problem

for her, and that the reason she started the rows was to bring excitement to an otherwise dull life. Finding new outlets for their pent-up energy and changing the focus of their relationship by incorporating other interests worked well.

Action plan

The couple learned how to deal with anger better and improved two other areas of life. The first was sociability. They started going out more often and got to see other couples regularly. The second was to establish some common ground other than sex. Within a year, they began a joint business venture and poured their energies into their business instead. A follow-up session with the therapist showed that the rows had virtually ended.

HOW TO DEAL WITH ANGER

THERE IS A FOUR-STEP method for resolving a partner's anger:

1. Begin with self-disclosure or by offering reassurance.
2. Invite your partner to respond and to explain his or her problem.
3. Reply to what your partner has said.
4. Negotiate a solution to the problem.

When dealing with your partner's anger, begin by acknowledging that your partner is angry and that you take his or her anger seriously and consider it important to both of you. In the course of discussion, try to keep calm and follow a few basic rules:

• Always be honest with your partner: never patronize or use subterfuge.
• Show your sincerity by behaving in a warm, empathetic manner.
• Listen carefully to your partner – don't interrupt, and do invite him or her to say more.
• Indicate that you have heard their complaints by repeating what they have said occasionally, and by using encouraging body language such as nodding.
• Don't look or behave like an interrogator. Sit casually.
• Do find at least a partial solution to the problem, otherwise you will go over the same ground again and again.

Adapting to life with a baby

WHEN A MALE is used to being the focus of his partner's attention, the switch to parenthood can be difficult. He suddenly finds himself in competition with his own youngster. This is dismaying for the new young mother, who suddenly sees her husband as a demanding small boy. Not a very sexy viewpoint of one's former lover, especially when you are struggling at the same time to keep up with the demands of a new baby, as Jennifer discovered when she gave birth to her first child.

The case

Nigel and Jennifer had enjoyed an active sex life with each other prior to the birth of their first baby, but the couple's sex life changed greatly after the birth. Caring for the infant left Jennifer too tired for imaginative lovemaking. She expected Nigel to understand, and had assumed that her new family life would be like that of her parents – her father helped her mother raise their children. Instead, Jennifer found herself having to pacify Nigel with sex activities that were solely for his pleasure. Denied the regular sexual treats he was used to, Nigel felt like a small unhappy child and concluded, wrongly, that Jennifer had switched her love from himself to the baby.

Therapist's assessment

A common problem following birth is that new mothers experience major hormone withdrawal: one of the casualties of this is sex drive. It does not mean that a new mother no longer wants sex, but it might mean that she finds it much harder to respond and almost impossible to take the initiative. Nigel, like many new fathers, needed to learn that for the first few months after childbirth Jennifer found it hard to be sexual, and that this had nothing to do with being unloving. Both Jennifer and Nigel also needed to realize that their attitudes to parenthood and their expectations of family life came from their very different backgrounds. Once they had discussed and understood their differences, they began to tune in to each other's feelings. Nigel began to accept Jennifer's new role as a mother and make allowances, and as a result Jennifer felt happier and made more time for intimacy with Nigel.

Action plan

Nigel needed attention that made him feel special – something he had previously achieved through sex. The plan was for him to experience this through non-sexual activities. Jennifer prepared exotic feasts, bathed and cuddled him and, when her energy returned, gave him erotic massage. In order to make this worthwhile for Jennifer, Nigel had to accept the idea of "giving to get". In return, he understood that the more he did to help Jennifer out in the home, the better she would feel and the more she would want to give him sexually.

UNDERSTANDING EXPECTATIONS *exercises*

WHEN YOUR EXPECTATIONS do not coincide with your partner's, the first thing to do is to clarify your beliefs and expectations together. Look at the areas where you and your partner disagree and work out why, by studying the following points:

- Ask your partner to identify any distortions that he or she sees in your expectations.
- Think back to your early beliefs about life – did any of your "distortions" have obvious origins in your childhood?
- Ask yourself if your relatives may have held the views that influenced you in these areas and ask, "Are these views relevant to me today?"

NEGOTIATION EXERCISE

If you feel comfortable with your personal expectations then you can begin to negotiate:

- Make sure your expectations are realistic and reasonable.
- Tactfully make your wishes clear.
- Listen to your partner's views.
- Be willing to compromise and make changes too.

Rediscovering intimacy

ONE OF THE MOST COMMON PROBLEMS to beset couples who have been married for some years is to feel distanced or unconnected. If you have previously relied on a lot of physical closeness, it comes as an unwelcome shock to realize that you are living in an undemonstrative relationship. It may be a lack of sex that bothers you, or a dearth of touch and cuddles. If you feel loving towards your partner but feel that the intimacy is lacking, you will probably want to improve the situation, as Catherine and Peter did.

The case

Catherine and Peter had been married for several years, and since the birth of their second baby had spent more and more time apart. They had developed separate social lives and different interests, and it wasn't uncommon for them to hardly see each other and to go to bed at different times. Each felt that they were drifting apart, and missed their former intimacy. The couple no longer made love often, and Peter seemed to have almost given up the little gestures of love that Catherine found very important. Yet they had a happy history and two children to think about, so it was important to sort the problem out.

The couple came to counselling to see if there was any way in which both relationship and sex life might be rescued. Catherine said that with each birth, Peter had become more and more demanding, and she ended up by classing him as "one of the children". He would lie on the bed and expect Catherine to undress him, just as a child would. It was hard, she pointed out, to feel sexy towards one of the children. Peter said he thought Catherine was simply no longer interested in him.

Therapist's assessment

This couple had been affected by the change of status that many people sense when becoming parents. Peter had been reduced to a type of helpless babyhood because he couldn't help but see his wife as a mother, and Catherine responded accordingly by no longer feeling sexual.

Both Catherine and Peter needed to rediscover the lover in the other, and see each other as equals within a grown-up relationship. Peter needed to understand that his behaviour was like that of an overgrown child, and that it was unsurprising that Catherine had lost interest in sex. Catherine needed to give off more positive body signals so that Peter felt valued as a lover.

Action plan

Therapy consisted of getting the couple to do sensual "homework" together, to literally put them in touch again with their sexuality. It also involved teaching Peter about the signals his almost infantile body language was giving out, and encouraging Catherine to be more positive – to make a point of telling Peter regularly how much she loved and appreciated him. He began to believe this, and because he felt better he stopped being so demanding. Instead, he took responsibility for himself and started pampering his wife instead of demanding that she look after him. The approach worked very well, and within a fairly short period of time, their distance was a thing of the past.

BODY LANGUAGE IN THE BEDROOM

WE CAN LEARN a lot about how intimate and close our partner is feeling towards us through observing his or her body language:

- People who are looking for intimacy hold their arms open wide, making their body available to the other person.
- Those nervous of intimacy might sit on the edge of the bed, look down with a frown, with their cheek resting on their hand, and their arms pressed close to their body.
- People not wanting intimacy at all might produce an actual "barrier", such as a tightly wrapped dressing gown or a newspaper held up to the face.

Learning to assert yourself

MANY WOMEN AND SOME MEN are very poor at "getting themselves heard" and being assertive. The outcome of this can be a store of resentment that eventually surfaces in unexpected ways. In Miriam's case, she flatly refused to try for a baby. Yet neither she, nor her husband, could understand what this was all about. Sometimes talking about things isn't enough. You have to step in and take strategic action, and do something so different that it stops you short.

The case

Harry wanted a baby, and Miriam refused point blank, although she wasn't sure why. She began to resist having sex, and was reluctant to have any kind of physical intimacy with Harry. Harry was a well-meaning individual, but he did most of the talking in the relationship, and seemed to take Miriam for granted, steamrollering her into decisions. Harry wanted to move to a house on a new estate several miles from town, while Miriam was keen to remain in town where she worked and had many friends. Although she tried to explain this to him, he wouldn't listen properly, and would just sweep her objections under the carpet.

Therapist's assessment

At the first session it became rapidly obvious what the problem was, because Miriam could not get a word in edgeways. Eventually the therapist intervened, handed over a bunch of keys to Miriam, and told the couple that only the holder of the keys might talk. For the first time, Miriam was able to say how swamped she felt by her husband. And how angry she was. She also came to realize the connection between her anger and her sex strike. Miriam felt overwhelmed by her husband's ebullience, and her refusal to have a baby seemed her unconscious method of getting him to "back off".

The therapist felt that long before this couple got to baby-making they needed to completely re-work how they lived each day. It was not easy altering Harry's habits. In his family, he explained, everyone talked all the time and this didn't bother his brothers and sisters. However, with a discussion controlled by the counsellor, they managed to have numerous constructive conversations where both talked and listened equally. Harry finally listened properly to his wife's objections about the move.

Action plan

Although this couple practised a little sensual massage to help them begin their sex life again, it was the relationship as a whole that needed improvement, in particular their method of communication. The couple

found the "Holder of the keys" and the "May I?" exercises (see below) extremely useful, and they managed to use these to communicate effectively at home.

The outcome of the therapy was that the relocation plans were changed, and the couple found a new home in town. Within about nine months, Miriam finally felt in control of her life enough to agree to start a family.

"HOLDER OF THE KEYS" AND "MAY I?" *exercises*

BELOW ARE TWO EXERCISES that help to improve communication when one partner is considerably more vocal and domineering than the other:

"HOLDER OF THE KEYS"
A bunch of keys is given to the person whose turn it is to speak. His or her partner must listen carefully, and is not allowed to interrupt. When the speaker has finished, he or she passes the keys over so the other person has a chance to speak.

"MAY I?"
Conversations should begin with the words "May I?" In this way, the speaker is forced to think before talking, and has to wait for a reply. This effectively offers control to the quieter, less forthcoming partner.

Overcoming grief

THE LOSS OF A BELOVED PARTNER usually affects people extremely deeply, often for a long period of time. Individuals tend to respond to bereavement in a number of ways: some mourners suddenly turn promiscuous; others do the opposite and withdraw from intimacy. A number of people find that although they may be very attracted to a new partner, they are unable to consummate the relationship.

The case

Andrew had been married to his wife for 15 years before she died, and had been faithful throughout the marriage. After some time of being alone, he formed a relationship with Sarah, and was keen to consummate it. However, he found that he couldn't even though he wanted to. At the crucial moment, he would feel guilty and his erection would deflate. He knew that there wasn't anything wrong physically, because he was still capable of getting an erection and achieving orgasm when he masturbated. Although he was able to bring Sarah to climax with his hands, he felt miserable and worried about the situation.

Therapist's assessment

We establish clearly defined patterns of lovemaking in a long-term relationship, so sex can feel strange if attempted with someone new. New patterns are, of course, created with new partners. But the mind plays odd tricks, and Andrew's was telling him he was being unfaithful to his deceased wife. A loss of interest in sex is just one way in which the bereaved person demonstrates how attached he has been to the person who has died. It is a sign that there is still a need to let go of the sadness inside.

Action plan

Andrew needed to give himself a bit more time to grieve and to get used to being with Sarah without rushing things. One way of achieving this was to concentrate on loving and non-penetrative sex, such as erotic massage, until Andrew really felt ready for intercourse. Being expressly forbidden by the therapist to have intercourse had the paradoxical effect of turning Andrew on. Within a few months, he and Sarah were having intercourse, and his erection problem was solved. Interestingly, he and Sarah continued with the erotic massage and orgasm without intercourse as well. Another effective way of kick-starting the system of arousal and erection would have been to have taken Viagra before intercourse (see p.207).

SEXFACTS

THE EFFECTS OF GRIEF

Grief can affect your sexual response in several ways. Sexual desire may decline or even cease for a time. Some women find their periods stop. Others find that their periods become incredibly heavy and "flood". There may be no desire for a new partner for months or even years. Or, like Andrew, there may be much desire but very little performance. These are all normal responses.

FOUR STAGES OF GRIEF

THERE ARE RECKONED TO BE FOUR stages that bereaved people pass through before completing their grieving. These consist of the following:

1 Numbness and disbelief – these are the mind's natural defences against the initial shock of losing a lover.

2 Intense emotional pain, sometimes manifesting itself as physical pain, emerges next.

3 A period of intense anger and guilt follows as you try to come to terms with the unexpectedness of loss.

4 Recovery. The slow re-entry to a normal social life happens eventually, provided you have grieved enough.

Discovering orgasm

WE TAKE IT FOR GRANTED these days that we all understand everything there is to know about sex because the subject is so widely written about. However, any sex counsellor will tell you that this isn't the case. Every new generation has to find out for the first time how to make love so that the male is able to last longer and the female can climax. Jerry and Tina learned this by discussing their problem with a sex therapist.

The case

Jerry was Tina's first lover. The couple had been lovers for six months, and insisted that they could talk about anything together. They were dismayed by the fact that during all this time, Tina hadn't managed to have an orgasm. Jerry felt very inadequate because of it and thought he must be a poor lover. Tina seemed to know little about her sexual response and was more concerned for Jerry's feelings than her own. Although the couple insisted that they knew the facts of life, when questioned about how sex actually worked, they turned out to be surprisingly ignorant, and each had much to learn.

SELF-MASSAGE

IF YOU ARE FAMILIAR with your own body you are much more likely to climax. To help you discover your sexual response, follow these steps over a period of several days, or even weeks, in relaxed, private conditions:

1 Have a warm bath, then massage your body afterwards with warm oil everywhere except the genitals. Focus on any good feelings your touch may arouse, and try to enlarge these areas of good sensation.

2 After your warm bath, do the same as Step 1 but this time include the genitals, massaging just as you would the rest of your body, remembering to keep doing what feels good.

3 Spend a little less time on the whole body and a little more time on the genitals. You're building on sensual arousal rather than orgasm at this stage.

4 Again, spend time massaging the genitals after your warm bath, but this time you're aiming at achieving orgasm. If orgasm doesn't arrive using your fingers, then include a vibrator in your genital massage (see pp.142–43).

Therapist's assessment

It turned out that Tina (who was only 18) had never masturbated and had only experienced orgasm once during a dream. Jerry, although older (22) and sexually experienced, had hang-ups about certain sex acts. For example, he hated the idea of performing oral sex on a woman, although he didn't mind the idea of oral sex being done to him. It became clear that the couple had two problems to be tackled. The first was that Tina needed to overcome her ignorance of her body's sensual responses and learn to masturbate. The second was that Jerry was sexually inhibited himself and although he didn't admit it, this inhibition was affecting his self-confidence. In his heart of hearts, he doubted his ability to be an exciting lover. This made him all the more reluctant to experiment because he unconsciously reckoned new moves would fail.

Action plan

Tina was set "sexual homework" to carry out over the next few weeks. In the privacy of her bedroom, she set out to discover her body, how self-massage felt, and how genital massage worked. She found it difficult to experience an orgasm by using her fingers alone, but graduation to a vibrator helped the process, and she began to climax much more easily. Jerry was then asked to do a day of exploration in the form of sexual mapping with Tina (see p.75). This enabled him to become more comfortable with Tina's body, especially her genitals. Next, he was asked to learn how Tina stimulated herself with the vibrator. The young couple discovered that they could incorporate the vibrator with intercourse and both felt a lot happier and more satisfied with their sex life.

Coping with infidelity

THE 21ST CENTURY is giving rise to some sophisticated relationship experiments. Perhaps the trickiest is the open partnership, where you know that at least one of you has sex with someone else. It may surprise you to learn that even open relationships must conform to a structure. One vital ingredient is the agreement to put the primary partner first. Nevertheless, it takes oceans of self-confidence to weather the insecurities such a set-up induces – as Lucy was finding out.

The case

Lucy had settled for a relationship with Chris where she knew he occasionally had sex with other women. She didn't like it, but maturely accepted that Chris still had a lot of growing up to do. Recently, Chris's job had changed so that he was forced to live part of the time in New York. Lucy, for her part, was about to go away on a business trip herself, and became very anxious about leaving Chris. She couldn't stop crying and was incapacitated. This imminent change in lifestyle triggered Lucy's latent insecurity and she told him that she now wanted an assurance of fidelity and a commitment for future marriage or she would have to split from him. Chris, who insisted he loved Lucy, felt unable to give these promises. He was too young to marry, he argued, and too young to settle down. However, he didn't want to lose Lucy.

Therapist's assessment

Any woman would find such a situation hard, but Lucy's background of parents who divorced and a stepfather who disliked her meant that she was especially needy. As long as there was the stability of their joint home she had been able to cope, but rapid change with both of their jobs had knocked her for six. Her life felt unpleasantly transient, and there seemed nothing solid for her to fall back on at times when she suspected Chris might be with someone else.

Chris had not paid enough care and attention to the relationship to "balance the books". So far, Lucy had kept her anxieties at bay by seeing Chris return home to her after his trips. Now her impending departure had somehow upset the balance. It was clear that the couple had reached a "make or break point" over the tricky subject of sexual freedom. Although she wanted a promise of monogamy from Chris, she was able to understand during counselling that a less dramatic approach might be possible.

Action plan

Chris agreed not to see other women for the immediate time that Lucy would be away, which helped calm her present fears. Counselling helped Chris see why Lucy's background gave real ground for insecurity, and as a result he decided to sell her a share in his apartment so that she felt she had security in her "relationship investment". He also paid in work (on building a new kitchen) into their home to give Lucy reassurance that he was committed to their relationship without marriage. These moves gave Lucy the feeling of "grounding" she had previously lacked, and the couple recovered their happiness. Chris did eventually settle down, although this process did not happen immediately. An exercise which helped the couple work out what were their true priorities was the "I should" exercise (see below).

"I SHOULD" *exercise*

THIS EXERCISE IS USEFUL when you and your partner have agreed to make some changes to the pattern of your relationship but are finding them hard to implement. It helps you understand your priorities and to put plan into action:

1. Each write a list of the actions you think you ought to take to bring about the changes you've agreed on.
2. Number them in order of difficulty.
3. Act on your respective lists, starting with the easiest and working your way up to the most difficult.

Erections in later life

MANY OF US OPTIMISTICALLY ASSUME our sexuality will remain the same for the whole of adult life. It comes as a shock, therefore, to discover that it alters as we age. Often this becomes a cause for depression. Yet sexual change is inevitable for all of us and if you are prepared for it, you tend to deal with it better. One regular change for both women and men can be that actual physical sensation becomes lessened, as was the case for Charles, who began to experience erectile dysfunction.

The case

Charles and Audrey had been married for 30 years. Their sex life had been a source of satisfaction for most of that time, but now the couple had become anxious. Audrey reported that Charles seemed no longer able to make love. Although he could get a preliminary erection, he couldn't sustain it. Lately, it was getting difficult to even start an erection. He was worried and frightened by this turn of events and she, although no longer as sexually driven as she had been in her youth, missed the intimacy of intercourse. The couple had heard of the newer sex aids and drugs. Would any of these help, they wondered?

Therapist's assessment

The first thing to discover was what was going on in Charles' body, so he was referred to a doctor specializing in sexual medicine. After careful examination, history taking, and blood tests, it was established that Charles was in good health (his blood pressure was fine), although his testosterone count was down (but no more than was normal for his age) and physically he was of course aging. Because of this, he might need much stronger stimulation than Audrey had been used to giving him. Older men regularly need harder, firmer stimulation of the penis for it to have the same impact as in former, more sensitive years. Another possibility that needed exploring was that Charles may have a problem called venous leakage.

WARNING

NEVER USE RUBBER BANDS as a penis ring. Medically designed penis rings can be bought from reputable pharmacies and chemists (see p.207).

SEX FACTS

VENOUS LEAKAGE

Venous leakage describes a problem where the blood flows into the penis during arousal causing an erection, but then flows out of the penis, leaving it limp. Normally, there is a kind of "automatic locking system" at the base of the penis that "locks" the blood flow in and maintains the erection. With age, the locking system deteriorates so that the blood slowly drains out of the penis thus deflating the erection.

Action plan

Charles was asked to take Viagra before intercourse (see p.207). This medication is often used as a diagnostic tool for identifying venous leakage. While most men find that Viagra will give them longer, more sustained erections, if a man has venous leakage the blood flow simply drains out of the penis again in spite of the drug.

In Charles' case, the Viagra showed that he did indeed have venous leakage, which meant the medical profession now knew what was going on and were able to prescribe correctly. Charles was advised to use a medical ring. This clamps around the base of the penis tightly enough to keep the blood flow in the erection but not so tightly that it is dangerous. In addition, Audrey was taught how to stimulate Charles by hand, and how to squeeze his penis harder, which made turn-on much more pleasurable. A combination of stronger stimulation and use of the penis ring meant that this couple's sex life was restored.

Communicating under stress

IF YOU LOSE SIGHT of what's happening in your partner's life, your relationship can suffer greatly. Any external pressures that he or she may be experiencing outside the home will have repercussions on you. Exam panic, for example, frequently turns people off sex. If you don't understand the connection between your partner's stress and lack of sexual interest, you might feel personally rejected. In order to have an accurate picture of your partner's emotions, it's vital to cultivate the quality of empathy.

The case

When Diana returned to full-time education as a mature student and studied for her degree, she found the anxiety about achievement and examinations troubling. A side-effect of this stress was that she could not raise much enthusiasm for sex with Bill, her husband. Bill complained that she was preoccupied, tense, and irritable with him for wanting her attention. The end result was that Bill and Diana's sex life had virtually ceased. Diana was tired of Bill's lack of understanding; Bill was fed up with being ignored and criticized.

Diana pointed out that her exams were only eight weeks away, and that afterwards all stress would be removed and everything would get back to normal. Bill didn't understand, and he accused her of being obsessive about her work and was convinced that she was giving him a deeper, more sinister message.

Therapist's assessment

Stress notoriously lowers testosterone levels and depletes sex drive. Bill needed to understand that Diana's temporarily diminished libido was normal for her circumstances and was a response to external factors rather than having anything to do with him. However, his tantrum-style behaviour made things worse: not only did it make him seem childish, which turned Diana off yet further, but his anger was frightening, and fear often makes many women sexually "frozen". For her part, Diana needed to understand just how bereft and uncertain Bill was feeling. Once she could sympathize with these emotions, she would feel much warmer towards him.

Action plan

In therapy, Diana was encouraged to tell Bill how much she loved him and was still attracted to him. She was also encouraged to give him lots of kisses and cuddles at home to make up for the bereft feelings he was clearly experiencing. Bill needed to understand how his temper tantrums affected Diana's feelings and her ability to feel sexy towards him. So that Bill could get a visual idea of what she meant, the couple did the "Hot and cold" exercise

(see below). Bill came away from therapy understanding that he had been equating lovemaking with sex (a common misbelief) and that just because there was less sex, it did not mean he was loved less. Before long, the couple were making love again.

HOT AND COLD *exercise*

THIS IS A USEFUL METHOD of judging whether you have gone far enough towards meeting your partner's needs when negotiating. When you have an issue to discuss, stand a few metres apart from each other and place a chair between you. As your partner talks, move nearer to the chair if you feel positively towards him or her, i.e. "hot", and move away from the chair if you feel unsympathetic, angry, or distant, i.e. "cold". Reverse the exercise when it's your turn to speak. Since you can both literally see how "hot" or "cold" the other person is feeling, you should be able to understand each other better and therefore communicate more effectively.

Balancing mismatched libidos

THE UNEVEN SITUATION of mismatched libidos – when one person desires more sex than his or her partner – is particularly eroding. The person who wants sex feels as if he or she is always in the position of a supplicant, while the one who appears to be "denying" sex gives the impression of being a passive controller. In Faye's case (see below), she began to feel that she must be sexually unattractive to her partner, while Robert began to question his virility.

The case

Faye and Robert had fallen in love and enjoyed a good sex life for two years. Yet now that the couple were married and living together full time, Faye was disturbed to find that they didn't make love nearly as much as she had expected, or indeed wanted. After a year, Faye was worried enough to seek professional advice. "I'm lucky if we have sex once a week," she confided. "For two healthy people in their twenties, just married, that doesn't feel right."

The difficulty was the fact that Faye frequently found herself keen to have sex, yet six times out of seven was turned down. This does not do a lot for the ego. "I'm wondering if he feels he made a mistake in marrying, or even if he has another lover? I'm getting awfully depressed," she said. Robert, who looked uneasy and guilty, assured Faye that he certainly didn't have or want anyone else, and that he felt content with Faye but just didn't feel that sexy.

Therapist's assessment

When we looked at Robert's sexual history, a pattern emerged. Although Robert had masturbated, he didn't do so until his early twenties, and then not very often. He had had one sexual relationship before Faye, in which the young woman he had been with had left him for another man. Far from having or wanting another lover, Robert was really not very interested in sex at all. Some people naturally like a lot of sex, others naturally don't. Robert fell into the latter category. He and Faye were suffering from a problem of mismatched libidos and, not surprisingly, this created difficulties.

Action plan

Faye found it comforting to learn that she was not personally responsible for Robert's lack of interest. However, she was still left with a lot of sexual energy that had nowhere to go. Several options were offered to Robert and Faye but, of course, it was up them to choose whichever seemed preferable. These options were:

- Faye might pleasure herself regularly, through masturbation or by using a vibrator, while Robert held her lovingly
- Robert and Faye might agree to undertake a "sex contract" (see below)
- Robert might like to seek medical advice about his low sex drive and see if he might be a candidate for testosterone supplements

In the event, Robert decided to seek medical advice as well as subscribing to the "sex contract" idea. Testosterone did increase his sexual desire, although not by a major amount, but the contract made each of them feel as if they had a bit more control over the situation than previously. This is because a contract gives you some choice in circumstances where previously you may have felt there was none.

THE SEX CONTRACT

MANY COUPLES find that a contract makes them feel that they are both getting a fair deal. In Robert and Faye's case, the rules of the sex contract were as follows:

- On three days of the week he chooses whether or not to have sex.
- On three nights of the week she chooses whether or not to have sex.
- The seventh night is left optional.

Controlling premature ejaculation

PREMATURE EJACULATION is generally a young man's problem. Most mature males don't have this difficulty; indeed, some men can last longer and become better lovers as they reach middle age. When young, most individuals with the problem have either needed to get sex over and done with quickly, or have done so once or twice by accident. They then somehow find themselves trapped in a pattern of over-rapid orgasm. Fortunately, premature ejaculation is one of the easiest sex problems to overcome.

The case

Caroline and John were a young couple and each other's first lover. When they arrived at the sex clinic, John was complaining that Caroline never experienced orgasm when they made love. When pressed about what actually happened between them, it soon became clear that the reason that Caroline was not climaxing was because John had his orgasm within about six thrusts of penetration.

Therapist's assessment

Ignorance about sexual needs meant that the couple had not realized that Caroline needed a lot more sexual attention before being ready for penetration. Caroline herself had never masturbated. John had tried masturbating himself to climax in advance of intercourse so that on a second occasion he would be slowed down, but this meant that either he found it difficult to get aroused for a second time or, if he did, that his climax happened just as quickly. When asked about how he first ever experienced orgasm, John revealed that it was in hurried circumstances, where he was fearful of being discovered. He had subconsciously "trained" himself to come quickly, and now he would have to alter his sexual pattern.

Action plan

The object of therapy was to slow John down and speed Caroline up. Caroline embarked on a self-discovery programme to learn her sexual response pattern (this involved experimenting with self-touch, see pp.70–71), and the couple explored mutual masturbation and vibrators together. John experienced pride when he managed to give Caroline her first orgasm this way. He and Caroline learned how long it took to get her close to climax, and the pair incorporated this timing into their lovemaking.

However, John still climaxed too fast for satisfactory intercourse. He and Caroline next learned sensate focus massage (see p.203), and Caroline practised applying the squeeze technique to John at the point of no return, both during massage and during controlled sexual intercourse. Other methods or treatments that help premature ejaculation are as follows:

- Beautrais manoeuvre (see p.99)
- Pressing the Jen-Mo point (see p.123)
- If you are young, climaxing once in advance of the sex act, although this may not necessarily work
- In acute cases, opting for drug therapy in the form of medically prescribed beta-blocker drugs

---

SEXFACTS

PSYCHOLOGICAL CAUSES

The causes of premature ejaculation can be complex and may not have anything to do with early sexual experience. Therapists occasionally see the following scenario: a female, previously anorgasmic, finally learns how to climax. When she lets her man know, he becomes a premature ejaculator. He has subconsciously been maintaining a feeling of superiority over his partner, and when the reason for this is removed he feels threatened. As a "defence measure" he retreats into premature ejaculation.

Rekindling sexual excitement

IT APPEARS TO BE NORMAL to experience less desire for a beloved partner after several years of living together. This lessened desire does *not* in most cases indicate lessened love; instead, the nature of love changes from intense passion of the early days to tender affection. For many couples, this state of affairs is fine. However, occasionally one partner suddenly craves more, and his or her thoughts begin to stray. Fortunately, there are now behavioural programmes that couples can embark on to improve loving.

The case

Marion and George had been happily married for 12 years. George worked as an insurance broker, and Marion was a homemaker and part-time accountant. Everyday life was routine, but the couple liked it like that. Unfortunately, there was one flaw – the number of times this couple had sex during the past few years had dwindled. This had only recently become a problem when George realized that he was getting very sexually attracted to a work colleague. Since the colleague had done absolutely nothing to lead him on, he decided that his lust might be down to sexual boredom; the constant predictability of sex at home was giving him yearnings for something else. And, since the marriage was generally a good one, he had discussed the problem with his wife. Both decided to go to counselling.

Therapist's assessment

In therapy, George and Marion expressed their willingness to do absolutely anything to change. The trouble was in knowing where to start. When they learned that most couples fall into a sex pattern within the first six months to a year of a sexual relationship, and subsequently stay in it, this was both comforting and dismaying, since it was the sex routine that seemed no longer enough for George. But listening to all the other aspects of this couples' life made both the therapist and the couple realize how little else in the way of novelty of any sort was experienced – the couple hardly ever went out in the evenings, preferring to eat in and watch television instead of going to the movies or visiting mutual friends. They all came to the conclusion that this marriage needed shaking up a little.

Action plan

The couple needed to re-make intimate connections and to undertake more activities together. Apart from being asked to find an enjoyable joint mutual project to take them outside the home, they were also advised to follow a marital harmony programme as well as a "re-learning sex" routine (see below). Interestingly, they reported that the marital harmony programme was most effective, because it stirred up tender emotions and put them in touch with the youngsters they had once been.

Marital harmony programme
You are asked to reminisce about:
- Early meetings
- First romantic feelings
- What appealed about the other when you first met
- What you liked about him or her as the early weeks went by

You are asked to say something positive about your partner at least three times every day – for the rest of your married life!

RE-LEARNING SEX

CLAIR HAWES, a clinical psychologist from Vancouver, suggests concentrating on the small things that give sex meaning, such as the following:

- Being sensitive to each other's mood during intercourse
- Carving out private time for intimacy
- Deliberately giving each other's body more loving stimulation, possibly in the shape of a sensual massage

Understanding selective impotence

THE MIND IS A STRANGE and powerful organ. Even though you feel passionate desire for a partner, there are no guarantees (if you are a man) that you can be actively sexual. This is because erections are at the mercy of the autonomic nervous system. Put simply, you can't will an erection: it needs a blend of desire, erotic stimulation, and relaxation. Sometimes memories of a "significant other", just at the crucial moment, are enough to put a dampener on the proceedings, as Jeremy and Gloria discovered.

The case

Jeremy was concerned because although he could still make love to his wife of some 25 years, he was impotent with Gloria, his mistress. He was frustrated and angry by this state of affairs, since he certainly did desire Gloria, but his erection would disappear most inconveniently. The reason why Jeremy had wanted this extra-marital relationship was because he and his wife had been each other's only lovers and suddenly, in middle age, he had panicked. He didn't want to go to his death feeling that he had missed out on a major part of life, and was determined to experience sex with another woman. He was equally adamant that he wanted to stay in his marriage. Jeremy attended counselling on his own, although Gloria had expressed her willingness to attend with him.

Therapist's assessment

When asked what actually happened during lovemaking, Jeremy described thinking about his wife at the point of penetration and, not surprisingly, it put him off. He was angry with himself, but insisted that he did not feel guilty about seeking another sex partner. He had been thinking about taking Viagra to get him over this situation, and asked the therapist if it would be wise.

It's not up to the therapist to make moral judgments, but it is important that the client understands his or her feelings in order to make careful decisions. Jeremy had little insight into the cause of his selective impotence. He may not have felt guilty (although this was debatable), but unconsciously he may have felt that he was risking his marriage, and his loss of erection was acting as a kind of warning system. Despite this, he still came to the conclusion that it was important for him to be able to make love to Gloria.

Action plan

The therapist asked Jeremy to draw up a list of priorities (see below). Interestingly, at the top of the list was his marriage. Despite this, Jeremy still decided to take Viagra so that he could have sex with Gloria. Although Viagra helped him to sustain an erection, his relationship with Gloria did not last long, partly as a result of Jeremy feeling he had satisfied his sexual curiosity, but also because Gloria sensed his lack of real involvement with her. A follow-up session with the therapist a year later showed that Jeremy was much happier about his marriage. He was asked to draw up a new list of priorities, and this one no longer included "catching up with my sex life".

PRIORITIES *exercise*

THE CLIENT IS ASKED to make a list of ten priorities. He or she is then asked to number the priorities in order of importance, from one to ten. The purpose of the exercise is to get life's objectives clear so that subsequent behaviour does not sabotage the really important issues. If you put marriage at the top of the list, it means you would be wise to safeguard it, even though you also want other life experiences. However, if you put sexual adventure at the top, this might indicate you are unconsciously moving away from your marriage.

Dealing with a partner's depression

IF ONE PARTNER starts to suffer from depression, the "dark cloud" hangs not just over the head of the sufferer, but it often floats over to other members of the family, having a negative affect on everyone in the household. Depression often causes an otherwise good sex life to dwindle or cease altogether (see pp.204–205). If you have little insight into your partner's moods, you won't realize that it's their depression that's causing the problems, and the odds are that you'll start thinking that *you* are at fault.

The case

Maria believed that she was to blame for her husband Julio's lack of sexual interest. She had tried all the tricks in the book to entice him, such as dressing up in sexy black underwear and trying to seduce him, but that hadn't helped. Julio remained sullen and unresponsive. Now Maria felt depressed, and thought that she had lost her powers of attraction. She loved her husband deeply and felt entirely at fault. Maria attended counselling without Julio, who refused to accompany her.

Therapist's assessment

When Maria was asked about the other things that might be going on in Julio's life, she described a man beset with oppressive responsibility. Julio was worried that his business was failing. He had been desperately trying to improve sales, knowing that the livelihood of several members of his family depended on it. Maria said that she had done her best to be supportive, but now Julio refused to talk about anything at all to her. The more she described him, the more it became apparent that here was a man who was so depressed he could hardly speak, let alone feel sexy. Unfortunately, Maria had had no insight into Julio's worries. She could only see the waning sexual interest and was concerned that he had lost interest in her.

Depression has a direct effect on sexual desire. It affects hormonal balance, and actually lowers testosterone levels so much that the sufferer can no longer feel sexual. The good news is that as depression lifts, sexual desire returns. Once Maria learned that it was not she who was at fault but external factors that were causing the problems, her own depression lifted and she was able to act.

Action plan

The first move Maria made was to stop pestering Julio for sex. Instead, she offered him support and sympathy and offered any help she might give in getting the business problems sorted out. The simple expedient of refraining from adding to the pressures in her husband's life helped to steer their relationship back on course. Once things had settled down, and Julio began to feel more in control of his life, his sex drive slowly returned and the couple resumed their sex life.

DEALING WITH SEXUAL DEPRESSION

A MAN WHO IS WORRIED about depression-related impotence could do the following:

- Check there is no underlying physical cause for his symptoms by having a medical check-up
- Reassess his lifestyle to find ways of reducing stress
- Practise self-stimulation; unlike intercourse, masturbation involves no real or imagined pressure to perform, and can build sexual confidence

If depression is linked to fears about a relationship, seeking counselling might be the most direct way to find out exactly where you stand with your partner. It will also provide practical methods to help you improve your relationship. If depression becomes acute or persistent, it is important to seek medical help.

Restoring sexual confidence

FREQUENT CRITICISM OF A PARTNER is an extremely common way of killing off a previously good sexual relationship. It may destroy the criticized person's confidence to such an extent that he or she retreats inwards and becomes quite incapable of responding joyfully to sex and many other aspects of life. Continual criticism is a kind of verbal abuse, a vocal weapon of brutal control. It has almost certainly been learned within the family of origin and is used (erroneously) to feel superior.

The case

Leon and Michele had been married for three years and came to the sex therapy clinic in great distress. Michele complained that Leon had completely destroyed her confidence by continually criticizing her in bed. Unsurprisingly, this had the immediate effect of making her withdraw. She had not felt anything sexual for the last six months, and now tried to avoid sex whenever possible. She had, she said, been perfectly happy about her sexuality prior to the relationship with Leon, but currently felt so destroyed by her husband's remarks that she wanted a divorce.

Therapist's assessment

Sexual criticism can be peculiarly destructive for both men and women. The act of sex is of necessity an extremely intimate one, where each individual displays themselves at their most vulnerable. Criticism therefore strikes at that inner vulnerability. The most confident people can be destroyed by being told that they're bad in bed. But Leon didn't just criticize his wife, he criticized everyone. It turned out to be his way of dealing with the world. Why did he do it? He had inherited the idea from his father, who had done the same. Both Leon and his father had felt insecure and inferior. Making someone else feel bad was their way of feeling superior.

When a habit is ingrained, it's extremely difficult to "unlearn". However, when Leon understood what he was doing he became despairing, because he realized that he was likely to repeat his behaviour. As a result, he became highly motivated for change.

Action plan

There were two routes this couple needed to take in order to give them any real hope for the future. The first (and imperative) route was for Leon to go into psychotherapy and examine his inferiority feelings and his ingrained self-defence method. The second was for the couple to do the "Acting as if" exercise (see below).

In order to give these two routes any possibility of working, the couple also needed to make a time commitment to each other. Overcoming a lifetime of criticism was not something that would improve overnight. Although Michele was reluctant to give this commitment, she did eventually agree to stay with Leon for another six months. And at the end of that six months she agreed for a further six months. Leon and Michele also agreed on a code word that Michele was to use the minute Leon went back to his destructive behaviour. On hearing the word, Leon agreed that he would stop immediately. This at least guaranteed Michele some respite.

A year later, Leon was making huge efforts to change, and Michele felt better enough to acknowledge his efforts and appreciate them. The "Acting as if" programme had also made a major improvement.

ACTING AS IF *exercise*

THIS MEANS THAT A COUPLE (or an individuals) are encouraged to behave "as if" something were true. For example, you may be encouraged to carry out sensate focus exercises (see p.203), acting "as if" you really wanted to do them. The idea behind this is that you will, with some luck, gain good feeling from the experience and will want to repeat it.

Overcoming inhibitions

THERE IS A SMALL MINORITY of women who suffer from "global inhibition" — that is, an overall inability to feel sexually excited. Sex research has not yet pinpointed the reasons for such behaviour, but explanations offered are that it is the result of upbringing, genetic inheritance, or an unusual balance of sex hormones. The real problems arrive when such a woman goes into a sexual relationship. She may find it very hard to respond sexually, with the result that her partner may become discouraged.

The case

Jean and Gary had been dating since Jean was 15. Now that she was 17, the couple were having a sexual relationship. However, all was not well. Gary was complaining that Jean seemed very unresponsive. Since the couple were intending to marry, both of them felt this was something that needed to be investigated. Gary, at 21, had had other sexual relationships and knew that Jean's behaviour "wasn't quite right" as he put it.

Therapist's assessment

Gary was a well-meaning young man but without great psychological skills. Although he didn't mean to criticize, his comments were interpreted as criticism with the result that Jean felt ashamed and unconfident. However, when Jean described what the couple actually did in bed it didn't sound as if she were over-modest, just a little shy. She found oral sex pretty unacceptable and didn't particularly like Gary stimulating her, but was perfectly happy to stimulate him in just about every way. She did get sexually excited, but not for very long. Sooner rather than later she would reach an automatic "cut-off" point where all feeling dwindled.

Jean's mother was a quiet, shy woman who had deferred to her husband in almost everything. It's possible that Jean had "learned" timid behaviour from her mother, but there's also the possibility that she had inherited a tendency to be tentative and undemanding. Jean had been a nervous child, and her mother had been very protective. She had held Jean back rather than encourage her to cope with the real world by taking action, which may involve risk.

Action plan

Since it was almost impossible for the therapist to ascertain the origin of Jean's meekness and lack of sexual interest, the problem had to be approached in two ways. The first was based on the assumption that Jean learned her behaviour from her mother. She was asked to perform a simple assertion exercise (see below), and to experiment with using a vibrator. With many women, these avenues are enough to trigger them into sexual life. Once people have experienced orgasm, their behaviour tends to alter.

Jean, however, did not respond to this "homework", although Gary manfully assisted her. This meant that Jean might be one of the tiny percentage of women who suffer from a kind of "global inhibition". No one quite knows what causes this, but the most prevalent theory today is that it is possibly a chemical imbalance. Jean was prescribed a drug called phentolamine, which works on the sexual brain centres with the result of lowering inhibition. This made a difference, and Jean did acquire sexual response — enough to see her through to having a climax. Gary began to relax and the relationship improved greatly.

ASSERTION *exercise*

MAKE A LIST OF TEN THINGS you want to achieve and number them in order of difficulty. Then, starting with the easiest, work your way up the list. If at any time you get stuck, go back a step. The joy of the exercise is that as you begin to achieve you gain a sense of satisfaction and your confidence grows. Many women with sexual inhibition find this new self-confidence enough to make them determined to act in a way they might have previously feared.

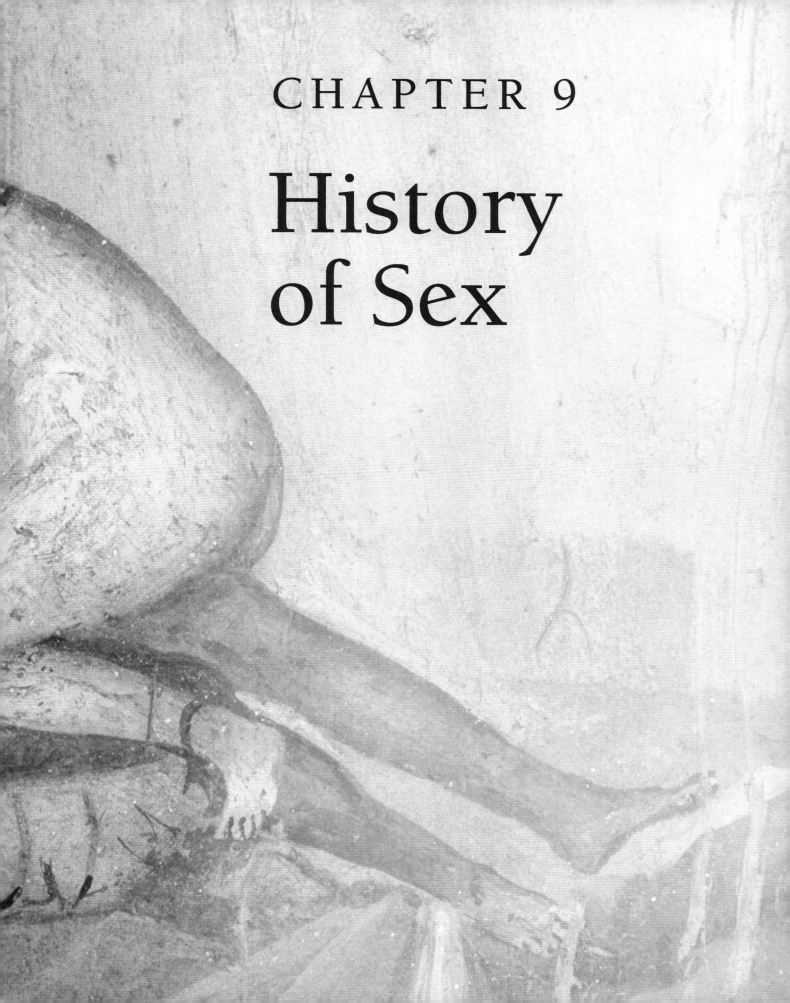

CHAPTER 9
History of Sex

sophisticated

CREATIVE

UNINHIBITED

permissive

PRE-HISTORY

HOW SEXY WERE OUR very earliest ancestors?
The truthful answer is we don't really know.
We know that the Cro-Magnon people, who
lived in Eurasia around 30,000–10,000 BC, were
physically much like us, and that their brains were
much the same. Whether their attitudes towards
sex were in any way similar to ours, however, is
almost impossible to tell.

Across the world, paintings, carvings,
and engravings have been discovered
that provide us with certain clues
about the lifestyle of early peoples.
Of course, there are hundreds of
possible interpretations of these works
of art, and we can only guess what
they signified in terms of cultural
beliefs. But it does appear that sex
played an important part in the
lives of our ancestors.

have been found in North
Africa showing men
copulating with giraffes,
elephants, and rhinos
(which would be
physically almost
impossible) suggests

Early sex drawings

The Cro-Magnons were hunter-
gatherers who made use of
caves as homes and ritual sites.
Thousands of years later, some of
these sites have been rediscovered,
complete with the images their
occupants painted on the walls.

The pictures show a variety of
sexual activities, including intercourse
with animals. It is not clear, however,
whether this was common practice. It
appears that our earliest ancestors may
have associated sex with magic: the
men in these cave paintings are
usually wearing animal masks and are
generally considered to be shamans,
priests, or healers, perhaps performing
some kind of ritual to move into the
spirit world. The fact that engravings

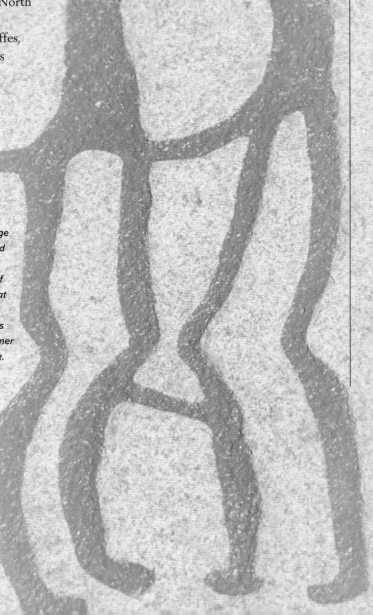

*THE LOVERS, a bronze age
rock carving from around
1,000 BC, was found in
the Bohuslan Province of
Sweden. It is thought that
the figure on the left is
male (with an erect penis
and sword) and his partner
(with long hair) is female.*

that these images are not true to life. Instead, they may depict mythical beings or perhaps symbolize human domination over beasts.

The Venus figurines

Small Palaeolithic statues of the female form, all sharing the same characteristics, have been found across an area of Europe stretching from France to Russia. These female figurines, known as Venuses, were made with highly exaggerated breasts, stomachs, and buttocks but have no facial features, and often no feet. The most famous figurine is known as the Willendorf Venus, named after the Austrian town in which she was found (see right).

THIS CAVE PAINTING from Les Trois Frères caves in France depicts a shaman dressed in a goat skin pursuing two animals, possibly with sexual intent. The painting dates from c.15,000–10,000 BC.

It is likely that these figures are fertility charms. For prehistoric people, life was tough and short, and reproductive success therefore a concern. In 20,000 BC, a woman's childbearing years were limited.

While we cannot be sure about the religious beliefs of Cro-Magnon people, it is clear that Venus figures from a later period had religious significance. By c.6,000 BC, an agricultural way of life had developed in Iran, India, and the Mediterranean, and a definite cult had emerged concerned with a Mother Goddess. The cult was not just about the fertility of individuals, but rather the fertility of the land they farmed and the cycle of birth, life, and death. Archaeologists have discovered shrines in Turkey containing terracotta images of the Goddess giving birth (sometimes to a bull or a ram!).

The nature of sexual practices in later history is clearer, with the advent of writing, especially in ancient Greece and Rome (see pp.246–47).

LANDSCAPED SEX

FERTILITY MONUMENTS on a massive scale show the importance of sex in the lives of ancient Britons. Silbury Hill in Wiltshire – an enormous man-made mound dating back to 2,600 BC – is thought to represent a pregnant Mother Goddess. Another prehistoric monument is the Cerne Abbas Giant, a huge naked man carved into a chalk hillside in Dorset. Infertile couples still make love on the giant's penis in the hope of conceiving a child.

THE WILLENDORF VENUS was carved some time between 22,000–18,000 BC. Her skinny arms rest on massive breasts; her tiny legs almost vanish under the mass of her belly and buttocks. Her hair is apparently shaped into curls, though some people have suggested she is wearing a ceremonial cap. She is just over 10cm (4in) tall.

CLASSICAL SEX

THE COLOURFUL MYTHOLOGY of the Greeks has horses seducing nymphs and maidens, and Eros firing arrows of passion into young men and women. In the sophisticated, decadent society of ancient Rome, the ruling classes enjoyed an immense variety of sexual diversions, and many of their sexual exploits – especially those of the emperors – are notorious.

THIS ROMAN CLAY MEDALLION is one example of the explicit sexual imagery that was commonly used in classical art.

Men and women in ancient Greece led very different lives. Women had no rights, were under the rulership of their male kin, were kept in segregated parts of the house, and were considered as breeding stock. While a husband could not be divorced for adultery or pederasty, and could keep concubines as secondary wives, a wife would be harshly punished for being unfaithful.

In ancient Rome, attitudes to sex were extremely liberal – at least for the upper classes. This sexual freedom extended to wealthy women, provided they were not too public about their activities. Some, such as the emperor Claudius's notorious wife Messalina, had dozens of sexual partners.

Prostitution

In ancient Greece, in addition to prostitutes who sold their services for cash, there were professional female companions known as *hetaeras*. *Hetaeras* were educated, cultivated, and accomplished, and they received gifts rather than money. While many offered sex as part of their services (those who did often insisted on anal intercourse as a contraceptive measure), some were nothing but friends to their rich and powerful clients.

In Rome, prostitutes, female and male, were readily available for those who wanted a change from their spouse or regular lover, or who required some special services. The major cities included "red-light districts", and to this day visitors to Pompeii can view the sex scenes luridly depicted on the wall decoration of one of the houses.

PRIAPUS, THE GREEK GOD of fertility and horticulture, and protector of domestic animals, is always represented with a huge penis – a threat to trespassers and thieves.

HISTORY FACTS

EARLY ADVERTISING
A pair of leather sandals belonging to a Greek prostitute has survived over the centuries. Studs on the soles imprinted the message "Follow me" into the earth as she walked.

GREEK VASE PAINTING often depicts popular sex positions. According to Aristophanes (438–380 BC), the one shown here is kubda. Lordo *is similar except that the woman leans back on the man's chest. In* keles *(racehorse), the woman sits astride the man.*

Sexual culture

Like the Greeks, the Romans enjoyed erotic art, often decorating dishes and vases with sex scenes, and they made couches, tables, and chairs with phalluses for arms and legs. They generally used the same sexual positions as the Greeks, but they had rules about who did what to whom. For example, it was felt unnatural for a woman to be on top, although many surviving examples of erotica show this "forbidden" position.

Roman sexuality has a cruel element not found in ancient Greece. The Roman Games often included acts in which women prisoners were raped by animals. And although incest was a crime, the rulers got away with it: Caligula bedded his three sisters, and Nero slept with his mother. Roman sexuality is often associated with the orgy. This wild overdosing on sex, food, and drink originated as a religious feast linked to ecstatic cults, such as those of Bacchus, although in time the religious connotations lost their significance.

In the sexually segregated world of ancient Greece, masturbation was considered a healthy way of relieving sexual tensions, and the dildo (*olisbos*), usually made of olivewood padded with leather, was extremely popular as a substitute for a man.

Given the status of women in ancient Greece, it is perhaps surprising that the most famous classical sex manual was written (in the 2nd century AD) by a woman, Philaenis of Samos. Only fragments of the book survive, but it is thought that it may

have included material on lesbian acts. No such handbooks survive from ancient Rome, although it is highly likely that they did exist.

Homosexuality

For the Ancient Greeks, homosexuality involved an elaborate social rite, especially between an older man and a youth. The elder was expected to help educate and protect the younger, and teach him the ways of the world; the younger man's role was to satisfy his mentor's sexual appetites. Lesbians, called *tribades*, were also in evidence. The most famous of these was the poet Sappho, whose home island Lesbos gave us the term "lesbian".

Both homosexuality and bisexuality were acceptable in ancient Rome, and many of the emperors enjoyed bisexual relationships. Julius Caesar's enemies called him "Every woman's husband and every man's wife".

THE PHALLUS was an important icon in classical society. The relief on the side of this monument in Delos depicts Dionysus (known by the Romans as "Bacchus"), the god of wine and intoxication.

CHRISTIANITY AND THE MEDIEVAL AGE

AS POWER IN EUROPE passed from the Roman Empire to the Christian Church, a liberal attitude to sexuality was replaced by a more austere doctrine. Despite this, the remnants of older traditions persisted at the fringes of society.

With the retreat of the Romans in the fifth century AD, some of the pre-Roman traditions of the indigenous people were revived. Among these were the customs of the Celts, whom Romans viewed as a barbaric people and the Christians viewed as pagans because they worshipped elements of nature, such as woods and streams. The Celts had a much more open view of sexuality than the Christians. Celtic religious men (druids) worshipped in sacred groves, often of oak trees, and sexuality played a central role in their religious ritual. Children were brought up in an environment free of the strictures of either Church or Empire, and sexual experimentation at an early age was accepted. In one account by the writer Drodorus, the druids are described as "offering their bodies to one another without further ado. This was not regarded as at all harmful; on the contrary, if they were rejected in their approaches, they felt insulted."

The Christians

The Celtic view of sexuality stood in direct contrast to the teachings of early Christianity. By the time of Pope Leo I (440–461), an organized Christian Church was gradually spreading all over western Europe in a hierarchy of bishops, provinces, and dioceses.

DESPITE THE MORAL MESSAGE *behind much Christian iconography, Christian art is often explicitly sensual, as is apparent in this depiction of Adam and Eve.*

HIERONYMUS BOSCH'S complex allegory of the deadly sins (lust is shown here) is typical of medieval imagery in its association of sexuality with the basest human instincts.

As the Roman Empire crumbled between the fifth and seventh centuries, the local church became the focal point of many communities, and the influence of the Christian Church's codes of conduct increased. There were strict guidelines for sexual behaviour: chastity, particularly for women, became a prerequisite; adultery, masturbation, and homosexuality were all declared sinful; and only sex within marriage in order to have children was acceptable. Saint Paul had declared that celibacy was preferable to marriage, and sex in all its forms became synonymous with sin and the fall of Adam and Eve. Early Church Fathers such as Saint Jerome and Saint Augustine successfully linked sex with a failure to obey God. (It took several centuries, however, to convince the priesthood to give up sex, and the promiscuous cleric was a stereotype of medieval art and literature.)

In contrast to the austere rules governing Christian sexuality, older, more liberal traditions survived. One such is the practice of maypole dancing performed throughout many centres in Europe, usually at the beginning of May (a festival called Beltane). This is the last remnant of pre-Roman phallic worship, and it had originally involved parading a giant penis through the centre of the town. Other examples are erotic carvings, including those of Sheila na Gig, the goddess of fertility in Celtic mythology. She is often shown holding her vagina open with both hands in an attempt to allay the power of death. Strangely, this pagan figure appears on Christian buildings, where she is portrayed as a female demon to ward off evil. Many of the figures found on pre-16th century churches and early monasteries in Ireland, England, Scotland, and Germany, were removed during the 19th century.

The Crusades

Among the most influential events of the late medieval period were the Crusades. This counter-offensive against the incursions of Islam, which began in 1096, and the pilgrimages to the Holy Land that it spawned, brought Europeans into contact with a different culture. From this period dates the concept of Courtly Love, based on the Islamic idea of Pure Love. This manifested itself in the form of a dashing knight wooing a high-born and virtuous lady, a figure that in many cases would be unattainable.

The crusaders also brought back to northern Europe many exciting sex practices from the Arab world. From the 14th century, this opening up to influences from other parts of the world led to a loosening of restrictions in sexual matters. The reaction to this would come in the form of Puritanism.

COURTLY LOVE is portrayed in this illustration from the Romance of the Rose (1487–95), which shows the difficulty of expressing chaste love.

INDIA AND ARABIA

THE WESTERN WORLD owes much of its present-day sexual sophistication to the ideas and practices that hail from the very early civilizations of the East. In India, sex was being written about from as early as the 7th century BC. Arab culture also had a major influence on European sensuality.

The *Kama Sutra*, the famous 4th-century Indian sex classic, gives us a very good idea of how one of the most ancient civilizations practised sex. Sex was thought to be one of the great activities that could provide young men with a feeling of balance and well-being, known as *moksha*. Although women, of course, took part in this sexual activity it was for men that the *Kama Sutra* was devised.

Written by a Brahmin (Hindu priest) called Vatsyayana for young wealthy men of high caste, the *Kama Sutra* is more than simply an early sex manual. In addition to its famously explicit depiction of sex positions, it

EITHER ORIENTAL ILLUSTRATORS had a lively sense of humour or lovers were far more athletic than they are today. It takes great strength and stamina to make love in this position.

FAMOUS POSITIONS OF THE KAMA SUTRA

THE *KAMA SUTRA* is most famous for its depiction of sex positions, perhaps because these parts of the manuscript were most fascinating to Western minds.

THE SUSPENDED CONGRESS

The man leans against a wall, the woman puts her arms around his neck, and he lifts her by holding her thighs or by locking his hands beneath her bottom. She then pushes off with her feet firmly against the wall so that she is controlling intercourse.

THE SPLITTING OF A BAMBOO

From the basic man-on-top position the woman brings up one leg and wedges it over her man's shoulder. Then she brings this leg down and raises the other. "Splitting the bamboo" like this makes the vagina squeeze the penis, increasing the sensation for him.

THE CONGRESS OF A COW

Emulating the mating of animals can be particularly erotic for many men and women. Here the woman bends over so that her hands touch the ground.

contains a great deal of interesting information about other issues concerning love and manners, such as courting a young wife while she is only a teenager, coping with more than one wife, using magic potions and aphrodisiacs, and the value of food, music, and perfume in the art of seduction.

Tantric sex

Many of the ideas that are explored in the *Kama Sutra* are echoed by tantric sex (see pp.120–21), which came to prominence about four centuries later. The word "tantra", or "tantrism", is derived from the Tantras, a number of Sanskrit religious texts written in the 5th century AD. From these come particular systems of meditation practised in Hinduism and Buddhism.

Tantrism encapsulates the idea that the universe can be divided into male and female forces, and the object of tantric practice is to unite these male and female elements within the body. This idea embraces not just the sexual act, but just about every part of civilized life, taking in art, religious belief, and philosophy. There are many ways in which tantra can be explored and experienced. But one central belief links all these other parts together – the notion of ecstasy, which can be achieved through the sex act.

Arabian sex practices

The Christian knights who departed to fight the infidels during the Crusades (see p.249) met with standards of hygiene, luxury, and sensuality never known before in colder and more brutish Europe. Happily for their women back home, they imported these, and suddenly Europeans were bathing, using perfume, and generally discovering a far greater sensuality than they had hitherto experienced.

The Perfumed Garden

This was a sex manual written a long time after the Crusades by an enlightened and knowledgeable Arab called Sheik Nefzawi. In the male-dominated North African culture of the late 15th century, in which *The Perfumed Garden* was written, such a book would have been kept strictly hidden from the womenfolk.

The book was compiled as a manual of practical sex advice for men. In evocative and sometimes poetic language it describes what a man can do with his wife or mistress. Although it appears barely to touch upon the woman's personal experience, it becomes clear when you read through the original translation that Sheik Nefzawi was exceptionally knowledgeable about sex and that he gave advice that could entirely benefit the man's female partner.

SOME OF THE EARLY drawings of sex poses were intended to be more amusing than informative. This position would be nearly impossible.

PLEASING
THE WOMAN

ACCORDING TO SHEIKH NEFZAWI, the man deserving of success with females is "the one who is anxious to please them". In physical terms, when he is close to women "his member grows, gets strong, vigorous, and hard; he is not quick to discharge, and after the trembling caused by the emission of the sperm, he is soon stiff again. Such a man is relished and appreciated by women; this is because the woman loves the man only for sake of coition."

CHINA AND JAPAN

As in India and ancient Rome, sex in ancient China and Japan was seen as an art. It was considered a special experience that should not be spoken about publicly otherwise it would lose its special power. This appreciation of the arts of love is most clearly seen in the lovemaking of the Tao and the elaborate rituals of the geisha.

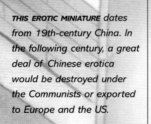

THIS EROTIC MINIATURE dates from 19th-century China. In the following century, a great deal of Chinese erotica would be destroyed under the Communists or exported to Europe and the US.

Ancient China and the Tao

Ancient China had a considerably more relaxed view of sexuality than the country did in later centuries. From about 200 BC, China produced some of the earliest sex manuals. They followed the Taoist view of sex (see pp.122–23), based on the principle of yin and yang, opposing male and females forces. Yin, the female principle, was seen as inexhaustible, while yang, the male principle, was limited. Balance could be achieved by the male refraining from ejaculation, and rules governed how often a man should ejaculate in order to maintain sexual power.

Confucianism

From the late 10th century AD, Confucianism had an increasingly strong hold over Chinese society and prescribed the "proper conduct" of virtuous women. The sole purpose of marriage was to produce male heirs, and only an individual's paternal relations were considered important. Strict rules governed the make-up of the family, with the roles of the sexes strongly differentiated. A married man could be accused of adultery only if he committed the act with a married woman, while a married woman would be accused of

adultery regardless of whether the man was married or single. In the higher reaches of society, men and women were separated during childhood, making all but the most ritualized of contact between the sexes impossible.

Footbinding

Around the middle of the 12th century, the practice of female footbinding began among court dancers. It spread throughout the court and then to the aristocracy. The process involved using tight bandages to force a child's feet to bend back on themselves and to cease proper growth, effectively crippling women by preventing them from walking naturally. The stilted, mincing movement it produced was considered graceful, and was believed to keep the vagina tight. The real result was diseased and extremely painful feet. Bound feet and the consequent inability of the woman to do any work were a prerequisite of high social status.

Around the same period the rise of the mandarins, a political priesthood, led to increasing control over family life and intolerance of non-conformity. While polygamy was practised among the aristocracy, promiscuity was frowned upon among poorer people. The individual's morality was strictly controlled by the state and by its representatives at every level.

THIS COLOUR WOODBLOCK PRINT by the Japanese artist Torii Kiyonaga (1752–1815) is entitled Women of the Gay Quarters. *It shows geisha entertaining their clients in a tea house.*

Japanese pleasures

Like China, Japan was a conservative nation where contact between the sexes was highly ritualized. Homosexuality was illegal in mainstream society, yet it was considered acceptable within the samurai (as an older man and younger acolyte relationship).

With the Edo period (1603–1867) came the rise of the merchant class and the associated urban lifestyle of the "floating world" (*ukiyo*), which revolved around the pleasure-seeking centres of the theatre, tea house, and brothel. Here, high-ranking officials mixed with merchants and aristocrats. In the early 1600s, the rulers of Japan legalized prostitution in the red-light districts known as the *yoshiwara*. At the same time there also developed the culture of the geisha – not prostitutes but beautiful, refined, educated women who entertained their wealthy clients with conversation, dance, poetry, and singing. The geisha were renowned for their exquisite kimonos and elaborate hair and make-up. Their houses and the tea rooms they frequented became famous centres of culture. Many hired artists to paint their portrait and spread their fame, and an entire school of elegant woodblock prints grew up around the most celebrated geisha. More erotic arts and services were provided by the *yujos*, the prostitutes who worked in the pleasure quarters. The tradition of the geisha, however, continued, and as recently as the 1920s there were as many as 80,000 geisha working all over Japan. Today, the remaining geisha exist primarily as a result of the tourist trade.

PICTURES OF THE FLOATING WORLD (Ukiyo-e) *portrayed aspects of the arts, geisha, tea houses, beautiful women, and brothels.*

EXPLORATION AND IMPERIALISM

FROM THE MIDDLE OF THE 15th century to the end of the 19th century, the explorations of Europeans brought them into contact with peoples and sexual practices far outside their usual experience. This was to have profound effects on the people they colonized as well as on the Europeans themselves.

The Europeans' colonization of new lands had a devastating effect on the indigenous population, for they brought with them many infectious diseases, such as smallpox, to which the indigenous people had no immunity. Within a century of conquest, the people of the Yucatan, in Mexico, for example, had declined from 25 million to 1.5 million. Conversely, Europeans fell victim to diseases brought back from the Americas. When Spain sent an army to besiege the city of Naples a new disease developed. It was said to have been brought from America by Columbus's sailors. The French dubbed it "Neapolitan disease"; the Spaniards called it "French disease". Syphilis was to become one of the scourges of society for the next 400 years.

A more one-sided exchange occurred in the 19th century. In its earliest phase, European exploration was largely limited to outposts, ports, and military bases. After 1815, however, the world opened up to European trade and with this trade went the mores of the European mainland and Christian suppression of sexual matters and sexual activity. Casual sex indulged in for mere pleasure was prohibited and declared "unnatural" by colonial laws. Much of the cultural erotica of the subjugated states, such as the erotic temple carvings of India, was considered obscene. Attitudes and appetites that are today considered natural were declared beyond the pale by the European colonialists, anxious to crush all "subversion".

SPANISH CONQUISTADOR Hernando Cortez entering Mexico (1519–20). As here, European depictions of South and Central Americans tended to emphasize their sensuality.

HISTORY FACTS

SEX BARTERING

When European sailors first arrived on the shores of the Polynesian Islands in the 16th century they were enchanted by the bare-breasted native women who would make love in return for an iron nail or a length of cheap cloth. Before long, however, many islanders realized the exchange rate was unfair and demanded hatchets, needles, and fishhooks in payment for sex.

PAUL GAUGUIN'S stylized depictions of Tahitian women reveal the artist's fascination with their sensuality. Formerly a wealthy stockbroker, Gauguin fled Paris in 1891, leaving wife and children behind for what he believed to be the sexual paradise of the South Pacific.

The Pacific islands

The difference between the attitudes of the Europeans and those of the people they colonized was perhaps most apparent in the Pacific islands. Early European travellers were amazed by the islanders' attitudes towards their bodies and sex. The climate meant that little clothing was required, and nudity (though sometimes only among family groups) was not uncommon. However, customs and attitudes did vary between islands. Polynesia, Micronesia, and Melanesia, for example, had very different sexual beliefs and customs; and while incest was acceptable among the Hawaiians it was illegal among the Maoris of New Zealand.

European priests tried to restrict the Pacific islanders' practice of using a variety of sexual positions, insisting that only the one they deemed godly and correct should be permitted – the one the natives contemptuously termed the "missionary" position.

Samoa

One of the most closely studied societies of the South Pacific in terms of its sexual life is that of Samoa. It was studied in the mid-20th century, when it appeared to have changed little since the 18th century. Samoan society was organized around family groups. Life was lived quite publicly, with children seeing birth, death, and sexual activity in the home. The Samoans regarded sex as an appetite to be satisfied and did not attach strong emotional significance to it. An absent husband would expect his wife to be unfaithful, and vice versa. Girls enjoyed a good lover without feeling obliged to fall in love with him.

Sexual relations outside marriage, conducted between people of the same age, were indulged in for pleasure, although this might lead to marriage. Couples would meet in "secret", called "meeting under the palms"; sometimes they would elope, although they would make sure that everyone was aware of the elopement well in advance. Rape occurred only rarely, but there was a form of it called *moetotolo* (night crawling). A *moetotolo* would sneak into a woman's house and enjoy the woman by pretending to be her lover. If caught, the *moetotolo* would become the subject of mockery and children would follow him about singing rude songs about him.

HISTORY FACTS

MAKING THE LINK

Until the 1930s, the Solomon Islanders did not make the connection between intercourse and conception. They held a hedonistic attitude to sexual matters, maintaining that sex was for pleasure while pregnancy was the work of ancestor spirits.

THE VICTORIANS

WE OFTEN THINK OF THE 19th century as a period of extremely conservative attitudes to sex. In fact, it was a time of great social upheaval in the West and one in which the advent of science – and particularly the influence of medicine – changed understanding of the nature of sex for good. Many of the beliefs and customs of this era persist in some form to the present day.

Towards the end of the 18th century, major economic changes occurred in western Europe. Industrialization and the growth of cities had led to dramatic overcrowding, and had disrupted patterns of social behaviour that had existed since the medieval period. This had a great impact on the way that people behaved sexually. Young people flocked to the burgeoning cities, often to encounter situations of immense poverty and squalor and an absence of the normal controls of sexual behaviour. Slums housed several people to a room, and the new metropolises offered abundant opportunities for sexual encounters. There was a genuine unease about the role of women, and images of women tended to fall into two categories: the good wife at home and the prostitute. Young women unable to make ends meet turned to prostitution, their trade hidden in the anonymity of the cities.

The family

In contrast to the squalid underground of prostitution and vice shone the image of the family unit. (In fact, while the wife was exhausted by numerous births, the husband would often keep a mistress or frequent prostitutes.) Attempts to impose family morality stifled discussion about sex. In 1802, the Society for the Suppression of Vice was formed and over the next century took out a series of prosecutions for obscenity. The result was ignorance of sex and even of basic anatomy. Marie Stopes (see p.259), interviewing an elderly man who in 1880 had been a young husband, claimed that when his wife had an orgasm he was "frightened and thought it was some kind of fit".

Science

Some improvement in information about sex came with the rise of science, although many writings on the subject were part guesswork. Victorian theorists, such as the philosopher and sociologist Herbert Spencer (1820–1903), believed that men were the active agents sexually, expending "catabolic" energy, while

VICTORIAN PORNOGRAPHY exploited all the props of the photographer's studio. Here, the set is dressed to evoke a kind of Arabian exoticism.

THE AWAKENING CONSCIENCE, *an allegorical painting by William Holman Hunt (1825–1910), conveys the stifling nature of Victorian sexuality. His model was Annie Miller, a young woman from the slums of Chelsea who became his girlfriend. The symbolism in the painting points to the figure being a "kept woman".*

IN THE LATE 19th century, Paris became a centre of hedonism, with revues such as the Folies-Bergère (first staged in 1866).

sedentary, passive women stored and conserved their "anabolic" energy. It was not until the 1850s that it was actually determined how the sperm fertilized the egg. The second half of the century saw a sudden explosion of scientific study as money from industry poured into the newly formed sciences.

Science also led to more precise classification of sexual behaviour and distinction between normal and abnormal behaviour: it was in the 1880s that the terms "heterosexual" and "homosexual" were coined. Other scientific changes were more practical. Condoms had been available in London since the 1660s, but from the late 18th century improvements in rubber led to their being widely used for the first time. They were a necessary weapon in the war against sexually transmitted diseases, which were spreading in epidemic proportions through many urban centres at this time.

Victorian pornography

The Victorian era was a Golden Age of pornography. In the late 18th century, France had led the world in pornographic literature, and de Sade's erotic novels, such as *Juliette*, had also contained political satire. But with the new century, the impetus passed to England and later the United States, where pornography became highly commercialized and popular titles were easy to obtain. With the advent of photography and cheaper printing methods, pornography took on a new dimension and became even more accessible. However, the prurience of Victorian attitudes persisted, and the end of the 19th century was dominated by voyeuristic "Through-the-Keyhole" style images.

SEX IN THE 20TH CENTURY

THE 20TH CENTURY SAW major changes in attitudes to sex over a relatively short period of time. At the beginning of the century, the view was very much a hangover from the previous century, when sex was considered unclean, and the subject was not discussed by decent, respectable people. There was no sex education, and people acquired information through hearsay, rumour, and old wives' tales.

THE BEADLE IN BURLINGTON ARCADE (1871) is bribed by a prostitute to "turn a blind eye" while she plies her trade.

In the 19th century, and into the early years of the 20th century, a carefully constructed double standard operated for men and women. Middle-class women were expected to be virgin brides, reluctant but compliant sexual partners, good household managers, and mothers. Men were expected to be breadwinners and the initiators of all sexual encounters in the marital bed. Men's premarital sexual experience was acquired from prostitutes, of which there were various types, from the upmarket courtesans that served the wealthy to those that walked the streets or worked in brothels.

The early sex experts
In the early 20th century, UK essayist Havelock Ellis (1859–1939) and German campaigner for homosexual and lesbian rights Magnus Hirschfeld (1868–1935) studied human sexuality. They treated the subject as just another aspect of behaviour rather than as a moral issue, and stated that homosexuality, transvestite behaviour, and masturbation were just different forms of sexuality and were not evidence of demonic possession or proof of moral turpitude.

Austrian psychoanalyst Sigmund Freud (1856–1939) had considerable influence on 20th-century views of human sexuality. He constructed an elaborate system to explain human behaviour based on his work with neurotic and psychotic patients (see pp.18–19). Freud's one-time colleague Alfred Adler (see p.18) also explored human sexuality around this time.

HISTORYFACTS

VICTORIAN PROMISCUITY
In the mid-19th century London had 80,000 prostitutes and New York 35,000. These were adult females, i.e. above the age of 13, although child prostitution was common in cities. Sexually transmitted infections and unwanted pregnancies were commonplace. As many as 75 per cent of men suffered from veneral diseases at some time in their lives.

HISTORYFACTS

MAGNUS HIRSCHFELD
In 1903, Hirschfeld carried out the first surveys of sexual behaviour. In 1925, he founded the first institute for sexual studies in Berlin. This was destroyed by Nazis in 1933.

Post World War I
World War I caused immense social upheaval, and the period between the two world wars saw a steady relaxation of social restrictions of sexual behaviour. During the war, women had gained a greater degree of financial independence, taking on work previously done by men now in the army, and men and women had begun to mix more freely. As a result, opposite-sex friendships emerged, especially among young people. While the Victorian chap had only his manly chums, the young man of the 1920s had female pals. Women smoked in public, flirted, used make-up, and began to show that they enjoyed sex.

ATTITUDES BECAME *increasingly liberal after the turn of the century. This illustration is taken from* Fantasio *(1928).*

These changes affected all society, but particularly the middle and working classes: the aristocracy had always been free and easy sexually, if only in private.

Sex began to permeate the whole of society as people began to enjoy greater personal freedom. Fashions became more risqué – long gowns and corsets were replaced with short skirts and silk cami-knickers – and literature, the movies, the theatre, painting, advertising, and music (especially jazz) were steeped in sex.

Divorce, which had previously been hard to obtain and considered a shameful social disgrace, started to become more common, and attitudes towards it became more tolerant. However, abortion and homosexuality were still crimes.

Family planning
As people enjoyed sex more often the illegitimacy rate increased, along with the demands for abortions and contraception. What people wanted was clear, readily available information about sex and contraception. In family planning, the US showed the way: Margaret Sanger opened the first

family planning clinic in 1916. She supplied diaphragms and advice. The first British family planning centre was opened in 1921 by Marie Stopes.

It must be remembered that birth-control aids and advice were offered to married couples only; they were not available to single people, co-habiting couples, or the young. And many people disapproved of such services reaching even mature married couples; in the UK and USA, legal action was taken to force family planning clinics to close (but without success).

MARIE STOPES

MARIE STOPES (1880–1958) was a gifted scientist and researcher who, in 1918, published *Married Love*, a sex guide written in clear, non-medical language. She followed this with *Wise Parenthood*, a guide to birth control.
The clinic that Stopes opened in London with her second husband, H.V. Roe, was the foundation stone of what became the UK Family Planning Association.

MARGARET SANGER

MARGARET SANGER (1879–1966), the sixth of 11 children, saw her mother die, worn out by repeated pregnancies. She decided to devote herself to helping women avoid that fate and trained as a nurse. In 1912 she began to write a sex education column "What Every Girl Should Know" in a New York newspaper. She also distributed a leaflet on birth control, which led to her prosecution under US law for sending obscene material by mail. She skipped bail and fled to London. On returning home she opened a birth control clinic in Brooklyn. The authorities closed it after nine days, and she was briefly sent to prison in 1917. She continued the fight, eventually winning the legal battle to set up clinics.

Post World War II

The end of World War II heralded even more social change than World War I had done. The rigid structure of society was broken down still further, and in the 1950s standards of living improved rapidly. People of all classes had more money and more leisure time. The biggest film stars were sex symbols, and the advent of television brought sex right into the viewer's home. Social attitudes changed. Homosexuality and abortion were decriminalized, although in the US laws varied from state to state.

The car played a big part in the sex life of young people; it wasn't just a machine for getting you from A to B – it was a private space that could be moved away from other people and serve as a bedroom.

All these sexual changes and activities did not go unobserved by sexologists. During the 1940s, 1950s, and 1960s Alfred Kinsey, and then Masters and Johnson, carried out major surveys of sexual attitudes and behaviour in America (see pp.20–21). Masters and Johnson moved on to helping those with sexual problems, especially impotence and premature ejaculation. Their work laid the foundation for the later sex therapists.

The permissive years

The greatest changes in sexual attitudes almost certainly took place in the 1960s, with the introduction of the contraceptive pill. The Pill was efficient and (for most women) had few significant side-effects. For the first time, men and women were able to enjoy sex purely for recreation and forget about unwanted pregnancies. This was a major alteration in sexual behaviour – sex was no longer something to be reserved for the solemnity of marriage.

People began to experiment with a great variety of alternative sexual relationships, such as swinging, group sex parties, and communal marriages (see pp.158–59), although in many cases jealousy and insecurity upset the experiment. Sexual communities appeared, run like country clubs for paying members to stay at over a

THE SUMMER OF LOVE in 1967 saw hordes of young people gather together in search of "free love" and drugs, and to herald the dawn of a new age in which materialism, warfare, and the patriarchal family would have no part.

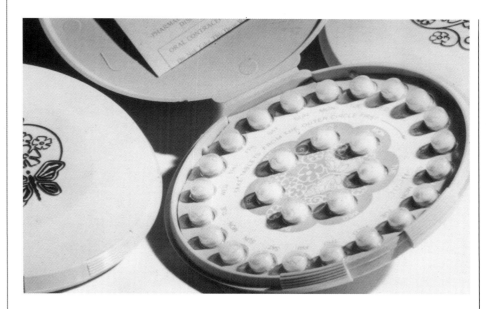

THE PILL was the contraceptive many people had dreamed of – a daily tablet that could be swallowed and forgotten about, freeing people from the fear of unwanted pregnancy.

weekend. The first was Sandstone, opened in California in 1968 and offering sex of all kinds, lectures, discussion groups, and workshops.

In the 1970s, sex shops offering all manner of bondage and S & M goods opened, as did both clubs catering for people with specific fantasies and a great number of gay bathhouses.

Sex workshops and therapy

Feminist views that emerged in the 1960s and 1970s affected marital partnerships and sexual expectations. Women wanted greater knowledge of their own sex organs and sexual responses; many had never experienced an orgasm and were not sure how to achieve one. Betty Dodson in the US and Anne Hooper in Britain conducted sexuality workshops introducing women to their own bodies and sexual responses.

Women used their newfound skills and men soon began to ask for instruction. Books on sex techniques appeared and were on open sale; Alex Comfort's *Joy of Sex* and Anne Hooper's *Ultimate Sex Guide* became bestsellers. Masturbation shed its negative image as unhealthy and

enfeebling, and Betty Dodson celebrated the wonders of solo sex in her book *Liberating Masturbation*, later titled *Sex for One*.

Sex therapy as a profession emerged in the 1970s and 1980s. Leading therapists in the US included Lonnie Barback, Helen Singer Kaplan, and William Hartman and Marilyn Fithian. In the UK, important figures in opening up the sexual debate were Martin Cole and John Bancroft.

Modern approach to sex

The arrival of AIDS in the early 1980s made many people shy away from sexual experimentation, although this change did not last for long. Today's surveys show that many people still risk infection through casual sex.

In recent years, drug companies have developed chemical cures to help men and women overcome a number of sexual problems – Viagra, for example, has proved highly successful (see p.207), as have hormone preparations (see p.203). In the past decade, there has been an emphasis on a healthy diet and exercise. Together, these factors are enabling people to remain sexually active for years longer than before.

DIGITAL TECHNOLOGIES, notably the Internet, have created whole new sexual worlds, including "virtual spaces", where you can create a "virtual you", whose gender and sexual preferences you can change at will.

FURTHER READING

Becoming Orgasmic: A Sexual and Personal Growth Programme for Women
by Julia Heiman and Joseph Lo Piccolo (Piatkus Books)

Dual Attraction: Understanding Bisexuality
by Martin Weinberg et al. (The Free Press)

Encyclopedia of Unusual Sex Practices
by Brenda Love (Abacus Books)

Erotic Passions
by Kenneth Ray Stubbs (Jeremy P. Tarcher)

Exploring Human Sexuality
by Karen Klenke-Hamel and Louis Janda (D. Van Nostrand)

Homosexuality
by William H. Masters, Virginia E. Johnson, and Robert C. Kolodney (Little, Brown)

How to be a Great Lover
by Lou Paget (Piatkus Books)

Human Sexuality and its Problems
by John Bancroft (Churchill Livingstone)

Human Sexual Response
by William H. Masters and Virginia E. Johnson (Little, Brown)

The Illustrated Manual of Sex Aids
by Evelyn Rainbird (Minotaur Press)

The New Male Sexuality
by Bernie Zilbergeld (Bantam)

Sex for One
by Betty Dodson (Crown Publishing)

Sexual Behaviour in Britain
by Kaye Wellings et al. (Penguin)

Sexual Behaviour in the Human Male
by Alfred Kinsey et al. (W.B. Saunders Company)

OTHER ANNE HOOPER TITLES BY DORLING KINDERSLEY

Anne Hooper's Kama Sutra
Illustrated with photographs of contemporary couples, this book presents all the arts of seduction and will inspire every reader to introduce more variety and excitement into sex. Here, in this unrivalled erotic masterpiece, you will find the key to lasting sexual fulfilment.

Anne Hooper's Ultimate Sex Guide
With exciting photos and clear illustrations, this is an irresistible book for everyone who wants to learn intimate erotic techniques and heighten their sexual enjoyment.

Great Sex Games
Expand your sexual repertoire and ovecome inhibitions with Anne's unique and imaginative guide to erotic sex games. There's something to suit everyone – you and your partner can discover how to live out daring fantasies and spice up your sex life.

Great Sex Tips
Heighten passion and enhance love-making skills with this adventurous guide to erotic tricks and techniques. Guaranteed to tantalize, the tips cover the full spectrum of sexual experience, from saucy seduction to spine-tingling foreplay and fantasy.

KISS Guide to the Kama Sutra & Kiss Guide to Sex
The Keep It Simple Series is your trusted guide through all of life's stages and situations. In both *KISS Guide to the Kama Sutra* and *Kiss Guide to Sex*, Anne walks you through the subject from start to finish, using simple blocks of knowledge to build your skills one step at a time.

USEFUL ADDRESSES

UK AND US

Sex toys and products

Ann Summers
www.annsummers.com
Shop online or book an Ann Summers party in your home. Check the website for addresses of UK high street stores.

Master U
PO Box 32759, London SE1 7FJ
tel: 08702 405737
e-mail: info@master-u.co.uk
www.master-u.co.uk
Mail-order leather and rubber bondage gear.

Passion8
4 Kilnbeck Business Park, Beverley HU17 0LF
tel/fax: 01482 873377
www.passion8.co.uk
Shop online for toys, books, and videos.

Sh! Women's Erotic Emporium
39 Coronet Street, London N1 6HD
tel: 020 7613 5458
fax: 020 7613 0020
e-mail: info@sh-womenstore.com
www.sh-womenstore.com
Toys and accessories for women.

Erotic art and literature

Amazon
www.amazon.co.uk
Look online for Amazon's excellent selection of erotic literature.

Cleansheets
www.cleansheets.com
Online magazine with news and reviews for writers and readers of erotic fiction and poetry.

Erotic Art
PO Box 6276, San Mateo, CA 944403-0991, USA
e-mail: info@eroticart.com
www.eroticart.com
Contemporary and antique paintings, sculptures, and books.

Information resources and discussion forums

After Glow
www.after-glow.com
Online magazine on love and sexuality.

Betty Dodson
www.bettydodson.com
Betty's website is devoted to erotic sex education, promoting sexual freedom, and liberating masturbation.

Go Ask Alice
www.goaskalice.com
A US-based question-and-answer website for all aspects of sexual health and relationship issues.

Nerve Magazine
www.nerve.com
Full-scale erotic discussion and personal anecdotes about sex.

Chat groups and meeting places

Most of the good Internet servers provide excellent general chat sites. Among the best are:
www.aol.com
www.netscape.com
www.altavista.com

Matchmaker
www.matchmaker.com
Online matchmaking and dating service.

SeniorNet
www.seniornet.org
A US-based general interest site for more mature citizens.

For people with disabilities

SPOD
286 Camden Road, London N7 0BJ
tel: 020 7607 8851 (10am–4pm Mon to Thurs)
fax: 020 7700 0236
info@spod-uk.org
www.spod-uk.org
Sex and relationship counselling and support for people with disabilities and their partners. The organization also supports carers and health professionals.

Lesbian, gay, and bisexual resources

Bi The Way
www.bitheway.org
A terrific list of lesbian, gay, and bisexual resources, discussion groups, and websites for the whole world.

London Lesbian and Gay Switchboard
PO Box 7324, London, N1 9QS
tel: 020 7837 7324
fax: 020 7837 7300
www.llgs.org.uk
Helpline for lesbian, gay, and bisexual people and their families, plus a database of pubs, clubs, organizations, and events.

Transsexual and transvestite resources

The Beaumont Society
27 Old Gloucester Street, London WC1N 3XX
tel: 01582 412220
www.beaumontsociety.org.uk
Weekend reunions, make-up finishing schools, a national information-line network, and a safe mailbox contact system.

Transformation Mail Order
409 Bury Old Road, Prestwich, Manchester M25 1PS
tel: 0870 743 2233
fax: 0870 741 7878
info@transformation.co.uk
www.transformation.co.uk
Visit the website for details of specialist retail stores in the UK or purchase online (deliveries worldwide).

Therapy and counselling

British Association for Counselling & Psychotherapy
1 Regent Place, Rugby, Warwickshire CV21 2PJ
tel: 0870 443 5174/5175/5182
e-mail: bacp@bacp.co.uk
www.bac.co.uk
Find a counsellor in your area.

British Association for Sexual and Relationship Therapy
tel: 020 8543 2707
e-mail: info@basrt.org.uk
www.basrt.org.uk
Information on accredited therapists in the UK.

Rape Crisis Federation
7 Mansfield Road, Nottingham NG1 3FB
tel: 0115 934 8474
fax: 0115 934 8470
e-mail: info@rapecrisis.co.uk
www.rapecrisis.co.uk
This organization will put you in touch with your local rape and sexual abuse counselling centre.

Relate
Herbert Gray College, Little Church Street,
Rugby CV21 3AP
tel: 01788 573241
helpline: 09069 123715
e-mail: enquiries@national.relate.org.uk
www.relate.org.uk
Counselling and psychosexual therapy for adult couples (married or unmarried).

Health issues

Herpes Viruses Association
41 North Road, London N7 9DP
helpline: 020 7609 9061
www.herpes.org.uk
Counselling for individuals affected physically or psychologically by herpes simplex.

Hysterectomy Association
Beech Mews, 51 Burton Road, Coton-in-the-Elms,
Derbyshire DE12 8HJ
www.hysterectomy-association.org.uk
Information and support for women having hysterectomies.

Terence Higgins Trust
52–54 Grays Inn Road, London WC1X 8JU
tel: 020 7831 0330
helpline: 020 7242 1010 (Midday–10pm every day)
fax: 020 7242 0121
e-mail: info@tht.org.uk
www.tht.org.uk
Advice and counselling for people with HIV/AIDS or those concerned with it.

Family planning

British Pregnancy Advisory Service
Austy Manor, Wootton Wawen, Solihull B95 6BX
helpline: 0845 730 4030
fax: 01564 794935
e-mail: info@bpas.org
www.bpas.org
Advice, counselling, abortion service, pregnancy testing, male vasectomy and female sterilization (and reversals) and emergency contraception.

Marie Stopes International
153–157 Cleveland Street, London W1P 5PG
tel: 020 7574 7400
fax: 020 7574 7417
e-mail: services@stopes.org.uk
www.mariestopes.org.uk
Well woman clinics, family planning, abortion services, and assistance with menopause.

AUSTRALIA

Sex toys and products

Intimate Toys
Melbourne, Templestowe, Victoria, 3106
tel: 1800 55 88 50
email: info@intimatetoys.com.au
www.intimatetoys.com.au
Shop online for toys, books, and videos.

For people with disabilities

http://members.ozemail.com.au/~pacetrav/
Online matchmaking and friend finder club for people with disabilities from around the world. The website also has links to related organizations and resources.

Lesbian, gay, and bisexual resources

Gay and Lesbian Switchboard (Victoria)
tel: 03 9827 8544 (Melbourne Metropolitan)
or 1800 631 493 (Country Victoria)
http://home.vicnet.net.au/~glswitch/
Counselling, referral, and information service. The helpline operates from 6pm until 10pm.

Hares and Hyenas
135 Commercial Road, South Yarra 3141, Victoria
tel: 03 9824 0110
fax: 03 9824 2839
www.hares-hyenas.com.au
Bookstore for gay, lesbian, and bisexual readers. Products can be ordered online.

Transsexual and transvestite resources

The Good Tranny Guide
www.tgfolk.net/sites/gtg/
Listings of transgender-friendly businesses, support groups, and contacts for medical and legal advice throughout Australia.

Therapy and counselling

Relationships Australia
www.relationships.com.au
This organization offers resources to couples, individuals, and families to help enhance relationships. It also provides listings of local relationship counselling centres.

Health issues and family planning

Australian Federation of AIDS Organisations
PO Box 876, Darlinghurst, NSW 1300
www.afao.org.au
Advice about AIDS issues and links to local organizations.

FPA Health
328–336 Liverpool Road, Ashfield, NSW 2131
healthline: 1300 658 886 (Mon–Fri 9am–5pm)
www.fpahealth.org.au
Listings of family planning centres and helplines across Australia, online factsheets on sexual health, and training programmes for health professionals and teachers.

INDEX

A

abdomen kneading, massage, 62

Adler, Alfred, 18, 32, 258

adolescents, 188–9

adrenaline, 16, 31, 80, 132, 154

affairs, extra-marital, 31, 236

age of consent, 189

aging, 92, 196–9, 205–6, 231

agnus castus, 177

AIDS, 159, 189, 223, 261

alcohol, 147, 206, 218

altocalciphilia, 156

amphetamines, 219

amputee fetish, 155

amyl nitrate, 147, 219

anal sex, 124–5, 178, 182

anal wands, 144

The Ananga Ranga, 105

anatomy, 44–7

andropause, 147, 196–7, 209

anger, 49, 224

angina, 212

animals, zoophilia, 157

anti-depressants, 205, 216

antihistamines, 217

antioxidants, 176

anxiety, 49

aphrodisiacs, 176, 178

appearance, 34–5

Arabs, 249, 251

arousal: delayed, 204

  female arousal, 49, 86–7, 90–1

  male arousal, 46, 86–7, 88

  prolonging, 74

arthritis, 212

Ashley, April, 161

asphyxia, autoerotic, 155

assertiveness, 227

B

asthma, 212

attitudes to sex, 22–3

attraction, 14–16

autoerotic asphyxia, 155

babies, adapting to life with, 225, 226

baby clothes, infantilism, 156

back massage, 60–1

back-to-front positions, 105

bacterial vaginosis, 178, 220

barrier methods, contraception, 185

bathing, 130–1, 178

Beautrais manoeuvre, 99

behaviourism, 18

bereavement, 228

beta-blockers, 208, 217

birth control, 184–7, 259, 260

bisexuality, 165

biting, 66

blindfolds, 144–5, 152

blood, vampirism, 157

blood circulation disorders, 213

blood-lipid control drugs, 216

blood pressure, 215, 216–17

body language, 17, 35, 226

body piercing, 150–1

bondage, 138–41, 144–5, 154, 155, 157

books, sexy, 137, 146

boredom, 132, 235

brain: fetishes, 154

  homosexuality, 169

  sex role differences, 24, 25

breasts: arousal, 90

  breast-feeding, 195

  cancer, 179, 181, 217

  massage, 62

"brewer's droop", 147

butt plugs, 144

C

cameras, 148, 158

cancer, 179, 181, 217

candidiasis, 178, 220

candles, 57

caning games, 140, 141

cannabis, 219

cap, contraceptive, 185

casual relationships, 30–1

Celts, 248

cervical smear test, 181

cervix, 47, 51

changing sex, 161

chemicals, and sexual response, 16, 49

childbirth, sex after, 194–5, 227

children, gay parenting, 165

China, 252–3

chlamydia, 221

Christianity, 248–9

Cinderella fetish, 155

circling: massage, 59

  pelvic, 174

circumcision, 45

climax *see* orgasm

clingfilm bondage, 157

clinics, sexual health, 180

clitoris: cunnilingus, 78, 79, 119

  erotic massage, 64, 74

  masturbation, 71, 77, 94

  orgasm, 20, 91

  stimulation, 46–7

  transsexuals, 161

  vibrators, 142–3

clothes: erotic, 146, 148–50
rubber and leather, 153, 154, 157
transvestites, 160
clubs, 159, 167, 261
cocaine, 219
cock (penis) rings, 143, 207, 231
cohabitation, 158–9
communal marriage, 159
conception, 187, 257
condoms, 182, 183, 185, 189, 257
confidence, restoring, 238
Confucianism, 252–3
contraception, 184–7, 189, 259, 260
cosmetics, 148, 178
counselling, 202, 207, 224–39
crabs, 222
criticism, loss of confidence, 238, 239
Cro-Magnon people, 244–5
Crusades, 249, 251
cunnilingus, 78, 79, 119
cystitis, 221

D

dating, 36–7
deep penetration, 102, 112
defilement fetish, 155
dehydroepiandrosterone (DHEA), 203
delayed gratification, 72
depression, 29, 49, 204–5, 237
desire *see* libido
diabetes, 213
diaphragm, contraceptive, 185
diet, 176–7

dildos, 143
doggy-style position, 109
domination, 138–41
dressing up, 146, 148–50, 160
drugs: anti-depressants, 205, 216
medicinal drugs, 216–17
penile injections, 207
phentolamine, 147, 212, 241
recreational drugs, 147, 218–19

E

ecstasy, 219
ejaculation, 44, 50, 89
injaculation, 123
multiple orgasms, 96
oral sex, 78
premature, 208–9, 234
retarded, 209
electrical toys, 144, 147
The Elephant position, 109
emotions, 49, 197
environmental factors, homosexuality, 168
epilepsy, 214, 217
erection, 44, 88
dysfunction, 206–7, 231, 236
Viagra, 147
erogenous zones, 73, 75
erotic literature, 137, 146
erotic massage, 64–5, 74
essential oils, 57
evolutionary psychology, 18–19
evolutionary theory, homosexuality, 168
exercises, sexual, 174–5
exhibitionism, 155
eye contact, 35

F

fabrics, sensual, 152
face-to-face positions, 100–3, 106, 110, 115
falling in love, 14–16
fancy dress parties, 149
fantasies, 48, 134–7
fatigue, 205
feathers, teasing with, 153
feet, 150
footbinding, 253
massage, 63
shoes, 150, 155, 156
fellatio, 78, 119
female anatomy, 46–7
female condom, 185
female-to-male transsexuals, 161
fertility, 51, 245
fertilization, 50–1, 187, 257
fetishes, 22, 25, 153, 154–7, 159
finger-tipping, 111
food games, 80–1
food supplements, 176–7
foreplay, 55–81
foreskin, 45, 178
French kiss, 67
Freud, Sigmund, 15, 18, 19, 20, 23, 168, 258
friction, increasing, 118
front massage, 62
frottage, 155

G

G-spot, 47, 95
games, 134–41
gays, 163–9
geisha, 253

gender dysphoria, 160
genetics, homosexuality, 168, 169
genital herpes, 189, 221
genital warts, 189, 221
genitals: anatomy, 44–7
  arousal, 88–91
  massage, 64, 74
  transsexuals, 161
ginkgo biloba, 177
ginseng, 177
glucosamine, 177
golden showers, 155
gonorrhoea, 221
Greece, ancient, 167, 246–7
grief, 228
group marriage, 159
group sex parties, 159

H

hair: hair fetish, 155
  scalp massage, 63, 131
heart disease, 212, 214–15
"heavy petting" 72, 188–9
hepatitis B, 221
herbal supplements, 177
heroin, 219
high-heel fetish, 156
Hirschfeld, Magnus, 258
history of sex, 241–61
Hite Report, 21, 130, 210
HIV, 182, 185, 223
homilophilia, 156
homosexuals, 163–9, 247
hormones, 16, 48–9
  andropause, 147, 196–7, 209
  casual relationships, 31
  contraceptives, 186
  erectile dysfunction, 207

homosexuality, 169
hormone replacement therapy,
  197, 205, 211
  oral contraceptives, 217
  in pregnancy, 190
  sex role differences, 24–5
  sexual problems, 203
  transsexuals, 161
  see also oestrogen; testosterone
hotels, 133
hygiene, 178
hymen, 47
hypertension, 215, 216–17

I

ice cubes, 80
illness, 212–15
impotence, 206–7
India, 250–1, 254
infantilism, 156
infidelity, 230
inhibitions, 27, 147, 210, 218, 229, 239
injaculation, 123
Internet, 158, 167
intimacy, 28–9, 226
intrauterine contraceptives, 187

J, K

Japan, 253
jealousy, 39
Kama Sutra, 57, 63, 66–7, 109, 116,
  250–1
Kaplan, Dr. Helen Singer, 87
Kegel exercises, 175
Kinsey Report, 20–1, 49, 96, 100,
  104, 164, 260
kissing, 66–7

kitchens, lovemaking in, 131
kneeling positions, 109, 112–13
kokigami, 156

L

L-arginine, 177
labia, 46, 47, 90
leather, 153
legs, sexual appeal, 24, 150
lesbians, 163–9, 247
libido, 18, 86–7, 90
  after childbirth, 194, 195
  bisexuality, 165
  increasing in later life, 204
  loss of, 202–3
  mismatched libidos, 233
  in pregnancy, 190–1
lice, 222
lighting, intimate atmosphere, 57
linseed, 177
living rooms, lovemaking in, 131
love, 14–16, 23
loving yourself, 32–3
LSD, 219
lubricants (lubes), 144, 211

M

magazines, 146, 189
magic mushrooms, 219
male anatomy, 44–5
male-to-female transsexuals, 161
mammography, 181
man-on-top positions, 100–3
marriage, 29, 41, 226, 235
massage: anal sex, 124
  during sex, 118
  erotic massage, 64–5, 74

feather massage, 153

sacral massage, 192

self-touch, 68–71

sensual massage, 58–63

setting the scene, 56–7

Masters and Johnson, 21, 23, 74, 96, 120, 165, 260

masturbation, 23, 68–71

female orgasm, 33, 71, 94–5

mutual, 76–7

in pregnancy, 192

vibrators, 95

materials, sensual, 152–3

medical check-ups, 180–1, 215

medicinal drugs, 216–17

meeting people, 36–7

menopause, 49, 196, 197, 211

menstrual cycle, 25, 49, 50, 51, 186, 211

mid-life sex, 196–7, 203

minerals, in diet, 176

mirrors, 136–7

missionary position, 100–3, 255

monogamy, 40–1

Mormons, 40

mud wrestling, 155

multiple orgasms, 96–7, 119

multiple sclerosis, 215

music, 57, 145

N

National Survey of Sexual Attitudes and Lifestyles, 164, 165

neck massage, 61

necrophilia, 156

nipples, 62, 68, 90

non-penetrative sex, 183

non-specific urethritis (NSU), 222

O

oestrogen: contraceptive pill, 186

functions, 49

hormone therapy, 203, 211

low levels of, 205, 211

menstrual cycle, 49, 50

phytoestrogens, 177

in pregnancy, 190

office sex, 133

oils, massage, 57, 58

older people, 177, 198–9, 205–6

open relationships, 230

oral sex, 78–9, 119

orgasm, 87

controlling, 98–9

discovering, 229

female, 20, 91, 123, 212

injaculation, 123

male, 44, 89, 92–3

masturbation, 69, 71

multiple orgasms, 96–7, 119

mutual masturbation, 76–7

in pregnancy, 191, 192

problems, 208–10, 234

timing, 119

orgies, 159

outdoor sex, 132

ovulation, 51, 184, 186

ovum, fertilization, 50–1

P

Pacific islands, 255

parenting, gay, 165

parties: fancy dress, 149

fetish parties, 159

swinging, 159

pedic lovemaking, 150

"peeping Toms", 157

pelvic circling, 174

pelvic-floor exercises, 175

pelvic-inflammatory disease (PID), 222

pelvic lifts, 174

penis, 51

anatomy, 44–5

arousal, 88

circumcision, 45

erectile dysfunction, 206–7

erotic massage, 64, 74

fellatio, 78, 119

implants, 207

masturbation, 69, 76

orgasm, 89

penis pumps, 207

rings, 143, 207, 231

squeeze technique, 208

surgery, 207

transsexuals, 161

The Perfumed Garden, 251

periods, 178

personal care, 178–9

phentolamine, 147, 212, 241

pheromones, 16, 118

phone fetishists, 157

phone sex, 133, 158

photography, 145

phytoestrogens, 177

piercing, 150–1

Pilates, 175, 199

The Pill, 97, 186, 260

podophilia, 155

pony-racing fetish, 156

poppers, 147, 219

pornography, 146, 257

positions: back to front, 105

face-to-face, 100–3, 106, 110, 115

Kama Sutra, 250
kneeling, 109, 112–13
man-on-top, 100–3
in pregnancy, 193
rear-entry, 94, 108–9, 111, 115, 193
side-by-side, 110–11, 193
sitting, 104, 106, 114–15
upright, 109, 116–17
woman-on-top, 104–7
positive thinking, 198
pregnancy, 189, 190–3
prehistoric people, 244–5
premature ejaculation, 208–9, 234
problems, 202–11, 224–39
progesterone, 49, 186, 190
progestogen-only Pill, 186
promiscuity, gay men, 164
props, 117
bedroom toys, 142–5, 146–7
sensual materials, 152–3
prostate gland: cancer, 181, 217
enlargement, 181
stimulation, 93, 125, 144
prostitutes, 246, 253, 256, 258
puberty, 24–5, 48
pubic hair, 64
pubic lice, 222
public-speaking fetish, 156
pulsar technique, orgasm, 93

R

reading out loud, 137
rear-entry positions, 94, 108–9, 111, 115, 193
recordings, 145
recreational drugs, 218–19

relationships: after childbirth, 195, 227
casual relationships, 30–1
contracts, 41
expectations, 40–1
falling in love, 14–16
gay relationships, 164–7
intimacy, 28–9
key issues, 38–9
learned behaviour, 26–7
marriage, 29, 41, 226, 235
meeting people, 36–7
problems, 224–39
singles cohabitation, 158–9
relaxation, 174, 205
renal failure, 215
reproduction, 50–1
resolution phase, 87, 88
restraints, 141, 145, 154
retarded ejaculation, 209
rhodiola rosea, 177
Roman Empire, 246–7, 248, 249
rubber, 153, 154, 157

S

sacral massage, 192
safer sex, 182–3, 189
sage, 177
salvia officinalis, 177
Samoa, 255
Sanger, Margaret, 259
saw palmetto, 177
scalp massage, 63, 131
scents, intimate atmosphere, 57
schizophrenia, 217
scrotum, 44, 45
self-confidence, 32–3, 34
self-touch, 68–71, 95

semen (seminal fluid), 44–5, 78, 89
sensate focus therapy, 120, 203, 208
sensual massage, 58–63
Sets of Nine exercise, 122
sex boosters, 146–7
sex-change surgery, 161
sex flush, 88, 91
sex therapy, 202, 207, 208, 209, 210, 224–39, 261
sexology, 18, 20
sexual behaviour, 20–1, 24–7
sexual exercises, 174–5
sexual mapping, 75
sexual response, 86–91
sexual splitting, 41
sexuality, 18–33
sexually transmitted infections, 178, 180, 182, 189, 220–3, 254
shampooing hair, 63, 131
shoes, 150
Cinderella fetish, 155
high-heel fetish, 156
shoulder massage, 61
showers, 130
side-by-side positions, 110–11, 193
singles cohabitation, 158–9
sitting positions, 104, 106, 114–15
"69" position, 119
smear test, 181
smegma, 178
smoking, 206, 218
soapsud massage, 65
spanking games, 140, 141
speed, 219
sperm, 44–5, 50, 89, 185, 187, 257
spermicides, 185
spinal injuries, 215
spoons position, 111
squeeze technique, 99

standing positions, 109, 116–17
sterilization, 187
stiffness, joints, 175
Stopes, Marie, 259
stress, 205, 232
string bondage, 157
striptease, 134–5, 136, 149
strokes, brain, 215
stroking, 72, 74, 120–1
submission, 138–41
supplements, food, 176–7
swinging, 159
syphilis, 222, 254

T

taboos, fantasy and, 135
tampons, 178, 220
tantric sex, 120–1, 251
Tao, 122–3, 252
tattoos, 150–1
teasing, with feathers, 153
teenagers, 188–9
telephone fetishists, 157
telephone sex, 133, 158
TENS machines, 144
testes (testicles), 50
  anatomy, 44, 45
  self-examination, 179
testosterone: andropause, 196, 209
  depression and, 49
  erectile dysfunction, 206, 207
  fatigue and, 205
  functions, 48
  hormone therapy, 147, 202, 203,
    211
  low levels of, 202
  sex role differences, 25
  in women, 48, 147, 210

textures, sensual, 57
Thai soapsud massage, 65
Thompson, Raymond, 161
threesomes, 158
thrush, 178, 220
tiredness, 205
toes, sucking, 150
tongue: oral sex, 78–9, 119
  tongue bathing, 75, 124
toys, 142–5, 146–7
tranquillizers, 217
transsexuals, 160, 161
transvestites, 160
trichomoniasis, 222
trichophilia, 155
tubal ligation, 187

U, V

ulcer/acid suppressing drugs, 216
underwear, 148–9
undressing, 134–5, 136, 149
upright positions, 109, 116–17
urination, golden showers, 155
urolagnia, 155
uterus, 51, 187
vagina, 51
  anatomy, 47
  arousal, 90
  cunnilingus, 79, 119
  G-spot, 95
  hygiene, 178
  pelvic-floor exercises, 175
  problems, 210–11
  secretions, 46
  vaginismus, 210
vaginosis, bacterial, 178, 220
vampirism, 157
vasectomy, 187

venous leakage, 206, 231
Venus figurines, 245
Viacreme, 147, 210
Viagra, 147, 207, 210, 231, 261
vibrators, 95, 142–3, 144
Victorians, 256–7, 258
virginity, 47
virtual sex, 158, 261
vitamins, 176, 177
voyeurism, 157
vulva, 46–7

W

washing, 178
web-cams, 158
wheelbarrow position, 117
woman-on-top positions, 104–7

Y, Z

yoga, 175, 199
yohimbine, 176
zinc, 176
zoophilia, 157

ACKNOWLEDGMENTS

AUTHOR'S ACKNOWLEDGMENTS

Anne Hooper would like to thank the following people for editorial assistance:
Kesta Desmond
Dawn Henderson
Jeremy Holford-Miettinen

PUBLISHER'S ACKNOWLEDGMENTS

Dorling Kindersley would like to thank Sh! Women's Erotic Emporium and Master U for the supply of materials.

Studio Cactus would like to thank Laura Seber and Aaron Brown for editorial help, John Sturges for proofreading and Hilary Bird for the index.

PICTURE CREDITS

The publisher would like to thank the following for their kind permission to reproduce their photographs:
(Abbreviations key: t=top, b=bottom, r=right, l=left, c=centre, BAL=Bridgeman Art Library, London/New York, MEPL= Mary Evans Picture Library, SPL=Science Photo Library)

7: BAL/Isoda Koryusai/Private Collection (bl); 8: Art Archive/National Museum of Prague (tr); 10-11: Getty Images/Juan Silva; 16: Getty Images/Dale Durfee; 18: MEPL; 19: Photodisc; 22: Getty Images/Kaz Mori (r); 30: Getty Images/James Darell (bl); 35: Photodisc (tr); 36: Getty Images/Michelangelo Gratton; 40: Corbis/Hulton-Deutsch Collection (br); 48: Getty Images/Jacques Copeau; 56: Photodisc (tr), Getty Images/Andy Whale (b); 57: Getty Images/Pete Turner; 60-61: Getty Images/Bruce Ayres (t); 155: Rex Features (bl); 158: Getty Images/Stone; 159: Getty Images/Deborah Jaffe; 160: Getty Images/Ross Kirton; 161: Rex Features (b, cr); 162-163: Getty Images/Ron Chapple; 164: Getty Images/Ghislain & Marie David de Lossy; 165: Getty Images/Bruce Ayres; 166: Getty Images/Greg Ceo; 167: Janine Wiedel; 168-169: Getty Images/Eric O'Connell; 170-171: Getty Images/Larry Dale Gordon; 176: Photodisc (tr, b); 178: Photodisc (tr, b); 180: Getty Images/Color Day Production; 188-189: ImageState; 190: Getty Images/Ebby May; 191: Digital Vision; 192: Digital Vision; 195: Getty Images/Laurence Monneret; 197: Getty Images/Simon Bottomley; 198: Photodisc; 199: Getty Images/Vincent Besnault; 207: ImageState (br); 212: Getty Images/Bob Thomas (br); 216: SPL/Colin Cuthbert (tr); 218: AKG (bl); 219: SPL/Michael Donne (cl); 220: Getty Images/Patrick Molnar; 221: SPL/Dr Linda Stannard, UCT (tr); 240-241: Corbis/Mimmo Jodice; 242: Art Archive (b), Getty Images/Hulton Archive (tl); 243: Art Archive/Musée du Louvre Paris (tl), Hulton Archive/Getty Images (b); 244: Werner Forman Archive; 245: AKG (tl), University Museum of Archaeology and Anthropology, Cambridge (br); 246: AKG (tr, bl); 247: AKG/Erich Lessing (t), Corbis/Roger Wood (br); 248: Art Archive; 249: Art Archive/Bodleian Library Oxford, Douce 195 folio 155v (bl), Museo del Prado Madrid (tr); 250: Werner Forman Archive; 251: Art Archive; 252: Corbis/Gustavo Tomsich; 253: BAL/Sigimura Jihei/Art Institute of Chicago, IL, USA (br), Torii Kiyonaga/Pushkin Museum, Moscow, Russia (tl); 254: Corbis/Bettmann; 255: BAL/Paul Gauguin/Hermitage, St. Petersburg, Russia; 256: Francis Frith Collection; 257: Art Archive (tr), Tate, London 2002/William Holman Hunt (tl); 258: MEPL; 259: Corbis/Bettmann (br), MEPL (tl); 260: Hulton Archive/Getty Images; 261: Hulton Archive/Getty Images (tl), Kobal Collection/New Line 1992 (br).

Jacket photo: Getty Images/Uwe Kreici
Illustrations: Richard Tibbits/John Geary

All other images © Dorling Kindersley.
For further information see: www.dkimages.com